Yhwh's combat with the sea

Carola Kloos

Yhwh's Combat with the Sea

A Canaanite Tradition in the Religion of Ancient Israel

G. A. van Oorschot   Amsterdam
E. J. Brill   Leiden
1986

ISBN 90 04 08096 1

Magistro venerato
Professori P. A. H. de Boer

CONTENTS

7

INTRODUCTION

The present study has resulted from the wish to investigate the influence which the Baal religion has exercised upon Yahwism. It is recognized nowadays, that Yhwh owes more to Baal than was formerly deemed possible, when the Ugaritic texts were not known. The extent of that influence is still controversial, however. Whereas some would limit it to certain poetical figures of speech, others consider the Baal religion to have influenced Yahwism at essential points.

In Part I of this study, Psalm xxix is examined. It is generally admitted, that the psalm contains elements which stem from the Baal mythology; but the question is once more: to what extent? I have the impression, that a discussion has too often been avoided when it was, in point of fact, required; it is simply declared, for example, that Psalm xxix is an ancient Baal hymn, whilst divergent opinions are passed by in silence. It has been my aim, therefore, to fill in this gap by discussing (as far as possible) all current opinions.

The outcome of my analysis – notably, that the psalm pictures Yhwh throughout as Baal – raises some questions, which are discussed next. Must it be assumed that the hymn expresses a genuine belief – as I imagine? Or does it express – just to mention one opinion – mocking contempt of the Canaanites and their god? In the case of the former, the Israelites worshipped a deity who shared certain fundamental traits with Baal.

We should, of course, beware of attaching too much weight to one single text. The assumption, that these Baal traits were indeed attributed to Yhwh by the Israelites, needs further confirmation. Such confirmation could be furnished by another text in which Yhwh functions as Baal – not some lines within a larger whole, but a self-contained unity of some length.

It seemed to me, that the Song of the Sea in Exodus xv might fulfill this condition. The song is examined in Part II of this study, by itself and in the context of the Reed Sea tradition. In my opinion, the Reed Sea story originates in the myth of the combat with Sea, which has been 'historicized', i.e. turned into pseudo-history, by the Israelites.

This process, by which a myth about gods is converted into a myth about the history of the nation, is by no means restricted to Israelite literature. In order to demonstrate the existence of such processes, I have chosen a chapter of ancient Roman historiography as an example; this may be used as an argument against those, who question the possibility of such a transformation of the myth. My investigation of the Reed Sea tradition has convinced me, that the deity of the Song of the Sea is not less of a Baal than the deity of Psalm xxix.

The presence of a hymn picturing Yhwh as Baal, and of a tale about Israel's history in which Yhwh functions as Baal, must lead to the conclusion, I think, that the Baal traits were an essential element of Yhwh's character – especially if it is taken into account, that the Reed Sea tradition plays an important rôle in the Old Testament. However, that conclusion stands or falls with the correctness of my interpretation of the texts. I hope that my analysis has been careful enough to carry conviction.

PART ONE

PSALM XXIX

I

ANALYSIS OF PSALM XXIX

Many single publications already exist on Ps. xxix, while the psalm is also treated in a great number of studies of a larger scope. My treatment will be especially directed at answering the question, how far Yhwh is represented in the psalm as Baal, as El, and as 'Yhwh himself'. This will involve a discussion of the relevant literature.

As heading the MT has *mzmwr ldwd*, rendered by the lxx with *Psalmos tooi Dauid*. That the Greek translators did not always know their Hebrew perfectly well and sometimes (mis)translated in quite a mechanical way, appears from Ps. vii, where *ldwd 'šr-šr* is translated with *tooi Dauid, hon èisen*, and from Ps. xviii, where *ldwd 'šr dbr* has become *tooi Dauid, ha elalèsen*. This absurdity makes it clear at once, that *ldwd* can only be understood as an indication of the supposed author of these psalms; then this will probably also be the case with Ps. xxix. However, what should interest us more is the addition made by the LXX to the MT heading of Ps. xxix: *exhodiou skènès*, on the last day of the Festival of Booths. Although, formally speaking, this direction for the use of the psalm cannot be held to say anything about the pre-exilic situation, the psalm might just conceivably have been connected with the Autumn Festival in that time also. For the moment, we shall leave this question aside; it will be discussed in connection with the 'Myth and Ritual' viewpoint (p. 112–113).

INTRODUCTION (VSS. 1–2)

Translation

1 Give to Yhwh, sons of El,
   give to Yhwh honour and strength,
2 give to Yhwh the honour of his name,
   bow down to Yhwh before the holy majesty.

Interpretation

bny 'lym

The term *bny 'lym* could be explained as 'sons of the gods', i.e. those who belong to the class of gods[1]; but I am inclined to follow H. D. Hummel, who proposes to read an enclitic *-m* in the expression.[2] At Ugarit, the assembly of the gods is called *dr bn il, mpḫrt bn il* (*KTU* 1.40 7–8, 17, 25, 33–34, 42 – partly reconstructed –; 1.65 2–3) as well as *p⟨ḫ⟩r bn ilm* (*KTU* 1.4 III 14). The expression is attested as late as the 8th and 7th century B.C.: the Karatepe inscription has *wkl dr bn 'lm* (*KAI* 26 A III 19), and the Arslan Tash plaque *wkl bn 'lm* (*KAI* 27 11). Apart from Ps. XXIX, *bny 'lym* occurs once more in the OT (Ps. LXXXIX 7).

The sons of El are the gods. In the Baal epic, El is called the father of several gods by means of the formula *ṯr il aby/k/h*, the bull El my/your/ his father. The standard name of Mot is *bn ilm mt*, Mot son of El. *KTU* 1.40 7, 16, 24, 33, 41 – partly reconstructed – mention offerings to the *ab bn il*, the father of the gods.[3]

According to W. Herrmann[4], however, the term *bn il*, and the terms for the 'assembly of (the sons of) El', do not denote (at least in the Ugaritic texts) the pantheon as a whole, but only a special group of gods, the circle of El. Herrmann bases his opinion on texts, in which other gods are enumerated beside the sons of El, as e.g. *KTU* 1.65; moreover, a *p⟨ḫ⟩r b'l* is mentioned next to the *dr il* (e.g. *KTU* 1.39 7). Furthermore, Herrmann points to *KTU* 1. 17 VI 28–29, where it is said that Aqhat will count the years *'m b'l*, and the months *'m bn il*; if *bn il* is taken as a plural, Baal would be excepted from these gods.

I think that Herrmann's conclusion concerning the *bn il* is not justified. The special mention which is made of the total sum of gods, next to a number of gods who are called by name, is a precaution: people wanted to make sure that no god was forgotten.[5] That is why they

---

1 Cp. Joüon (1923) 129 j; *GK* 128 v.

2 The *y* must then be considered as a secondary addition; perhaps it was added at a time when *'l* + *m* was no longer understood. See Hummel (1957) 101; Freedman (1960) 104–105; *CMHE* 45–46, 152.

3 This expression suggests that 'sons of El' was a *terminus technicus* for 'gods', because, if taken literally, it would be a rather strange way to designate El.

4 Herrmann (1960).

5 Herrmann admits this possibility in another article on the subject, in which he concedes that *bn il* may sometimes refer to all gods; see Herrmann (1982) 98–100.

would invoke one god too many, rather than erroneously pass one over. Thus, for instance, Hittite state contracts mention 'the thousand gods'[6]; this way of putting it is prudent as well as economical. H. S. Versnel[7] writes about this phenomenon in the Greek and Roman world, mentioning i.a. sacrifices and prayers in Mycenaean texts from Cnossos to 'all gods', sometimes next to individual gods.

The reference to the $p\langle h\rangle r$ $b'l$ is not clear; but as it occurs in combination with dr il, not with bn il, we cannot draw any conclusions concerning the latter.

As to the passage in the Aqhat epic, Herrmann drops this argument in his article in UF, saying that bn il may also be singular and a synonym of Baal. Indeed, this seems to be a possible explanation[8]; but even if bn il is plural, it does not follow that Baal is not counted among the bn il. Moreover, should bn il be a singular here, we may draw a further conclusion. We may then conclude from this text (seeing that Baal normally passes as the son of Dagan), that there was a tendency to regard El as the father of any god, whatever his descent according to tradition. In fact, the formula tr il abh is also used with reference to Baal (e.g. KTU 1.4 IV 47). The contradiction, when Baal is also called the son of Dagan, probably did not trouble the Ugaritans. Presumably the literal meaning of bn il was already fading away in their time.[9]

It could also be argued that Atirat, who is the wife of El, is regularly called $qnyt$ ilm, creatress of the gods, without specification of these gods. KTU 1.3 V 38–39, 1.4 IV 51, V 1 have ilm in parallelism with bn $atrt$. The context refers to the house of Baal every time, which he has to possess like the gods and like the sons of Atirat. In KTU 1.4 V 28 this formula is varied; we have here bt lk km ahk, a house for you like your brothers. His brothers, then, are 'the gods', 'the sons of Atirat' – which is in accordance with the idea that Baal is the son of El. Therefore, this text too pleads for the gods being conceived as one big family, the sons (and daughters) of El and his spouse.

A refutation of Herrmann's opinion seemed necessary in connection with the bny $'lym$ in Ps. XXIX.[10] This expression has been interpreted by

6 E.g. $ANET^3$ 206.
7 Versnel (1981) 13; see $Docs$ 303–312.
8 Cp. De Moor (1971) 42.
9 Cp. p. 16 n. 3.
10 It is also a counter-argument against Rendtorff (1966), 288, who uses Herrmann's findings as an additional argument, that El cannot be regarded without qualification as the head of the pantheon.

J. L. Cunchillos[11] as having to do in some way especially with El.[12] Cunchillos, who has written a substantial monograph on Ps. xxix (307 pages), regards the *bny 'lym* in the psalm as an 'Elistic' datum (in contrast to 'Baalistic' and 'Yahwistic' data in the psalm). The expression *bny 'lym* is one of the indications, according to Cunchillos, that the author of Ps. xxix wanted to identify Yhwh with El. It should be stressed that it does not seem to be the representation of Yhwh amidst other gods who are paying homage, which has given rise to this opinion. On the contrary, Cunchillos (following H. Cazelles[13] and Th. H. Gaster[14]) repeatedly compares this scene with Enuma Elish (VI 140–144: the honouring of Marduk by the other gods); moreover he states expressly that the title *mlk* (and the homage which accompanies it), in Ps. xxix as also, often, in Mesopotamia and Canaan, is given to the highest god who has earned this position by his struggle with the powers of chaos. This does not point to ideas connected with El. Surprisingly enough Cunchillos at the same time calls the idea of a king-god surrounded by a court of subordinate heavenly beings a theme connected with El, and regards Yhwh's title *mlk* in Ps. xxix as a sign of the intention to assimilate Yhwh to El. How this is to be rhymed with the earlier-mentioned statements is not made clear; anyway, one gains the impression that it is not in the first place the homage given to a highest god, which has caused Cunchillos to think of such an assimilation, but, quite literally, the expression *bny 'lym*. This term is put by him on his list of 'Elistic motifs', where the 'paying of homage' is missing (as is the title *mlk*). Moreover, Cunchillos keeps hinting that it is important to the interpretation, whether *'lym* was felt as the proper name El or not. This appears from the following:

At Ugarit, Cunchillos states, *bn ilm* referred to the circle of El (although he adds that it does not follow that the term had the same meaning in Israel: there it perhaps simply meant 'all gods' – apart from Yhwh). Against the opinion of F. Stolz[15], that Ps. xxix (because of *'l* in vs. 3) was originally dedicated to El, Cunchillos argues that *'l in vs. 1* and vs. 3 need not be a proper name; apparently he thinks that 'sons of El' can only pay homage to El himself, while gods in general can honour

11 Cunchillos (1976) Chs. I, IV, VIII.
12 According to Herrmann, the term has become a *terminus technicus* in the OT, which need not necessarily be connected with El.
13 Cazelles (1961).
14 Gaster (1946/47); Gaster (1961) 443–446. Gaster's important theory will be discussed below (p. 99–100).
15 Stolz (1970) 152–155.

other gods than El. In this light Cunchillos's remark becomes understandable, that if the original hymn intended to represent Baal as the head of the pantheon, *bn ilm* must have been an appellative.[16] In other words: 'sons of El' cannot be the subordinates of Baal, but '(sons of the) gods' can. In another passage Cunchillos suggests that, if the hymn was originally dedicated to Baal, vss. 1–2 could have meant that the gods from the circle of El had to put their power into the service of Baal (and after the Yahweization of the hymn, that they had to give their aid to Yhwh against Baal); this would then have to be seen against the background of the growing influence of Baal and the diminishing importance of El. Again we observe that in the opinion of Cunchillos 'sons of El' naturally praise and obey only El; when they do not, there must be a special reason for it, such as a shifting of allegiance.

Now although Cunchillos uses the argument against Stolz, that *'l(ym)* need not be a proper name in vs. 1 (and vs. 3), he nevertheless feels free to produce the expression *bny 'lym* as a witness to Yhwh's identification with El by the author of Ps. xxix. As was the case with the (last-mentioned) suggestion about Baal, Cunchillos invents a dogmatical reason for the connection of the 'sons of El' with another god than El; it is now not so much a shifting of allegiance (by the gods, ergo by the maker of the hymn), as a purposeful melting together of two gods by the author. It should be noted that Cunchillos places Ps. xxix within the framework of the 'tactics' of Yahwism to identify Yhwh with El.

Against this theory I would observe that the 'sons of El' can be brought together with any god, since they are simply 'gods' (see above); it is not necessary to take *'lym* (*ilm*) as an appellative instead of a proper name, to arrive at this meaning. The term can in no way be regarded as an 'Elistic' motif: neither as an indication of an original dedication of the hymn to El, nor of a shifting of allegiance from El to another god, nor as an attempt to identify Yhwh with El.

The OT shows more traces of the belief in heavenly beings, other than Yhwh.[17] They play, however, no rôle of importance, and most often even their name has been changed (apart from Ps. LXXXIX 7; note also *'lm*, Ex. XV 11, and the archaizing *'l 'lym*, Dan. XI 36; *bny 'l coni*. Dt. XXXII 8.[18]

However, this does not mean to say that these gods have never been a

---

16 Only *ilm* must be meant.
17 See Cooke (1964); De Boer (1973).
18 See below (p. 207 n. 12).

reality in Israel, as is, for instance, maintained by F. C. Fensham.[19] Fensham states that, although traces of the Ugaritic conception of the *bn ilm* are still to be seen in Ps. xxix, the Israelites saw in the *bny 'lym* only 'angels', because it was impossible for them to believe in lesser gods in heaven. Possibly however, thus Fensham, at first *bny 'lym* in Ps. xxix was intended as a figure of speech, to denote that the gods of Canaan must worship Yhwh. Amongst these idols of Canaan was Baal himself. This does not mean, Fensham remarks, that the existence of idols was acknowledged, but that figurative language in a poetic form was used, to persuade faithless Israelites or Canaanites to accept Yhwh as god and not Baal.

I find this alleged 'impossibility' for the Israelites to have accepted other gods next to Yhwh hard to believe. Monotheism is not something that drops out of a clear sky; cp. the chapters written by H.-P. Müller and F. Stolz in the volume on monotheism edited by O. Keel.[20] Müller writes that the monolatrous disposition of the patriarchal narratives does not exclude occasional references to pairs and triads of gods nor contact with anonymous groups of numinous beings; furthermore, the first commandment is only a part of the *pre*history of monotheism. Stolz observes, that only with the exile does the evolution of monotheism enter into a completely new phase, which he calls 'Der allgemeine Durchbruch des Monotheismus'.

Of course a strong priestly class, devoted to the defense of a nationalistic ideology, can do much to carry through a monotheistic program; the writings of the OT testify to this. One can only guess how far the 'man in the street' kept pursuing his own religious needs; anyhow the OT testifies to these mishaps also. A just parallel seems to me to be the situation after Christianity had become a state religion: pagan gods continued to be revered nonetheless, because no authority of church or state was able to suppress the old habits completely. The only successful policy was, to adopt the old gods as saints.

One must, in my opinion, turn the argument the other way round; not: the Israelites cannot have believed in more than one god, therefore *bny 'lym* meant 'angels', not gods, but: *bny 'lym* means 'gods'; their appearance in an Israelite psalm suggests that the Israelites, at the time of origin of this psalm, reckoned with the existence of other gods than

19 Fensham (1963).
20 Cp. Lang (1981); cp. also the illuminating remarks made by Hartmann (1980) on 'Monotheismus', 'Monolatrie', 'Henotheismus' and 'Henolatrie'.

Yhwh. For the maker of this psalm these gods must have been 'real'; otherwise the scene of vss. 1–2 would have no point. 'Figurative language', which is thought to express that non-existent idols are called upon to worship Yhwh, seems to me beyond the grasp of most people.

But even if we remove the non-existence of the *bny 'lym* out of Fensham's theory, the remainder is unsatisfactory. To begin with, I cannot see how the maker of Ps. xxix could have had especially Baal in view when using the expression *bny 'lym*. Fensham's argument for this is, that in the Ugaritic texts the supremacy of Baal over the *bn ilm* is stressed; their adoration of Yhwh thus implies a degradation of Baal. But then, one may ask, what about the supremacy of El? The message of Ps. xxix would be rather obscure too: why not address Baal himself, when in fact he was meant?

Fensham will answer to this, that in the main part of the psalm Yhwh is represented in the same way as Baal. This fact in itself is thought by many authors (including Fensham) to express a polemic against the Baal religion, because the psalm would stress that it is Yhwh, not Baal, who possesses those qualities. I shall come back to this in the next chapter; for the moment it may suffice that this (together with the supremacy of Baal over the *bn ilm*) must have caused Fensham to think, that Ps. xxix 1–2 speak of a transfer of allegiance of the *bny 'lym* from Baal to Yhwh.

But this whole idea of a transfer of allegiance seems to me to be a wrong interpretation. The point is, that the *text itself* does not say anything about it. A theory like Fensham's could only be based on data outside the text, for instance, that at the time of origin of this text a movement existed in Israel, which made propaganda, i.a. by way of psalms, to abjure Baal and put Yhwh in his place. This is indeed what Fensham seems to think, as he calls Ps. xxix a 'missionary poem' or an 'evangelizing psalm', written to convert Canaanites or apostate Israelites. Now what is wanting is some indication that, at the time when polemics were carried on against the Baal cult (as by the prophets Elijah and Hosea), psalms were indeed being used as a weapon in these polemics. Fensham may think this probable; anyhow, the discussion would have to be based on historical data outside the text, as long as the text itself is not explicitly polemical.

Perhaps it seems self-evident to those who see a polemic in Ps. xxix 1–2, that the *bny 'lym* are the gods of a non-Israelite people; the polemic would then consist of the picture of the Israelite god being elevated above foreign gods.

I would counter to this that there is no indication, that the *bny 'lym* were 'foreign gods' to the Israelites. Moreover, the worship in itself does not express any degradation of the worshippers. That Ps. xxix 1–2 imply a degradation of the *bny 'lym* as compared to their former (non-Israelite) status, is explicitly postulated by W. Schlisske.[21] It should be noted however, that also outside Israel the *bn ilm as such* have never been anything else but an anonymous group: the heavenly population over against their king(s).

Schlisske stresses the fact, that outside Israel the *bn ilm* formed a council, whereas in Ps. xxix their consultative function has disappeared: here their only task consists of worshipping Yhwh. The *Vorlage* of the psalm presumably made mention of the council (Schlisske bases this on the conjecture of Th. H. Gaster, who supplies in vs. 9 *qhl qdšym yhllh*, thus contriving to have an antecedent to *klw*), but the adapter abridged the text, so that only the worship of the *bny 'lym* remained, as a proof of their total loss of power.

It is interesting to note how P. C. Craigie[22] theorizes the other way round: there is a continuous line of development from Ex. xv 1–18 to Ps. xxix, amongst other things because Ex. xv 11 mentions the *'lm*, whereas in Ps. xxix this concept has been worked out more fully. Whilst Schlisske assumes a development consisting of an abridgement (implying a 'demythicizing' of the traditional material), Craigie assumes an extension in the course of time. Of course both theories are completely gratuitous.

As to Schlisske's theory: even if Gaster's conjecture is right, the reconstructed text does not express an advisory function of the *qhl qdšym* any more than a simple mention of the *bny 'lym* (without a term for 'assembly') does: the task of the *qhl* would be only: to praise. No term indicating the 'council' could suggest an advisory practice in the given context, the 'council' being only a term to express 'the sum' of gods. Even leaving aside Gaster's reconstruction, the idea that the *bny 'lym* in Ps. xxix would have lost their power, because formerly they were a consultative body, does not reckon with a perfectly possible multifunctioning of the *bn ilm*; a citizen may advise *or* applaud his king. The occasion on hand impels the *bny 'lym* to worship, not to debate; a degradation is therefore out of the question (or one would have to suppose that a context like that of Ps. xxix could not have occurred outside Israel).

21 Schlisske (1973) 47–54.
22 Craigie (1972).

One argument of the 'polemics' party remains to be considered, which is based on the translation of *hbw ʿz* in Ps. XXIX 1. Both H. Cazelles and J. L. Cunchillos have explained this expression as an intention to devaluate the *bny 'lym*. I shall discuss this below, in connection with the explanation of *hbw ʿz*.

In any case, the OT knows of the concept of other gods next to Yhwh; Ps. XXIX clearly retains the idea of a god being honoured by the other gods, which is, as Gunkel[23] first observed, a well-known feature of Near-Eastern hymns. Already from the fact that Gunkel mentions, in this respect, hymns to Marduk, Sin and Amon-Re it becomes clear, that there is no reason to see in the 'giving of *kbwd*' in Ps. XXIX a reminiscence of ideas connected with El, as has been done by some.

kbwd

W. H. Schmidt[24], discussing the influence which the concept of Yhwh's kingship underwent from that of the kingship of El, mentions in this regard texts in which Yhwh is pictured enthroned amid a court of heavenly beings (I Kgs. XXII 19; Is. VI 1–2), and texts in which homage is paid to Yhwh as king-god (Ps. XXII 29–30; XXIX 2; XCV 6; XCVI 9; XCVII 7; XCIX 5, 9; Zech. XIV 16–17); especially the term *kbwd*, connected with Yhwh, would point to influence from the concept of the kingship of El (Ps. XIX 2; XXIV 7–10; XXIX 1–2, 9; Is. VI 3; Jer. XIV 21; XVII 12). Baal is also king but, Schmidt observes, there is no assembly of Baal (*KTU* 1.39 7 *p⟨ḫ⟩r bʿl* is an uncertain text[25]), and Baal does not receive homage, such as the gods pay to El. Ps. XXIX thus combines, according to Schmidt, a representation of Yhwh as Baal (vss. 3–9b) with a representation of Yhwh as El – which would plead against considering Ps. XXIX an ancient Baal hymn; on the contrary it would suggest an origin of the psalm in Israel, where El and Baal characteristics were combined in the picture of Yhwh.

23 Gunkel (1926) *ad locum*, with literature.
24 Schmidt (1961) 20–21, 23, 47.
25 Mullen (1980), 117 n. 14, points out that on the basis of line 12 most scholars reconstruct *p⟨g⟩r bʿl*, body/corpse of Baal. When Mullen writes, however, that the other (supposed) occurrences of the expression (*KTU* 1.41 16; 1.87 18) are also reconstructions, he is partly wrong. Mullen has apparently not used the *KTU* edition. In this edition, which is based on a fresh examination of the tablets, the text of 1.87 18 reads *il.w pḫr b**[; the end of line 17 is lacking. Thus, *pḫr* is clearly legible; the *b* is damaged, but recognizable, according to Dietrich-Loretz-Sanmartín.

C. Westermann[26] distinguishes between an Israelite and a Canaanite component of the concept *kbwd*. Israelite: the honour which one pays to Yhwh by an act, the honour which is due to Yhwh, recognition, sometimes: atonement (when his honour was injured); this implied that history was seen as the domain in which Yhwh's *kbwd* became manifest. Canaanite: the cultic honour, the honouring of the glory of the god who sits enthroned in his temple, the glory of God which manifests itself in nature (e.g. Ps. XIX 2; LVII 6, 12); this went back to the concept of the *kbwd* of El and belonged especially to the Jerusalem cult. Texts like Ps. XXIV and Is. VI, Westermann observes, show a connection with the Jerusalem temple, where elements from the Canaanite cult were preserved, notably the concept of the *kbwd* of El. In Ps. XXIV 7–10 Yhwh is called *mlk hkbwd*, while vss. 1–2 mention his work of creation; in Is. VI 5 Yhwh is called *mlk*, while according to vs. 3 the whole land is filled with his *kbwd*. Ps. XXIX, thus Westermann, shows the Canaanite use of the term *kbwd*: the cultic honour (vss. 1–2, 9) and the glory of God which manifests itself in nature (vs. 3; cp. vss. 4–9).

Before I answer to this, I want to make a remark about the use of the term 'cultic honour'. In my opinion this term is out of place in the case of Ps. XXIX; its use should be restricted to the homage paid by man, as in the variation on Ps. XXIX 1–2, found in Ps. XCVI and 1 Chron. XVI. Ps. XCVI 7–9a and 1 Chron. XVI 28–29 repeat Ps. XXIX 1–2 almost literally, the alterations being the changing of *bny 'lym* into *mšpḥwt 'mym* and the adding of 'bring an offering and come into his fore-courts/before him'. The 'families of nations' testify to a demythologizing of these lines, by a writer who apparently took offence at the idea of a company of gods around Yhwh. Only with this change can one speak of a cult proper, as also appears from the 'offering' and the 'forecourts'. The scene in Ps. XXIX is, of course, situated in the heavenly palace (see vs. 9).[27] One could speak here of 'cultic honour', I think, only in an indirect way, that is to say if one imagines the psalm being sung by human worshippers, who put their praises into the mouths of the gods.

26 Westermann, *ThHAT* I, 803–806.
27 I cannot share the opinion of Loretz (1974), 191–195, who regards vss. 2, 3b and 9c as glosses, by which the scene is transferred to the Jerusalem temple, where Yhwh's *kbwd* is present. The 'stichometric analysis', on which the determination of glosses is based, implying the counting of the number of consonants in each unit, does not seem to me a sound base for text-criticism. By itself it is not clear why the so-called glosses would have to be connected with the Jerusalem temple; anyhow, if they are not glosses, there has not been a transfer of the scene from the abode of the gods to the place of human worship.

24

Thus, there are two claims made for *kbwd* in Ps. xxix: it is thought to stem from a Canaanite complex of ideas connected with El as king because 1) the deity receives *kbwd* from the other gods; 2) the *kbwd* of the deity is seen in nature.

Now it seems to me rash to conclude, just because maybe some texts picture Yhwh as El while at the same time mentioning his *kbwd*, that every text which speaks of the latter (in one of the so-called 'Canaanite' senses) must necessarily represent Yhwh as El. This contention would stand on more solid ground if the *kbd* of El were indeed a concept which is found in extra-biblical texts.[28] In fact, it is not.

There are some personal names in Amorite with the root *kbd*, but not with the element *il*: *ka-bi-da*, *ka-bi-da-ia*, *ka-bi-it-ta*, *ga-bi-da-nu-um*, *ka-ab-tu-ka-a-bi*, *i-bi-iš-ga-bi-id*, *mu-ut-ga-bi-id*.[29] At Ugarit, *PTU*[30] lists as personal names *ka₄-bid-na-na* (a theophoric name according to *PTU*, where the second element is explained as the Mesopotamian goddess Nana(ya)), *kabid(DUGUD)-ia-nu*, *ma-ar-ka-bu-di*, *bin-ka-bu-di-ya*, and *bn kbd*. The names containing the element 'son' may be theophoric (see below); the element *il* however is absent.

Punic inscriptions contain, apart from the name *kbdt* (22 times), two theophoric names with this root: *kbdmlqrt* (*CIS* I 364 5–6; 2416 2) and *kbd'štrt* (*CIS* I 5945 2–3).[31] Furthermore, *kbd* as a noun occurs in Neopunic, in the combination *skr kbd*, glorious memory (*KAI* 123 4; 161 5), and in the expression *bkbd t'ṣmty*, in my (his) great honour (?) (*CIS* I 6000 bis 7).[32]

When we look at the occurrence of the verb *kbd*, to honour, there are, apart from Ugarit, two cases to be noted: the Kilamuwa inscription (*KAI* 24 14–15) and *EA* 245 39; in both cases the object is constituted by human persons.[33] Possibly, the verb is found on a ceramic vessel from Hazor's stratum VI (IDAM 72–116, 8th century), where J. Naveh[34] reads *lmkbdym* instead of *lmkbrm*. Naveh takes this to indicate that the container belonged to the food-servers. Anyhow, a connection with El is not shown by this.

28 OT texts – see Ps. xix 2 *kbwd 'l* – can furnish no proof, as *'l* is commonly used as a designation of Yhwh in the OT.
29 Gelb 304, 579, 589, 612, 626.
30 *PTU* 44, 52, 148, 159–160, 167.
31 Benz 131, 330.
32 *DISO* s.v. *kbd* II. Possibly, *bkbdt 'ṣmty* should be read in *CIS* I 6000 bis 7, to the honour of my (his) bones; see *DISO* s.v. *t'ṣmh*.
33 *DISO* s.v. *kbd* I.
34 Naveh (1981).

In the Ugaritic texts, the substantive *kbd* occurs with the meaning 'liver', 'inside'. It might have another meaning in *KTU* 1.123 21, which reads *kbd il gb/d*.[35] J. C. de Moor[36] takes *kbd* to be the name of a deity in this text; he translates 'Kabidu, who is the god Gabi[du?]'. If *kbd* is a deity, this may also explain some of the personal names. The existence of a deity called *kbd* is also assumed by F. de Meyer[37], who however does not regard *kbd* in *KTU* 1.123 21 as a divine name, but as a liver which is offered to the deity. P. Xella renders the text with '*kbd* del dio del *gb* (?)'; he suggests that *kbd* might refer here to an 'honorific gift'.[38] The text is too obscure, however, to justify conclusions concerning the 'glory of El'.

The verb *kbd* (d-stem) in Ugaritic means 'to honour', literally 'to make heavy' (cp. the adjective *kbd*, heavy); part. ni. 'valuable'. This verb is found in a formula, which survives in Ps. XXIX; it contains the verbs 'to bow down' (*yšthwy* or *tšthwy*) and 'to honour'. The formula is also preserved in Ps. LXXXVI 9, where the *gwym* are the subject; furthermore in Ps. XCVI 7–9a and in 1 Chron. XVI 28–29, already mentioned above. A relic of the formula is found in Ps. XCVII 6–7 (the '*mym* see the *kbwd* and the '*lhym* are requested to bow down) and in Ps. CVI 19–20 (they bowed down to an image and exchanged their *kbwd* for the image of a bull). In the Ugaritic texts, the formula sometimes has the form of an exhortation (to messengers), just like in Ps. XXIX. As the subject as well as the object of this formula are always gods, we are now in a position to judge claim 1, viz that the deity is represented as El in Ps. XXIX because of the *kbwd* paid to him by the other gods.

It should be noted, then, that the object in this formula is not exclusively El: against five times El (*KTU* 1.1 III 25; 1.2 III 6; 1.4 IV 26; 1.6 I 38; 1.17 VI 50–51) we have once Mot (*KTU* 1.4 VIII 28–29), twice Anat (*KTU* 1.1 II 16–17; 1.3 III 10), and twice Ktr w Hss (*KTU* 1.1 III 3; 1.3 VI 19–20).[39] This formula describes the greeting, when a visit is paid by a god (or by divine messengers) to another god. The one who pays the visit does the homage, but can in his turn be honoured on

35 This is the reading of the *KTU* edition. In *Ugaritica* V, an additional *d* is read after *kbd*.
36 De Moor (1970) 201 no. 125.
37 De Meyer (1980).
38 Xella (1981) 218, 370. The meaning of *gb* is not wholly clear; according to Xella, 365, it was a part of the palace which was reserved for the cult. See also the discussion of the term by De Tarragon (1980), 100–101.
39 Partly reconstructions.

receiving a visitor. The case of El is only an exception in as far as El does not pay visits. Moreover, mention is never made of honour paid to El by all gods together.

Apart from the formula, *kbd* (d-stem) appears twice more in the Ugaritic texts, sc. *KTU* 1.17 V 20, 30. In this passage Ktr w Ḥss visit king Danel, who asks his wife to 'give the gods food and drink, serve them and do them honour (*kbd*)', whereupon his wife fulfills this request. This is the sole case in the Ugaritic texts of the verb *kbd* being used of humans honouring gods; but it has nothing to do with the cult, only with common hospitality. Neither is it El who is thus regaled.

For these reasons, I cannot see an unambiguous reference to El in the request to the gods, to give *kbwd* and to bow down to Yhwh. Of course, El was the head of the pantheon, while Yhwh is the highest god present in Ps. xxix. But I think that this is not enough justification to see in the scene of Ps. xxix 1–2 a reminiscence of El. I would prefer the following view: when Yhwh became the most important, and in the long run even the sole god for the Israelites, he naturally assumed traits which at Ugarit belonged to El, for instance being the president of a heavenly council (1 Kgs. xxii 19–22; Ps. lxxxii; Job i–ii). The texts that we have are apparently mostly from a period when the decline of the other gods had become a fact. We are well acquainted, therefore, with the El-like traits of Yhwh; but we must not forget that he need not necessarily have had those from the beginning: that assumption needs proof, especially when we observe that the El-like traits are balanced by other aspects. Now if we see Ps. xxix in the light of the OT as a whole, we are apt to jump to conclusions: we are used to regarding Yhwh as the supreme god, in which quality he is a successor of El, and we see this picture confirmed by the scene in which the *bny 'lym* pay homage to Yhwh. Our fault is, then, to have taken the OT as a whole. I want to stress that, methodologically speaking, the only thing that is correct is, to consider if the *paying of homage* makes Yhwh a successor of El. This is not so, as I hope to have shown above. When one nevertheless feels inclined to regard Yhwh's elevation above the gods in Ps. xxix as a sign of his 'El-ship', he is influenced, in my opinion, by the occurrence of El-like traits in other parts of the OT.

A god who does receive homage from other gods, and in a more meaningful way than as a simple greeting, is, contrary to what Schmidt says, Baal. In Ps. xxix the deity is represented as king (vs. 10; the homage is paid in his palace, vs. 9). Baal too is honoured as king. This is done by the following words: *mlkn.aliyn.bʿl.tptn/in.d ʿlnh* (*KTU* 1.3 V

32–33), spoken by Anat; in *KTU* 1.4 IV 43–44 the same words (with the insertion of *w* before *in*) are spoken by Atirat: The victor Baal is our king, our ruler (or: judge); there is no one above him. It is interesting to note what E. Lipiński[40] writes about these words. He calls them an attestation of loyalty ('profession de fidélité') in front of a third party; as parallels he adduces Is. xxxiii 22 *ky yhwh špṭnw yhwh mḥqqnw yhwh mlknw*: For Yhwh is our ruler, Yhwh is our commander, Yhwh is our king; Enuma elish V 151–152 *pa-na-ma be-lum ma-a-ru ⟨na-ram-ni⟩/i-nanna šar-ra-ni*: Before, the lord (i.e. Marduk) was our beloved son; now, he is our king; and the words of the conquered adversaries of Asarhaddon[41] *an-nu-u šar-ra-ni*: He is our king. It seems to me that the scene in Ps. xxix is comparable with this. The gods, in paying homage to Yhwh, recognize his 'eternal kingship' (vs. 10); this resembles the formal pledge in the examples quoted above.

The supposition remains that Yhwh's *kbwd* in nature is a concept which goes back to a Canaanite conception of the glory of El (of course such a conception could have existed although it was not termed *kbd*). I find this questionable. For one thing, Westermann uses the terms 'creation' and 'phenomena of nature' rather indiscriminately. It is not the same thing at all when Ps. xxiv 1–2 speak of the earth being Yhwh's possession because he has created it, and when Ps. xxix describes a theophany in a thunder-storm. The thunder is the mode of Baal's manifestation, not of that of El.

But apart from that, the picture of El as manifesting himself especially in the work of creation is misleading. Of course, the epithet *qn 'rṣ* (e.g. *KAI* 26 A III 18) testifies to El's creatorship[42]; but El is at least as much a god who is concerned with the events in the lives of gods and men, as the epics of Baal, of Keret and of Aqhat confirm. This state of affairs is aptly described by F. M. Cross[43]: 'The one image of 'El that seems to tie all of his myths together is that of the patriarch. Unlike the great gods who represent the powers behind the phenomena of nature, 'El is in the first instance a social god. He is the primordial father of gods and men, sometimes stern, often compassionate, always wise in judgment'. One

---

40 Lipiński (1965) 389–391, 432.
41 Borger 44 l. 77.
42 It is to be noted, however, that we cannot be absolutely sure that the epithet refers to El's creation of the earth; it might refer to his possession of it. Cp. *DISO s.v. qny* I, II, and the literature cited there.
43 *CMHE* 42.

might also recall *KTU* 1.128 14–16, where El is called *il brt* and *il dn* (cp. Judg. IX 46).[44]

With his distinction between an 'Israelite' and a 'Canaanite' component of the concept *kbwd*, Westermann seems to have fallen prey to the presupposition, that 'nature' is the speciality of the gods outside Israel, and 'history' that of the Israelite god. Anyway, we find in the OT both the *kbwd* which is seen in creation and the *kbwd* which is seen in the events in the life of man. To isolate herein a specifically Israelite part, and to call that which remains 'influenced by Canaanite ideas', seems to be based on a preconceived notion. After the important study of B. Albrektson[45], who however deals only with Mesopotamian and Hittite material, N. Wyatt[46] has tried to remove such prejudices as may exist on this subject with respect to the West Semitic world.

We have one more study to consider, in which the existence of the concept of the 'honour' of El is defended, be it not expressed by the term *kbd*. I am referring to an article by B. Margulis[47], in which it is argued that the main theme of Ps. XXIX is the *kbwd* of Yhwh. The psalm describes, according to Margulis, how the divine *kbwd* (which is manifest in the form of a fiery storm-cloud) makes its way from the Sinai-region to the temple in Jerusalem, where it is finally enthroned. The psalm has its origin in the Jerusalem cult, Margulis observes, because the temple of Solomon is mentioned in vs. 9; an additional argument is the previous existence, at this temple, of a Canaanite *kbwd*-theology centered around the royal cult of El (cp. Gen. XIV 18–20). Margulis thinks that there is a direct line of development from this Canaanite *kbwd*-theology to its subsequent Israelite manifestation.

For the notion of the honour of El Margulis refers to *KTU* 1.108 1–3[48]; this text reads:

1 [ ]*n.yšt.rpu.mlk.'lm.w yšt*
2 ⟨*il*⟩*gtr.w yqr.il.ytb.b 'ttrt*
3 *il tpẓ.b hd r'y*

---

44 Laroche (*Ugaritica* V, 515), however, suggests the translation 'El des sources' for *il brt*. – On the concept of the 'covenant', theological as well as secular, an interesting article has been written by Kitchen (1979).
45 Albrektson (1967).
46 Wyatt (1979).
47 Margulis (*Bibl* 1970).
48 See also Margulis's treatment of this text in *JBL* (1970).

In the translation of Margulis:

Lo! (the?) Rapha, eternal king, imbibes
(the gods) imbibe *gṯr*;
(While) the Honour of El sits (enthroned) in Ashtaroth
El rules in (H)/Edrei.

The concept *yqr* = *kbwd* is also found, Margulis observes, in personal names in Amorite[49] and Ugaritic[50]; furthermore he points to *yqr* = *kbwd* in late biblical and in middle Hebrew. I may note in passing that the personal names do not contain the element *il*.

Leaving aside for the moment Margulis's interpretation of Ps. xxix as a whole, I want to put a question-mark to the 'Canaanite *kbwd*-theology' connected with El. Unfortunately *KTU* 1.108 is a problematical text. As to the identity of the subject(s) of lines 1–3, a difference of opinion still exists. A survey of opinions (and of their subscribers) can be found in an article by M. Dietrich and O. Loretz.[51] Now we might give to Margulis the benefit of the doubt and assume that the deity is El; but even then his proposition is questionable. I find the solution of Virolleaud in *Ugaritica* V (followed by many authors) preferable, viz to connect *gṯr w yqr* and to take these words as epithets of the preceding *il*: (le dieu) fort et majestueux. (For *gṯr* cp. Acc. *gašru*, strong; the root *yqr* is common Semitic and has, as an adjective, the sense of 'valued', 'honoured', 'precious'.) Then we have the parallelism *rpu mlk 'lm//il gṯr w yqr*. Even more weighty as an argument is the parallelism *il yṯb b 'ṯtrt//il tpẓ b hd rʿy*, which would be destroyed with Margulis's division of the lines; this should be a sufficient reason to take *gṯr* and *yqr* together. (C. E. L'-Heureux[52] takes *gṯr*, like Margulis does, to be a kind of drink, but he saves the parallelism of the following lines by combining *gṯr* and *yqr*, giving to *yqr* the sense of 'highly valued wine'.)

Of course one could remark that, even with Virolleaud's translation, the epithet *yqr* is applied to El (always assuming that the deity *is* El). Only we then do not have a hypostatization of the Majesty of El – which is not a minor point in Margulis's theory. I may remind the reader of the 'fiery storm-cloud', which is, according to Margulis, the form that Yhwh's *kbwd* has taken on (he accordingly translates Ps. xxix

49 Huffmon 214.
50 *PTU* 145.
51 Dietrich-Loretz (1980) 171–172.
52 L'Heureux (1979) 169–172.

9c–10 with 'The "Honour(-cloud)" of Yahweh is enthroned'; I shall come back to this below[53]).

Dietrich-Loretz are opposed to the pairing of *gṯr* and *yqr*, on grounds that fail to convince me (that this would be the only occurrence of this pair, and that *yqr* occurs nowhere else in the Ugaritic texts as an adjective). Their solution is, to take *yqr* as a verbal form ('es verweile', of a verb *qrr*), of which the following *il* (twice) is the subject. But with their interpretation the parallelism *il yṯb*//*il ṯpẓ* (etc.) remains intact; it plays indeed an important rôle in their argument.

Lastly I want to draw attention to an interesting article by S. Ribichini and P. Xella, who take *yqr* as the Yaqaru who founded the dynasty of Ugarit.[54] Their translation 'e *Yqr il* risiede in 'Aṯtarot, il divino *ṯapizu* (risiede) in Edrei' neglects, however, the parallelistic structure. Nonetheless it is worth mentioning that *il yqr* occurs on the list of the deified kings of Ugarit (*KTU* 1.113 26).

Thus the least one could say about the supposed concept of the 'Honour of El' is, that it is based on very uncertain textual evidence. Moreover, if this concept indeed formed a part of the Canaanite 'theology', it is surprising that no other texts speak of it.

The conclusion, therefore, must be that a connection of Yhwh with El cannot be demonstrated from the words *hbw kbwd*. This assumption could only be based on the fact that some texts, which speak of Yhwh's *kbwd*, apparently belonged to the cult of the Jerusalem temple, where El seems to have been worshipped in pre-Israelite times; but it remains a mere hypothesis.

A theory also exists, according to which the term *kbwd* can be associated with the theophany of the storm-god. This will be discussed in connection with the expression *'l-hkbwd* in Ps. xxix 3.

The Ugaritic formula, consisting of the verbs 'to bow down' and 'to honour', has undergone minor changes in Hebrew (also at Ugarit the formula was subject to variations in number, gender and mode of the verbs): in Ps. xxix the sequence of the two verbs has been changed, and the verb *kbd* is circumscribed by the substantive *kbwd* + the verb 'to give'; moreover the Ugaritic formula is longer: it contains, apart from *y*/*tštḥwy*, two other verbs meaning 'to bow down' (*hbr* and *ql*; these do not interrupt the sequence of *y*/*tštḥwy* and *kbd*, however). As to the other OT passages containing this formula see above, p. 26. It is to be

53 P. 56; cp. p. 61.
54 Ribichini-Xella (1979) 154–156.

noted, that Ps. LXXXVI 9 stands closer to Ugaritic; here the sequence of the two verbs has not been changed, and 'to honour' is rendered by the verb *kbd*. The change we observe in Ps. XXIX, the further change (sc. of the addressee) in Ps. XCVI and I Chron. XVI, and the larger deviations found in Ps. XCVII and in Ps. CVI, testify to the freedom, with which the Hebrew poets handled the traditional material. S. Gevirtz[55] calls our attention to this phenomenon; in his article lists are presented of standard parallel pairs, which show that, though often the sequence in Hebrew is the same as in Ugaritic, it is sometimes reversed. When discussing the poetic form of Ps. XXIX (in the next chapter), I shall return to the subject of the development which Hebrew poetry presents as compared to Ugaritic. The fact of this development should not obscure the dependency, however. When, for instance, Fensham and, following him, Cunchillos mention *kbwd* as an example of something typically Israelite in Ps. XXIX (which they seem to take as a contraindication to a Canaanite background of the psalm), because the substantive *kbd* is not found in Ugaritic in the sense of 'honour', they overstress the new development at the cost of the likeness. Philologically and poetically Hebrew has brought something new in this case, but it is an old formula which has been used.

The formula is extended in Ps. XXIX with *'z* and with *kbwd šmw* as additional objects of *hbw*. The latter does not present a difficulty (although it did to the LXX and the Vulgate, which translate *šmw* as a dative): the 'honour of his name' must be the honour, due to his name, i.e. the honour due to him. O. Grether[56] states, that especially in the psalms and in the later prophets the 'name' is often used to indicate Yhwh himself, mainly with verbs expressing praise or scorn. E. Lipiński gives examples of such a use of the 'name' in Accadian psalms, also mainly with verbs expressing praise.[57]

hbw 'z

The expression *hbw 'z* is less clear at first sight. I do not think that Lipiński[58] is right when he takes *'z* to mean 'gloire', because it is often paralleled by *tp'rt*; cp. too the expression *'z whdr* (Prov. XXXI 25) over

55 Gevirtz (1961).
56 Grether (1934) 38–39.
57 Lipiński (1965) 312–314.
58 Lipiński (1965) 115.

against *kbwd whdr* (Ps. VIII 6). In my opinion *hbw 'z* is best explained by the comparable expressions in Dt. XXXII 3 and Ps. LXVIII 35.

Dt. XXXII 3 *ky šm yhwh 'qr' hbw gdl l'lhynw*: for I shall exclaim the name of Yhwh, give greatness to our god.

Ps. LXVIII 33 *šyrw l'lhym zmrw 'dny*: sing of God[59]), chant the Lord; 35 *tnw 'z l'lhym*: give strength to God.

The context in these passages indicates, that 'to give greatness' or 'strength' means 'to praise', indubitably by exclaiming that the god is great c.q. strong.[60]

This reminds one of the ancient Roman religion, viz of the term *mactare* = to sacrifice. Whereas the construction of this verb in classical Latin has become *mactare* + acc. (the object, that which is sacrificed) + dat. (the one to whom the sacrifice is offered, the deity), it was in older Latin *mactare* + acc. (the object, the deity) + *abl. instrumenti*; the meaning was 'to strengthen by'. Cp. Cato, De re rustica 141 (prayer of the farmer to Mars) *Mars pater... macte hisce suovetaurilibus lactentibus immolandis esto*: Father Mars, be strengthened by these suckling *suovetaurilia* which are to be offered. (*Mactus* is from a root *ma/eg(h)* – , cp. *magnus*, *magis, maior* ⟨*magior*; accordingly it means 'made great, made powerful'.) This shows that the belief existed, that the deity was made strong (or great) by the sacrifice; of course a god who is strong is more capable of lending succour to man.

One may compare too Vergil, Aeneis I 704 *flammis adolere Penates*, commonly translated 'to kindle the (fireplaces of the) Penates with flames'; but note the commentary of Servius ad Aen. I 704: *adolere est augere* (i.e. to cause to grow), and especially Nonius Marcellus, De compendiosa doctrina (a lexicographical work) I, Lindsay 81, *Adolere verbum est proprie sacra reddentium, quod significat votis vel supplicationibus numen auctius facere*: *Adolere* is, properly speaking, a term having to do with those who sacrifice; it means: to make the god more powerful by votive offerings or prayers. Marcellus then refers to the expression *macte esto* and to Aen. I 704.

Perhaps those philologists indeed retained the memory of the proper etymology. Anyhow, in the case of *mactare* the original meaning seems

---

59 Cp. De Boer (1981).

60 Ps. LXVIII 36 adds *brwk 'lhym*, which signifies according to Wehmeier (1970), 117, that God is full of *brkh*. Toll (1982) translates *brwk* with 'Inhaber von Kraft'; he defends the meaning 'potency', 'power', for *brkh*. This meaning of *brwk* accords very well with my explanation of *tnw 'z*.

certain.[61] This magico-religious idea might form the background of the term *hbw/tnw ʿz*, although we may justly translate it with 'proclaim the strength (of God)'. The thought, that the power of God is augmented for the benefit of man, is expressed too by Ps. LXVIII: after 'give strength to God' follows in vs. 36 'the god of Israel, it is he who gives strength and might to the people'.

In Ps. XXIX this last thought is also present: Yhwh will give strength (*ʿz*) to his people (vs. 11). But the immediate sequel to *hbw ʿz* is the main part of the psalm, in which Yhwh needs strength for his own purpose.

To assume that 'to give strength' is done by proclaiming the power of the deity, implies, at the same time, a rejection of the explanation of H. Cazelles and J. L. Cunchillos. As I observed above, these share with Fensham the idea, that the *bny ʾlym* are in some way or other the adversaries of Yhwh. In their opinion *hbw ʿz* is an exhortation to the *bny ʾlym* to surrender their power to Yhwh (together with their *kbwd*, their glory, which is taken by Cunchillos in a concrete sense: the luminous splendour which surrounds the deity, which is a manifestation of his vital power[62]).

To explain *hbw ʿz* as 'surrendering one's power', however, seems impossible to me if it were only for the lack of a suffix to 'z (*your* might). This highly forced translation is again due to preconceived ideas concerning the religion of Israel. A further example of going beyond the evidence of the text itself is provided by Cunchillos, when he supposes that the way in which vss. 1–2 were understood by the Israelites must have undergone a development in the course of time. As a general idea this stems from Cazelles, who speaks of a 'relecture', i.e. a reinterpretation of the psalm in later times, but Cazelles does not apply it to vss. 1–2. According to Cunchillos, the thought that the *bny ʾlym* have to give their glory and might to Yhwh can only belong to an early stage of Israel's history, implying as it does that the *bny ʾlym* in fact possess these attributes. In a later stage this cannot have been believed by the Israelites. Now it is also possible – thus Cunchillos – to translate *hbw* with 'come!'. It is true that the interjectional function is only certain with the form *hbh*, but as there is, generally speaking, a fluctuation between the categories of imperative and interjection, this might also apply to *hbw*. In the time of the Deuteronomist, then, vss. 1–2 must have meant

61 Cp. Latte (1960) 45 n. 2.
62 For this sense of *kbwd* Cunchillos refers to Cassin (1968); this will be discussed below (p. 56–59; cp. p. 56 n. 130). See Cunchillos (1976) 35–50.

according to Cunchillos: Come! To Yhwh belong the *bny 'lym*; Come! To Yhwh belong the glory and the might; (etc.).

These *bny 'lym* are then conceived as the 'forces of nature', or the 'powers of creation', as Cunchillos alternately calls them. In between Cunchillos postulates yet another stage, in which *hbw kbwd* meant that the gods had to repent or to honour Yhwh (this 'repentance' is based on the meaning of *śym kbwd* in Josh. VII 19 and *tnw kbwd* in Jer. XIII 16).

Now in the first place I would say, that no method exists to make out whether a text has been reinterpreted, when commentaries on the text are wanting and the text itself has undergone no changes. Secondly, Cunchillos's idea is based on a theory about what the Israelites must have believed, such as the repentance of the gods, whereas this meaning of 'to give *kbwd*' could only be deduced from the context. The context in Ps. XXIX in no way suggests such a meaning. In the third place Cunchillos's view on grammar is too theoretical. The extensive treatment of the relationship between imperatives and interjections[63], in the course of which Cunchillos expresses the wish that more research be done on the subject, disregards the way in which the living language functions.

Grammar is only an attempt to describe a complex reality, but this reality does not always let itself be so easily forced into classifications. When we consider the case of *qwl*: this remains a substantive, even when it is used as an interjection ('a sound!...'). The only way to make out what is meant is a pause in the sentence. In a written text the punctuation may indicate this; without that, we can only guess what the author has meant. Usually we can make quite a good guess, but when both alternatives are equally probable, we shall never know (unless we could ask the author; but it is even possible that the author himself has forgotten what he intended). In the case of *qwl*, moreover, there is no difference as to the result: 'a sound... someone is calling!' and 'a sound of someone calling!' differ only in liveliness of diction. If both make an equally good sentence, it is impossible to say whether a word 'is' an interjection or not. This applies also to *hbh*: 'give up! your cattle!' (without punctuation to make it clear) cannot be distinguished from 'give up your cattle!'. It only becomes different if 'and I shall give you bread in exchange'

---

63 The relationship between substantives and interjections is also discussed, because *qwl* in Ps. XXIX has been taken by some to be the interjection 'hear!' – for which reason Cunchillos has compiled a list of cases in which *qwl* might have this meaning. See Cunchillos (1976) 63–65.

follows: then the second alternative makes the more fluent (and there-fore probably the intended) sentence.

In the case of Ps. xxix 1–2 the problem is born behind the writing-desk. There can be no problem, because an interjection here makes no sense. 'Come!' (literally 'give!', which might be elliptical for 'give that this happens') is used as an incitement. Now why should an incitement be used when only a statement follows (namely, that the *bny 'lym* belong to Yhwh)? I think that more common sense is needed, not more research.

bhdrt-qdš

The introduction of the psalm ends with the expression *bhdrt-qdš*. F. M. Cross[64] proposes to connect *hdrh* with *hdrt* in *KTU* 1.14 III 51, where it is paralleled by *ḥlm*, dream (l. 50). *Bhdrt-qdš* in Ps. xxix is translated by Cross with '(Yhwh) who appears in holiness'.[65]

In my opinion one had better depart from the Hebrew occurrences of *hdrh*, which point to the meaning 'majesty', 'splendour'.[66] Apart from Ps. xcvi 9 and 1 Chron. xvi 29, which have the same words as Ps. xxix 2, *hdrh* occurs in 2 Chron. xx 21 *mšrrym lyhwh wmhllym lhdrt-qdš*: men singing of Yhwh and praising the holy majesty, and in Prov. xiv 28 *brb-'m hdrt-mlk*: the splendour of the king is in a numerous people. When we assume the meaning 'majesty' or 'splendour' in Ps. xxix also, the ques-tion is how to translate *b*. I do not agree with A. Caquot[67], who trans-lates 'en lui donnant la Majesté sainte', which he supports with *KAI* 26 C III 16–18 *brk b'l... 'yt 'ztwd bḥym*: que Baal bénisse Azitawadda en lui donnant la vie, and with the Arabian expression (without a verb) *ana lakum bihi*: je vous l'ai apporté. These comparisons do not hold, because in both cases 'to give' is expressed by another word (*brk, lakum*[68]), not by

---

64 Cross (1950).
65 Donner (1967), 331–333, points to the fact, that a strict synonymity in the Ugaritic text would require the sense 'Traumgesicht, Vision'. Cross however answers that it concerns a divine apparition, whether seen in a dream or in the waking state (*CMHE* 152–153 n. 28).
66 There is thus a divergence in meaning from the Ugaritic *hdrt*, if its parallelism with *ḥlm* is indeed synonymous. Perhaps we should assume (with Gordon (1965), Glossary *s.v. hdrt*) a semantic connection '(divine) majesty' = 'theophany' = 'dream'.
67 Caquot (1956).
68 As dr. P. S. van Koningsveld of Leyden University kindly informs me, the word *za'im* or *ḍamin*, guarantor, is implied in the Arabian expression (the construction is:

b. In Ps. xxix there is no other word which contains the notion 'to give'.

In my opinion *b* in Ps. xxix 2 means 'on the occasion of', and tends to have the additional meaning 'because of' (both of these meanings are present in the translation 'before', given above). Cp. Neh. x 1 *bkl-z't*: because of all this.

It is not unusual in Hebrew that substantives occur in a masculine and a feminine form.[69] In Ps. xxix we have the masculine form in vs. 4, where it is said of the *qwl yhwh* that it sounds *bhdr*, with majesty. This suggests, that also in vs. 2 the 'holy majesty' refers to the voice of Yhwh; in this way we have a smooth transition from the introduction, which ends with *bhdrt-qdš*, to the main part of the psalm, which begins with *qwl yhwh*. It should be noted that the voice of Baal, which is the thunder, is also called *qdš*, in a passage which for several reasons can be compared with Ps. xxix[70], viz *KTU* 1.4 VII 25–52 (*qlh qdš*, l. 29 and l. 31).

Conclusions

The results of our investigation have thus far been mainly negative: there is no reason to suppose that the introduction of Ps. xxix pictures Yhwh as El; neither can it be shown that polemics are intended against the *bny 'lym*.

On the other hand, it has appeared that hymns, in which a god is praised as the highest deity by the other gods, are found in Mesopotamia (Marduk, Sin) and Egypt (Amon-Re); that the Ugaritic formula which has been adopted by the Israelite poet is used in connection with several gods; and that the Baal epic twice contains the formal pledge by Anat resp. Atirat that Baal is their king, who has no one above him.

Finally, we have noticed a connection between the introduction and the storm-theophany which follows, notably the words *bhdrt-qdš*; it will be shown below that also the word *'z* forms a connection between the introduction and the main part of the psalm.

zaʿim/ḍamin bi). The passage referred to by Caquot (Kitab al-Aghani² II 132, 1) is about a poet, of whom it is said 'I guarantee him to you'; that is, in view of the context, 'I promise to bring him here'. The only word in the expression, by which it is indicated that something is 'given', is the dative *lakum*.

69 See the examples given by Caquot; cp. also Ben-Asher (1978).
70 See below (p. 92–93).

Translation

3 The voice of Yhwh rises against the waters,
(the glorious god thunders)
Yhwh rises against the mighty waters.
4 The voice of Yhwh sounds with power,
the voice of Yhwh sounds with majesty.
5 The voice of Yhwh smashes cedars,
Yhwh smashes the cedars of the Lebanon.
6 He makes the Lebanon skip like a calf,
and the Siryon like a wild bull.
7 The voice of Yhwh slays (with) flames of fire.
8 The voice of Yhwh shakes the wilderness,
Yhwh shakes the wilderness of Qadesh.
9 The voice of Yhwh shakes mighty trees,
and makes woods bare.

Textual and grammatical notes

3 A comparison with vss. 5 and 8 (*qwl yhwh* + object without qualification/*yhwh* + the same object with qualification) strongly suggests that vs. 3b is an interpolation. It might be an explanatory gloss; it is also possible that this line originally belonged elsewhere in the psalm. In the second case, there is much to be said for the solution of E. Podechard[71], to read vs. 3b between vss. 9b and 9c; there is a close correspondence between vss. 3b and 9c: the thundering of the *'l hkbwd*, and the response, consisting in the call *kbwd*.

5 The piel *wyšbr* must be translated in the same way as the qal in the first line of this verse, because with transitive verbs it has a 'resultative' meaning; in the present case: 'to make broken', which can hardly be distinguished from 'to break'.[72]

6 The enclitic *–m* in *wyrqydm* as well as the form *kmw* instead of *k* are features which are comparatively rare in biblical Hebrew, but are well attested in Ugaritic. There are ten instances listed in *RSP* of comparisons, in the Ugaritic texts, with a double *kmw*.[73] When we furthermore

71 Podechard (1949), *Notes critiques* I 130; cp. Tournay (1956) 173–174.
72 Jenni (1968) 124–126.
73 *RSP* I II 289.

observe that the Siryon is commonly called 'Hermon' in the OT (apart from Ps. xxix, the name Siryon only occurs in Dt. iii 9, where it is stated that the Sidonians call the Hermon 'Siryon'; Siryon *coni*. 1 Chron. v 16), whereas the name Siryon is used in the Ugaritic texts, notably parallel to Lebanon[74], it follows that vs. 6 preserves an ancient usage of the language.[75]

7 The obvious solution would be to take *lhbwt ʾš* as the direct object of *ḥṣb*, as the existence of an *acc. instrumenti* in Hebrew is questionable.[76] Thus the LXX has *diakoptontos phloga puros*; the Vulgate *dividens flammas ignis*. The meaning of this however is not immediately clear.

In order to achieve a clearer meaning, the *NEB* translates *ḥṣb* in an irregular way: makes flames of fire burst forth.[77] S. Mittmann[78] comments that the psalmist seems to have had in mind the sparks which are thrown out of the rock by the activity of the stonecutter. Indeed *ḥṣb* is the technical term for hewing stones. It must be added that fire is a not uncommon phenomenon in theophanies (see e.g. Ps. xviii 9). One should note, however, that this fire is never produced by cutting up rocks. *Ḥṣb* can mean 'to manufacture', 'to produce', but only when the product is the result of hewing.[79] According to the established use of the verb, there are two ways in which the product is achieved: either it did not exist before, but is procured by modelling the rough material c.q. removing rough material (e.g. pillars or cisterns), or it did exist and is brought to light by hewing, notably copper out of the rock. As a consequence, Ps. xxix 7 would say, either that Yhwh, by hewing,

74 *KTU* 1.4 VI 18–21; in this passage 'Lebanon and its trees' is parallelled by 'Siryon and its choicest cedars'. On *Sa-ri-a ù La-ab-na-an* in the epic of Gilgamesh see below (p. 110 n. 52).

75 Surely this must plead against the opinion of Mittmann (1978), that vs. 6 is secondary.

76 Joüon (1923) 126 l; *GK* 117 s, t; 144 l, m (esp. n. 4).

77 Cp. Kraus (1978⁵) *ad locum*: 'sprüht Feuerflammen' (with the comment 'eigentlich: "zerspaltet"'). *HAL s.v. ḥṣb* II assumes the meaning 'to stir' (the fire), with reference to the Arabic root *ḥḍb*. Ps. xxix 7 is the only text which is cited, however.

78 Mittmann (1978).

79 The suggestion of Cunchillos (1976), 88–99, that *ḥṣb* might signify 'to cause to spring forth' (like water; thus in Is. li 2), 'to cause to overflow' (said of cisterns; thus in Dt. vi 11, Neh. ix 25 and 2 Chron. xxvi 10), so that Ps. xxix 7 (where *ḥṣb* would have no object) would lay stress on Yhwh's fertilizing force, does not take into account that, even if his translations were right, the notion of hewing is always present too; in fact, this would remain the basic notion. I cannot see how 'to hew' (without any addition) can suggest the idea of fertilizing force.

modelled the rough material (fire) in order to make flames out of it[80], or that the flames were hidden somewhere and were brought to light by Yhwh's hewing activities. Of course this is rather an absurd picture, especially if one imagines the dragon, which is able to produce fire spontaneously out of its own nostrils or mouth (cp. Job XLI 10–12) – and indeed Yhwh does no less, as appears from Ps. XVIII 9.[81]

It would seem that we are left with the alternative of an *acc. instrumenti*. Ex. XXX 20 has *rḥṣ mym*, to wash with water (cp. *KTU* 1.3 IV 42–43 *w trḥṣ ṭl.šmm.šmn.arṣ*, she washed herself with dew of heaven, with oil of the earth); Josh. VII 25 has *rgm 'bn*, to stone with stones. However, in these expressions the accusative might be explained as an internal object, which does not seem possible with our expression in Ps. XXIX 7. Fensham[82] thinks that the preposition *b* may have dropped out. Still, one would prefer to have an object to *ḥṣb*, as the statement is rather incomplete without it. There seems to me to be just a possibility that 'the voice of Yhwh slays flames of fire' is a reminiscence of a datum of Ugaritic mythology; on this, see below, p. 59–60.

8 The region of Qadesh Barnea is in the OT nowhere called 'desert of Qadesh'; instead, the names 'desert of Sin' and 'desert of Paran' are used. *Mdbr qdš* does occur, however, in the Ugaritic texts (*KTU* 1.23 65), where it might indicate the Syrian desert near Qadesh on the Orontes,

---

80 *BdJ* ingeniously adds the notion of 'arrows'; Yhwh 'taille des éclairs de feu' is commented upon with: God cuts himself arrows to pierce his enemies. The idea on which this translation is based (Yhwh sharpens his flashes of lightning into arrows) is the same as the notion of modelling fire into flames.

81 Del Olmo Lete (1980) suggests that *KTU* 1.3 III 20–31 might help to explain Ps. XXIX 7, notably the words 'wood' and 'stone' occurring there. The passage contains Baal's message that he will create the lightning; this is called 'a tale of wood and a whisper of stone', 'a murmuring of the heaven to the earth, of the ocean to the stars'. According to Gese (1970), 54, this is the stock formula for secret messages, conveying the notion that the whole cosmos has part in the message, except animals and men. Indeed the formula is also found in *KTU* 1.1 III 12–16, where El sends a message to Ktr w Ḥss – a message which has nothing to do with the lightning. It is true that this passage has lacunas; notably the words 'a tale of wood and a whisper of stone' are missing, but it seems likely that these words belonged to the standard verses. Del Olmo Lete also points to the characterization of the lightning as 'cedar(shaft)' in *KTU* 1.4 VII 41, and possibly as 'stone' in *KTU* 1.3 III 26; the interpretation of *abn* as 'stone' does not seem to me to be right, however (cp. below, p. 47 n. 107). But even if the lightning was characterized as wood or stone, I do not quite see how 'the semantic field here involved fits well into the image of "cutting" or "hewing" suggested by vs. 7 as an effect produced by Yahweh's "voice"', as Del Olmo Lete puts it.

82 Fensham (1963).

or else: the holy desert. It is more plausible that *mdbr qdš* in Ps. XXIX is a reminiscence of the Ugaritic expression, than that it refers to the southern region which is never called by that name.[83]

9 The form *yḥwll* can be explained in two ways:

1) *ḥll* poel: to pierce (Is. LI 9; Job XXVI 13; Prov. XXVI 10; *coni*. Ezek. XXVIII 9).

2) *ḥyl* (qal: to have labour-pains, to writhe, to tremble) polel: to bring forth (Dt. XXXII 18; Is. LI 2; Job XXXIX 1; Prov. XXV 23).

The form *'ylwt*, vocalized *ayyalot*, as in the MT, means 'hinds'; vocalized *elot* the meaning would be 'mighty trees'. As early as 1753 the emendation *elot* was proposed by Richard Lowth in his *De sacra poesi Hebraeorum*.[84]

Because 'to pierce' or 'to bring forth' hinds is obviously not the intended meaning, many authors have altered the attested meaning of *ḥyl* polel into 'to cause to bring forth'; cp. Vulg. *obsetricans*. To me however the emendation of Lowth seems preferable, as the reaction of animals is never described in storm-theophanies. We need not have recourse to the verb *ḥll* when we read *elot*[85], although this would be possible; the meaning 'to tremble' is so well attested for the root *ḥyl* (see for instance Ps. LXXVII 17 qal 'to tremble'; Job XXVI 5 polal 'to be made to tremble'; Job XV 20 hitpolel 'to tremble'; Esth. IV 4 hitpalpel 'to tremble'), that we may safely assume it for the polel also ('to cause to tremble'). I would prefer this solution, because of the variation *ḥyl* hifil (vs. 8)/*ḥyl* polel (vs. 9) – both having the same meaning –; this style-figure is (*mutatis mutandis*) also found in vs. 5 (*šbr* qal/*šbr* piel).[86]

As for the second part of the verse, there seems to me to be no need of an emendation. The only problem is the plural *y'rwt*, because the regular plural of *y'r*, wood, is *y'rym*; see however above, p. 37 and n. 69, on the occurrence of masculine and feminine forms of the same substantive.

---

83 Still less can the expression be held to contain a reference to the history of salvation, that is to say, God's aid given in the desert, as is assumed by H. Cazelles (1961).

84 Lowth (1753) *prael*. XXVII.

85 Thus Buttenwieser (1969²) 148: 'splits the oaks'.

86 Mittmann (1978) accepts the emendation *elot*, but keeps to the meaning 'to bring forth' for *yḥwll*, stating that 'die Stimme Jahwes ist ... nun eindeutig mehr als ein naturhafter und unartikulierter Donnerlaut; sie kommt dem göttlichen Schöpfungsworte gleich'. Apparently Mittmann prefers to explain this verse by other OT texts, in which Yhwh is a creator-deity, rather than by its immediate context, in which the awe and terror, inspired by the thunder-god, are described. The terror of nature is a common feature in descriptions of theophanies.

This phenomenon is also found in Ugaritic.[87] Moreover, the LXX has *apokalupsei drumous*, the Vulgate *revelans saltus*.

Ḥśp, to strip, to lay bare, occurs several times in the OT (see *KBL s.v.*). The translation 'drenches forests'[88] could be based on Ugaritic *ḥsp* (cp. Is. xxx 14; Hag. ii 16, where however the sense is 'to draw' water resp. wine, not 'to pour'); but this translation deviates from the LXX and Vulgate, and moreover does not fit in with the context (vss. 5–8), which describes the destructive effect of Yhwh's voice. (Cp. Am. i 2, Nah. i 4: the withering of the green as a concomitant of the theophany.)

Driver's proposition[89] to translate 'to bring kids (goats) to an early delivery' is based upon meanings of the two words which are not attested elsewhere in Hebrew, and is, moreover, not necessary.

Interpretation

Theophany motifs

The work of Jörg Jeremias[90] has greatly enlarged our knowledge of the *Theophanie-Gattung*. 'Theophany' is defined by Jeremias as the coming of the deity to judge and to destroy. The coming is described through the accompanying phenomena (storm, etc.); characteristic is the terror which it causes. A number of psalms and prophetic texts contains descriptions of a theophany, which stand like erratic blocks within the context; from their similarities it appears that it concerns an independent *Gattung*. In its original form the theophany-description contained two elements: 1) the coming of the deity; 2) the reaction of nature (cp. Judg. v 4–5; Ps. lxviii 8–9). The original form has been developed in different ways: one or the other (or both) of the two elements have undergone an enlargement, or have even become independent. Ps. xxix 3–9b is an example of the enlargement of the second member; the first member is only vestigially present through the thundering of the deity. As to the origin of the separate images, Jeremias points out the striking resemblance of the OT descriptions to those found in Mesopo-

---

87 *CML* 129: 'A considerable number of nouns of masculine form ... take the feminine plural termination; and a few have both this and masculine plural forms'. Cp. Gordon (1965) 8. 9.
88 Thus Strauss (1970); *CMHE* 154.
89 Driver (1931) 255.
90 Jeremias (1965).

tamic hymns, although he allows for some influence of Canaan also.[91]

Having given due praise to the work of Jeremias, F. M. Cross[92] observes: 'Nevertheless, he does not examine the *form* of Baʻl's theophany in the mythic cycle from Ugarit, the starting point in our view for the discussion of the early biblical theophany. He does not treat the transformation of the Canaanite *Gattung* in the early Israelite context. Jeremias therefore does not recognize... the primary connections of the battle with/at the sea with the theophanic form'. Cross then proceeds to expound his own view:

An examination of the 'Canaanite lore' (in which, by the way, Ps. xxix is also included by Cross, as he considers the psalm to be an ancient Baal hymn) shows that two patterns can be discerned, either in separate or mixed form. The first pattern is the march of the Divine Warrior to the battle against chaos (Yam or Lotan), with his terrible weapons (the thunderbolt, etc.). All nature convulses and languishes when the Warrior manifests his wrath. The second pattern is the return of the Divine Warrior from battle to his new temple on his newly-won mount, where he takes up kingship. His victory over Sea or the flooddragon is often alluded to, especially in his being enthroned on the Flood. When he manifests himself as victor and king in the storm, nature is awakened by the roar of his voice; the appearance of his storm-cloud is both awesome and fructifying. His rule is manifest in the fertility of the earth; animals give birth; mountains dance in festive glee and trees clap in their hands. Ps. xxix shows the mixed form: the terrifying as well as the fructifying effect of the voice of the storm-god on nature.

In hymnic descriptions of the theophany of Yhwh – thus still Cross – we find these same patterns and motifs. The first category includes virtually all of Israel's oldest hymns; in many of these the mythological theme merges with the motif of the march of the conquest, sometimes including the event at the Reed Sea.

The observations of Cross deserve our closest attention. Valuable as they are, they need, to my mind, some corrections. Let us consider the Ugaritic texts first.

The first thing that strikes us, then, with regard to the first pattern, is

91 Jeremias (1965) 88 n. 1: 'Vermutlich hat man sich den Sachverhalt so vorzustellen, dass die betreffenden Vorstellungen in Mesopotamien entstanden und von den vorisraelitischen Einwohnern Palästinas übernommen wurden, die ihrerseits Israel mit ihnen bekannt machten.'

92 *CMHE* 147 n. 1.

that the thunder is not mentioned in the passage narrating the battle of Baal and Yam (*KTU* 1.2 IV). Cross however calls our attention to a passage referring to an 'alloform' of this story, notably Baal's fight with the sea-dragon Lotan (*KTU* 1.5 I 1–5). We are told that, when Baal destroyed this monster 'the heavens withered (and) drooped like the loops of your (sc. Baal's) garment' (translation by Cross). Although Cross does not comment on his translation, the meaning of the words is by no means certain. A controversy exists as to the meaning of the separate words as well as the syntax. The text reads *ttkḥ ttrp šmm krs ipdk*. The root *tkḥ* has been translated by 'to wither' (and the like) because it occurs here in combination with *ttrp*, which is thought to be a td-form of *rpy*, to be slack, to droop (cp. Hebrew *rph* hitp., to show oneself slack or disheartened.[93]). The root *tkḥ* is also found in *KTU* 1.11 1–2 and 1.24 4, in combination with 'to embrace'; that is why others have interpreted it as 'to burn' (e.g. *CSH*[94]: the heavens are on fire). Driver tries to do justice to its combination with *ttrp* as well as to its sexual context, by translating 'to relax' in *KTU* 1.11 and 1.24.[95] According to De Moor[96], however, the latter passages point to a meaning 'to uncover'. In *WUS*, the root is associated with Syr. *škḥ*, to find.[97] Whereas some consider 'the heavens' to be the subject of *ttkḥ*, others regard it as a 2nd. person singular; e.g. Van Selms[98]: you set alight (sc. the heavens) or De Moor: you were uncovered.

The form *ttrp* has been thought to stem either from the root *rpy* or from a root *trp*, to be connected with Judeo-Aramaic *trp*, to be dissolved. Either 'the heavens' are considered to be the subject, or it is thought to be a 2nd. person singular (thus e.g. *WUS*[99]: you would sink down; Van Selms: you weakened the heavens).

In translating 'like the loops', Cross follows Albright's emendation of *krs* into *kr⟨k⟩s*; cp. also *CML*, Glossary s.v. *rks*, where it is translated by 'belt'. Indeed the verb *rks* occurs parallel to *asr*, to bind, but in a broken context (*KTU* 1.1 V 9–10, 22–23). If the reading *krs* is retained, one would arrive at the translation 'belly'[100], provided it is read as one word;

93 See *KBL* s.v. *rph*.
94 *CSH* 239–240.
95 See *CML* 121 and 125.
96 De Moor (1979) 640–642.
97 *WUS* s.v. *tkḥ*.
98 Van Selms (1975).
99 *WUS* s.v. *rpy*.
100 Cp. *HAL* s.v. *krš*.

the combination with *ipdk* (the meaning of which might be ascertained by a comparison with the Hebrew term *ephod*) would lead to the conclusion that *krs* refers to what in Latin is called *sinus*, the fold overhanging the belt of the garment. Perhaps we should then assume a haplography in the transmitted text: *krs* for *kkrs*, like the fold of your garment. However, *krs* could also be read as two words, *k* (like) and a noun *rs*. Thus, *CSH* translate 'like a drop of sweat' (cp. Hebr. *rss*, to sprinkle); Van Selms 'like a ruin' (Hebr. *rsysym*); De Moor 'like succulent meat' (Hebr. *rss*, Arab. *rašraš*).

Apart from being translated by 'your garment', *ipdk* has also been regarded as a verb (of which the following *ank* is the subject); thus e.g. Van Selms: I will swallow you (Hebr. *pyd*); De Moor: I shall consume you (Arab. *anfada*).

Thus, the only thing that seems to be certain is, that something is said of the heavens, probably that they 'became slack' (*rpy*) or that Baal 'dissolved them' (*trp*). This could indicate a reaction of fear, as is assumed by Cross (even if Baal is the subject, because Baal's fight with Lotan would be the cause of the fear). Another interpretation is given by Van Selms, however; in his opinion 'you weakened the heavens' means that Baal shot at the heavens with his lightning, with the result that this cupola got weak places where the rain could fall through. (Only, this image would deviate considerably from the image of the window in Baal's palace.[101]) Anyway, the passage cannot be called an unambiguous testimony of what is called by Cross 'the collapse of the cosmos in response to the battle of the divine warrior'. We must also note that the thunder is not mentioned in this passage.

In addition, Cross adduces a letter of Abimilki of Tyre to the pharao (*EA* 147), in which the pharao is described as follows (lines 13–15): *ša id-din ri-ig-ma-šu i-na ša-me ki-ma addi ù ta⟨r⟩-ku-ub gab-bi mati[ti] iš-tu ri-ig-mi-šu*, who utters his voice in heaven like Addu, so that the whole land trembles at his voice. The ideogram *[d]IM*, which in Accadian texts and in the Mari letters refers to Adad, is taken by Cross to refer to Baal, without any comment. Whether this assumption is right, is difficult to decide; cp. M. J. Mulder[102], who in discussing the meaning of the ideogram in the Amarna letters concludes (with Baudissin[103]), that 'on occasion' the sign for 'Hadad' was used to indicate Baal.

But if *[d]IM* in *EA* 147 refers to Baal, we have got an affirmation, that

101 Cp. below, p. 46.
102 Mulder (1980) 71.
103 Baudissin (1929) III 36 n. 1.

the 'trembling of the land' before Baal was indeed a literary topic. Cross omits to mention the fact, that in the letter of Abimilki it most probably concerns a piece of literature. It has been argued by A. Jirku[104] in a very convincing way, that the Amarna letters contain fragments of Canaanite hymns. It concerns passages which, by their poetic and religious tone, stand apart from their 'dry' context. That these are, in fact, quotations, appears from the fact that the same lines are sometimes found in letters from different senders (or in different letters from the same sender). The writers address the pharao (c.q. Egyptian official) with these quotations as if he were a god. Sometimes in these passages the 2nd. person plural is used instead of singular. This is to be explained by the circumstance that the hymn, from which the quotation was taken, was addressed to more than one god. In that case the writer has not taken the trouble to adjust the quotation, but there are cases in which he has done so. A good example is *EA* 169 7–8 (in Knudtzon's German translation because English does not show the difference) 'Du gibst mir Leben und du gibst mir Tod', as compared to *EA* 238 31–33 'Ihr gebt uns Leben und ihr gebt uns Tod'. Presumably *EA* 147 13–15 is also based on a Canaanite hymn. This is of importance, because we are dealing now with a theory about literary patterns. That people imagined the earth to tremble when the storm-god uttered his voice, is only to be expected; what we are at the moment concerned with is, whether this was expressed in a literary form.

Thus far the existence of the first pattern could not be demonstrated; nowhere in the existent literature is the thunder mentioned in connection with the battle with Sea or the dragon; maybe the drooping of the heavens is connected with the battle; and in the letter of Abimilki the reaction to the thunder is the trembling of the land. The motifs are demonstrable, but there is no clear-cut pattern.

Things grow even worse when we consider the passage in which Baal gives forth his 'holy voice' after having opened the window in his palace (*KTU* 1.4 VII 29–35). This should be the second pattern, as Baal is now seated in his palace after the battle with Yam. Indeed the idea of the fertilizing rain is present, because the window serves as an aperture for the rain to pass through. But the 'festive glee' of nature is totally absent; on the contrary, the reaction of nature is one of fright. From the damaged and not always comprehensible text this much appears: the mountains are afraid (ḫšy; cp. Arab. ḫašiya) and the high places of the earth

104 Jirku (1933).

46

shake (*ntt*, which is something Anat does with her feet in fury, *KTU* 1.3 III 32–33). First of all the earth is mentioned, but the verb is only partly legible.

Now Cross admits indeed that each theophany of the storm-god is also terrifying; but the point is, that the 'also' cannot be shown to have a complement: outbursts of joy on the part of nature are lacking in this text. Neither are they described anywhere else in the Ugaritic texts.[105]

The remaining instances of thunder and/or lightning in the Ugaritic literary texts should all be classed with the second pattern; but again we notice only motifs, not the pattern as it is described by Cross. *KTU* 1.4 V 6–9 and 1.19 I 42–46 are not descriptions of a theophany, but do show a connection between thunder/lightning and the rain. The first passage – just after El's permission to build a palace – states that Baal will appoint the time for his rains, his thunder and his lightnings[106] (cp. *KTU* 1.3 III 26–31, where, still before El has given his consent, Baal sends the message that he will create the lightning[107]); in the second passage a drought is described as the absence of the sweet voice of Baal. Finally we have *KTU* 1.101, where thunder and lightning are connected with Baal's being enthroned on the 'mountain of (his) victory'. This is also the sole text on which the existence, in Canaanite lore, of the motif of the enthronement on Flood could be based by Cross.[108] The tablet is much

---

105 Festive glee (dancing and hand-clapping) is not exactly what is being described in the passage adduced by Cross, in which El sees in a vision that 'the heavens are raining oil, the wadis run with mead' (*KTU* 1.6 III 6–7, 12–13) – which means that Baal has come to life again. Nor is mention made here of the thunder.

106 Cross translates this in the past tense, which does not seem in congruence with the story: Baal's ability to raise a fructifying thunder-storm is connected with his possession of a palace.

107 In all probability, the root underlying *abn* is *bny*, not *byn*. As to the translation 'stones of lightning', De Moor (1971), 107, is surely right in observing, that *abn brq* does not belong to the stock formula for secret messages, so that *abn* cannot be an apposition. Cp. above, p.40 n. 81.

108 Cross, it is true, bases this also on Ps. xxix 10 ('Yahweh sits enthroned on the Flooddragon'); moreover he takes vss. 9a ('Yahweh makes the hinds to writhe (that is, calve)') and 9b ('(the voice of Yahweh) drenches the forests') as evidence of the second pattern in Canaanite poetry. But, for one thing, there is not a scrap of proof that Ps. xxix was originally a Canaanite hymn dedicated to Baal; for another, I do not think that the flooddragon is meant in vs. 10 (see below, ad vs. 10). As to vss. 9a and 9b: if they are translated in this way, the description would switch rather unexpectedly from the destructive to the salutary effect of the thunder; and in a very haphazard way at that, if one reads – with Cross – vs. 9b after vs. 7 (after which vss. 8 and 9a follow). Cp. my comment ad vs. 9.

damaged, but the crucial lines are in a comparatively good state:

1 *bʻl.ytb.k ṯbt.ǵr.hd.r* [ ]
2 *k mdb.b ṯk.ǵrh.il ṣpn.bt⟨k⟩*
3 *ǵr.tliyt.šbʻt.brqm.* [ ]
4 *ṯmnt.iṣr rʻt.ʻṣ brq.y* [ ]

The text thus says that Baal is seated on his mountain, the divine Sapon, on the mountain of (his) victory. Then the text goes on to say something about 'seven lightning-bolts, eight supplies of thunder, a spear of lightning'; one can only guess at the verbs. (This is not followed up in l. 5 sqq by a reaction of nature.) The beginning is translated by Cross as follows:

> Baʻl sits enthroned, (his) mountain like a dais,
> Haddu the shepherd, like the Flood dragon,

to which he adds as a comment: 'Apparently Baʻl's mountain is compared with a dais, and with the (back of the) dragon'.

The meaning of *mdb* (obviously 'flood' or 'ocean', not 'flood-dragon') can be ascertained from its parallelism with *ym* (*KTU* 1.23 34–35); the root is PS *ḏwb*, to flow. But the translation given by Cross is awkward because of the (twice repeated) interruption of the sentence: it implies that, within the main sentence, two nominal sentences (*k ṯbt ǵr* and *k mdb*, sc. *ǵr*) are interposed, to be read as it were between brackets. In my opinion the lines are to be translated as follows: Baal is seated like a mountain sits (lit.: like the sitting of a mountain), Haddu the shepherd[109] (is seated) like the flood (sits). (The *idea* of *ṯbt* has to be supplied before *mdb*, but grammatically it is not needed.) The *tertium comparationis* seems to me to be the stability and eternal duration of this state.[110]

Resuming we may say with regard to the second pattern, that indeed Baal's being enthroned is connected with thunder and lightning, which in their turn are connected with the rain; the motifs of the enthronement on the flood-dragon and of the joy of nature, however, are absent.

---

109 *l. rʻy.*
110 Pope-Tigay (1971) , who I find give the same solution, are of the opinion that the simile concerns the height and width of mountain and ocean; gods are often pictured as beings of enormous size. I think, however, that the point of comparison is not the *ǵr* and *mdb* in themselves, but the *sitting* of mountain and ocean, which is not large but solid and eternal.

Only the terror of nature is described, when Baal utters his voice from his palace.

A diagram may show our findings. The diagram shows the following motifs:

1 battle with Sea or monsters;
2 thunder/lightning;
3 anxiety of nature (mountains, earth, heavens);
4 kingship;
5 fertility.

	1	2	3	4	5
KTU 1.2 IV	+			+	
KTU 1.5 I 1–5	+		?		
EA 147 13–15		+	+		
KTU 1.4 VII 29–35		+	+	+	+
KTU 1.101 1–4		+	+		
KTU 1.4 V 6–9		+		+	
KTU 1.19 I 42–46		+		+	

When investigating the occurrence of the patterns in the OT, we shall have to exclude for the present those texts which speak of the event at the Reed Sea. As we noted, Cross posits the existence of 'primary connections of the battle with/at the sea with the theophanic form'; moreover he states that the mythological theme 'merges with' the motif of the march of the conquest, sometimes including the event at the Reed Sea. The exact relationship between these different motifs will occupy us later on; for the moment it may suffice to say that I do agree with Cross on the existence of a connection between the battle with, and the battle at the sea, though of another nature than is assumed by Cross. For the present purpose we must restrict ourselves to the 'battle with Sea', as our starting point was the influence of this Canaanite motif on OT theophany descriptions.

As to the texts which mention only Yhwh's coming from the south (Judg. V 4–5; Ps. LXVIII 8–9; Dt. XXXIII 2) – which is interpreted by Cross as a reference to the march of the conquest –, there is even more reason to exclude those. Whereas the 'battle at the sea' is not included here because its relationship to the battle with Sea still remains to be demonstrated, the texts about Yhwh's coming from the south have, in my opinion, nothing to do with any sea whatever, neither the mythological one nor the Reed Sea.

Isolated references to the battle with Sea have of course to be left out too, as no patterns can be deduced from them.

As for the motifs in question: that of the 'enthronement on Flood' is absent (cp. p. 47 n. 108; next to Ps. XXIX 10, Cross adduces Ps. LXXXIX 10, but his translation rests upon an emendation which, apart from being unnecessary, is quite arbitrary).

In contradistinction to the Ugaritic texts, we now meet with the motif of the joy of nature.

The battle with Sea is sometimes only indicated by a slight reference, such as Yhwh's being elevated above the sea (Ps. XCIII 4), or by 'the waters' as an indication of Sea (Ps. XVIII 16). However, as already was demonstrated by Gunkel[111], it cannot be doubted that it concerns references to the primeval battle with Sea.

It also was Gunkel who observed, that Yhwh's 'rebuking' ($g'r$) of the sea was a topic of the myth. Now we may infer from Ps. CIV 7, where $g'rtk$ is used in parallelism to $qwl\,r'mk$, that, in point of fact, the thunder is meant by this verb (cp. Ugaritic $g'r$, to roar), so that we may take the occurrence of $g'r$ as an indication of the presence of this motif.[112]

The distribution of the motifs over the relevant passages is again best shown by a diagram. The numbers 1, 2, 3, 4, 5 indicate the same things as in the first diagram; number 6 indicates the joy of nature. Ps. XXIX is, for the moment, left out of consideration.

	I	2	3	4	5	6
Nah. I 3–6	+	+	+			
Hab. III 3–15	+	+	+			
Ps. XVIII 8–16 =						
2 Sam. XXII 8–16	+	+	+			
Ps. LXXIV 12–17	+			+		
Ps. XCIII	+			+		
Ps. CIV 1–18	+	+			+	
Ps. LXV 6–14	+				+	+
Ps. LXXXIX 10–19	+			+		+
Ps. XCVII 1–6		+	+	+		+
Ps. XCVI			+	+		+
Ps. XCVIII				+		+

111 Gunkel (1895) 91–111.
112 Cp. the commentary on Job XXVI 11 by Moses Ben Naḥman (13th century), who sees in $g'rh$ a reference to the noise of thunder. See Reif (1971).

It appears, that the Hebrew poets have combined the motifs in a free and easy way; to speak of two distinct patterns seems somewhat exaggerated (although Cross, it has to be admitted, also allows for a mixing up of the patterns). But a real step forward as compared with Jeremias's book is the observation that – in eight cases anyway – the battle with Sea forms part of what we may call 'theophany' motifs. The demonstration by Cross that the theophany has a positive side, is a gain; for it is not simply a question of how one wants to define 'theophany', but of a connection between its terrifying and its blissful aspects via the mythology of the storm-god.

In view of the fact that the OT passages are not narratives but lyrical compositions, we do not meet with a fixed sequence of the motifs in this poetry. Its being lyrics is also an explanation of the fact, that single motifs out of the whole series could be left out. The Baal epic, on the contrary, had to narrate the events in a fixed order, which is the reason why the 'Canaanite' diagram shows fewer combinations than the OT diagram does.

Before we return to Ps. xxix, I want to make a remark on the purport of what we concluded thus far. What we have been considering is: the combination of motifs in certain pieces of *literature*. To some, the establishing of a tie between Yhwh's kingship and his battle with Sea (or chaos) may seem *vieux jeu*; they will say that as early as 1922 a relationship between these two motifs (of which the battle with chaos represented the creation of the world) was assumed by Mowinckel, who thought them to belong to the articles of faith connected with the Autumn Festival. This theory still has many subscribers. Others are sceptical or firmly opposed to it. The conclusions drawn by me above are not as far-reaching as those of Mowinckel: they are concerned with only a limited number of motifs (whereas Mowinckel, with a view to the autumn celebrations, created an amalgam of a great many motifs found in the OT). As to Mowinckel's opponents: those who are opposed to theories which have remained hypothetical, need not be opposed to conclusions on a literary plane, concerning eleven literary texts (fewer texts and fewer conclusions than Cross would have it).

When we fit Ps. xxix into our diagram, the motifs 'thunder', 'anxiety of nature', and 'kingship' (vs. 10) can be marked. Just like Yhwh's *qwl* is used to indicate the thunder – in all, 24 times in the OT[113] –, the *ql* of Baal is used to indicate the thunder in the Ugaritic texts. In *KTU* 1.4

113 See Labuschange, *ThHAT* II, *qol* 4.

VII 29 and 31 Baal's thundering voice is called *qdš*; in Ps. XXIX the majesty (*hdr*, vs. 4; *hdrh*, vs. 2) of Yhwh's voice is also called *qdš* (vs. 2; cp. p. 37). Anticipating our discussion of vs. 10, I want to note that Yhwh is called king 'till eternity' (*l'wlm*) in this verse, just like Baal's kingship is called 'eternal' in *KTU* 1.2 IV 10 (*mlk 'lmk*). To my mind, all conditions are fulfilled to see in vs. 3 (Yhwh's voice '*l-hmym*) a reference to the battle with Sea.

'*l-mym rbym*

In fact, the term *mym rbym* has been shown by H. G. May in a thorough treatise[114] to signify, in many instances, the insurgent elements of the cosmos. Although May also points to texts where this meaning does not apply, and although occasionally I differ from him in opinion (for instance, Ps. XVIII 17 does not belong to the theophany of vss. 8–16, as May supposes, so that *mym rbym* in vs. 17 cannot be explained as the enemy against whom Yhwh is advancing), the examples adduced by May are manifold and convincing. Especially interesting for our subject are Ps. XCIII 4 and Hab. III 15, where *mym rbym* is used parallel to *šbry-ym*, the breakers of the sea (in the preceding verse these are called *nhrwt*, rivers, whilst *nhr* is also a name of Yam at Ugarit) and to *ym* respectively; these texts are obviously references to Yam (with a capital). May does not connect *mym rbym* with Yam especially; he only points out a general resemblance to Ugaritic, Hittite and Mesopotamic conceptions connected with the storm-god and his enemies. Indeed, it is impossible to regard *mym rbym*, in the OT, as a *terminus technicus* for Yam. But in the context of Ps. XXIX, in view of our cluster of motifs, it can only signify, as I think, Yam.

In the Ugaritic texts, a designation of Yam as *mym rbym* is not found. Nevertheless, *rb* is used as an epithet of gods; to Yam, it has been applied in *KTU* 1.3 III 39 (*il rbm*, the mighty god; the *m* must be a case of 'mimation'[115]). In Ps. XXIX, the best translation seems to be, not 'many', but 'mighty' waters.[116]

It is perfectly possible to translate '*l* in Ps. XXIX 3 with 'against' – not 'on', as the vast majority of the translations has it. Examples like Judg. XVI 12 and Job XVI 9–10 testify to this meaning of '*l*.

114 May (1955).
115 The translation given by *CSH*, 167, sc. 'le dieu des grandes (eaux)' is rather forced.
116 Cp. Berlin (1981), who concludes that *rb* means 'noble', sometimes 'mighty', but not 'large' in a quantitative sense.

The voice of Yhwh rises against the mighty waters; we may thus mark the motif of the battle with Sea too for Ps. XXIX. Vs. 3 is another example of the topic of the myth, the 'rebuke' which consists in the thundering voice of the deity (cp. p. 50).

A stylistic argument may reinforce my conclusion. Those who consider vs. 3 only to be indicating *where* the thunder-storm takes place (this sea is the Mediterranean, they sometimes state in their commentaries), have to put up with a considerably weakened sense of vs. 3, and rather illogical at that: this verse would then contradict the following verses, which describe the uproar on land. Of course one could riposte that the storm passes on from sea to land; but then the fact would remain that vs. 3 would contain rather a bleak statement as compared with the other verses: a mere indication of the place of action is not the same thing as saying how Yhwh's voice affects nature. Already from this incongruity (all kinds of effects being described on land, but no effect at all at sea) it appears, that vs. 3 does not stand on the same level as vss. 5-9b, so that it is not simply a thunder-storm passing from one place to another. That a distinction must be made between vs. 3 and vss. 5–9b also appears from the fact, that an interjacent verse (4) interrupts the supposed course of the thunder-storm. Thus, in my opinion, the text is built up as follows: the description of the theophany begins with stating against whom it is directed; it goes on to describe its quality (vs. 4), and ends with a picture of its effect on nature (vss. 5–9b).

My interpretation of vs. 3, although far from being generally accepted, is not new. In fact, Mowinckel was the first to translate vs. 3a with 'wider's Wasser' (vs. 3c, however, with 'über'm mächtigen Meer'). He comments, that the psalm refers to creation.[117] Gunkel, in his *Schöpfung und Chaos*, mentions this connection of Ps. XXIX 3 with the battle-myth (for him, as for Mowinckel, the Babylonian myth) only casually, translating 'über den Wassern'[118]; but in the fourth edition of his commentary on the Psalms, he refers to Mowinckel's interpretation.[119]

117 Mowinckel (1922) 47; cp. 48: 'Er (the poet) sieht, wie der Held Jahwä auf das wütende, tosende, brüllende Meer, das noch nie von den Strahlen der Sonne und der Sterne erleuchtet war, hinabfährt und seine donnernde Stimme wie einen Blitz über die dunkle Fläche hinausschleudert, und vor dieser Wunderstimme schrickt das Meer geschlagen zurück.'

118 Gunkel (1895) 107.

119 Gunkel (1926) *ad locum*: 'Das Gewitter (steht) über dem Meere; von dort her zieht es über das Land... Bei der Wahl gerade dieses Naturbildes mag die Erinnerung an den Mythus mitgewirkt haben, wonach Jahves Donner gegen das Urmeer losfuhr.' (after which he mentions Mowinckel).

In the epoch-making contribution of H. L. Ginsberg[120], it is proposed that Ps. xxix was originally a hymn to Baal, being only slightly modified for its use in the early cult of Yhwh. However, although Ginsberg perceived some 'pagan notions' in the psalm, he did not comment on vs. 3. It was A. Lods who suggested, in a discussion following on Ginsberg's paper[121], that vs. 3 might have to be translated with 'contro le grandi acque', signifying 'la lotta del Creatore contro il Mare Primitivo'. Remarkably enough, Lods saw in this reference to Yhwh's battle an instance of the Israelite modification of the pagan psalm. Both Lods and Ginsberg had apparently not seen the article of J. A. Montgomery[122], who, in a commentary on the text of Baal's fight with Yam, observed, that Ps. xxix 3 ('the voice of Yahweh is upon the waters') must be a reminiscence of this myth.[123] Then follows a period of silence; not even Gaster[124], who saw a general Near-Eastern 'pattern' expressed in Ps. xxix (on this, see below, p. 99), commented on vs. 3. Later on, it is occasionally remarked that Ps. xxix contains an allusion to Yhwh's combat with the waters[125]; but Cross – who translates 'on the Waters' –

120 Ginsberg (1938).
121 See the minutes, *ibid.*
122 Montgomery (1935); see esp. p. 270.
123 In 1969, Ginsberg remarks that the waters of Ps. xxix 3 are those of the Mediterranean sea.
124 Gaster (1946/47).
125 Schmidt (1961), 42 n. 141, remarks that Ps. xxix 3 and 9 are an 'Anspielung auf den Kampf mit dem Urmeer'. Stolz (1970), 152–153, comments on Ps. xxix 3 that 'without doubt' the theophany was 'anyway also' directed against the power of chaos (although he translates 'über den Wassern'). However, for Stolz it was not Baal who served as a model for this picture, but El (see below, p. 114–119; cp. also p. 55 n. 127). Some other authors reckoned with the possibility of this meaning of vs. 3; but they either supposed that the meaning had not remained the same in the course of time, or assumed several other meanings at the same time. Thus Cazelles (1961): in the oldest version vs. 3 meant that Yhwh dominated Rahab (there is, however, no reference to a battle); after the reinterpretation, consisting i.a. in the adding of vs. 10 – where *mbwl* means the deluge –, *mym rbym* came to signify 'the waters of Noah', so that then the psalm referred to the history of salvation. Deissler (1961): *mym rbym* might mean the waters above the firmament, or the clouds, or the Mediterranean; but because the term means the sea, the chaos, and (perhaps) the nations in Ps. xciii 4, it might also in Ps. xxix have this threefold meaning, because the Hebrews loved polyvalence. Dahood (1966) *ad locum*: *mym rbym* refers to the Mediterranean, but the original meaning of vs. 3 may have been 'against the waters'. Cunchillos (1976) 73–76: perhaps May is right in taking *mym rbym* in a mythological sense, that is to say, as referring to the historical enemies of Israel (*sic*); but this does not say that this meaning was present from the beginning: the author of the psalm may have thought of creation. In that case vs. 3a refers to the waters above and below the firmament (cp. Gen. 1 6–7), vs. 3c to the Mediterranean.

was the first to offer an explicit justification of the thesis, that Ps. xxix represents a 'recapitulation of his (Baal's) victory over Sea' – an argumentation which we have tested above with positive results.

Over and against this interpretation stands the explanation of *mym rbym* as the heavenly ocean on which, as appears from vs. 10, Yhwh sits enthroned.[126] My argument, viz that it would be illogical to consider vs. 3 as referring to the *place* of action, does not apply when the action is situated in heaven: also in that case (as with my explanation) a clear distinction is made between the contents of vs. 3 (Yhwh's voice sounds above the *mbwl*) and those of vss. 5–9b. I do not think this interpretation is right, however. In the first place, I would prefer to see the series of motifs filled up by the battle motif, which is the basic one. In the second place, we know of the use of *mym rbym* as 'the insurgent waters', but not of the term being used for the heavenly ocean.

If the battle-motif is expressed in vs. 3, the words *hbw 'z* in the introduction at once receive a significance which they would not have had otherwise. The strength must not be given to Yhwh for no reason at all, but because he needs it when he rises against Sea. Next to *hdrt-qdš*, the holy majesty of Yhwh's voice which is again mentioned in vs. 4 (*hdr*), the words *hbw 'z* form a link between the introduction and the theophany scene (cp. p. 37). This is one of the arguments against those who want to see a picture of El behind that of Yhwh in the introduction. If Yhwh uses his strength as a storm-god in the main part, then it is given to him as a storm-god in the introduction. This storm-god is the god who subdued Sea – which was not a function of El.[127]

To round off our discussion of the main part of Ps. xxix, we will consider the meaning of *'l-hkbwd* in vs. 3, and the possibly mythological background of vs. 7.

126 Duhm (1922²) *ad locum*; Kissane (1953) *ad locum*; Hillmann (1965) 132–133; Jeremias (1965) 31; Lipiński (1965) 209; Kraus (1978⁵) *ad locum*; Mittmann (1978) states at the same time, that according to the psalm Yhwh subdues the waters, and that he is enthroned on the 'great waters' of the *mbwl*.

127 The opinion, that the battle with chaos was a function of El in Jerusalem, will be discussed below (p. 113–123). Cp. also above, p. 18, on the opinion of Stolz (1970), 152–155, that *'l* is a proper name in Ps. xxix 3b, from which he infers that the psalm was originally dedicated to El. Stolz, who takes it for granted that the psalm was originally dedicated to a Canaanite god, calls it illogical if this god were Baal, because in that case the Israelite adapter would have replaced the name 'Baal' by the name 'Yhwh' in every instance but vs. 3b, where he replaced it by the name of El. However, the meaning 'god' is not only well attested for Ugaritic *il*, but also for Hebrew *'l* (see e.g. Ex. xv 11); in Ps. xxix 3b this seems to be the obvious translation.

On *'l-hkbwd*, Cross[128] comments that *kbwd* appears to be a *terminus technicus*, namely the aureole which surrounds the deity in his manifestations. This might be, according to Cross, a hypostatization of the 'glory' of the god, and could be compared with Accadian *melammu*, the aureole of gods, demons, and kings; in the OT, we meet with this use of *kbwd* in Ex. XXXIII 17–23, where Moses sees the back of the Glory after Yhwh has passed by. Alternatively, it could have originated in the fiery storm-cloud associated with the theophany of the storm-god; in that case *kbwd* might have been derived from *'nn kbd*, cp. Ex. XIX 16 (where however the MT reads *'anan kabed*, a heavy cloud, not *'anan kabod*). Although Cross considers the latter explanation the less likely, he nevertheless calls the appearance of the *kbwd* characteristic of storm-theophanies, as fire is a regular feature of them. Other gods than the storm-god may have had the 'Glory' – thus Cross –, but as appears from Ps. XXIX it was in any case an epithet of Baal-Haddu.

It this theory could be substantiated, we would have an additional argument against the assumption, that *kbwd* is a concept especially connected with El (cp. above, p. 23–31).[129] In my opinion, however, a special connection between *kbwd* and the storm-theophany cannot be shown to exist. E. Cassin[130], who ends her book on the Mesopotamic concept of *melammu* and related notions by pronouncing her impression, that the Hebrews expressed with *kbwd* some of the realities which were discovered behind the Accadian terms, does not only mention the devastating power of the *melammu*, which advances like a hurricane towards the enemy, but also many other aspects (health, sexual potency, beauty, fertility, etc.). Indeed, Hebrew *kbwd* can be also shown to have many aspects. Admittedly, the *kbwd* of Yhwh may be pictured as visible, directly or indirectly. But the question we must put to ourselves is, whether we ever meet with a thunder-theophany, in which *kbwd* is one of the visible phenomena. A survey of the potentially evidential texts may show that this is not so.

128 *CMHE* 153 n. 30; cp. 163–169.
129 On the other hand, it would confirm Margulis's explanation (see above, p. 29–31) of the *kbwd* as a hypostatization in the shape of a fiery storm-cloud. (This would not, of course, imply a confirmation of his theory of the enthronement of the *kbwd*.) Cp. also the opinion of Cunchillos (above, p. 34 and n. 62), that *kbwd* in Ps. XXIX 1 refers to the luminous splendour, which the *bny 'lym* have to surrender to Yhwh.
130 Cassin (1968) 7, 29, 69, 73, 80–82, 132–133.

Is. LVIII 8 'then shall your light break forth like the dawn... the *kbwd* of Yhwh shall be your rearguard' and Is. LX 1–2 '... your light has come and the *kbwd* of Yhwh has risen – *zrḥ*, which is commonly used of the rising of the sun – over you;... but Yhwh shall rise over you and his *kbwd* shall appear over you' compare the *kbwd* with the light of dawn and of a heavenly body respectively.

To quote the commentary of Westermann[131] ad Is. LX 1–2: 'As their background the verses have the old motif of Yahweh's epiphany. ... But great changes have come over it. ... The old concept of the epiphany, which presupposes that Yahweh does actually draw near, is almost entirely obliterated by that of a star's rising.' But these verses offer no proof whatever, that *kbwd* was of old used in the storm-theophany.

Ps. XCVII 6 'the heavens proclaim his justice, and all peoples see his *kbwd*' is preceded by a thunder-theophany; Ps. CIV 31 'may the *kbwd* of Yhwh exist forever; may Yhwh rejoice in his works' is followed by it. In the latter case, the 'forever' (*lʿwlm*) is hardly a fitting description of a fiery cloud in a thunder-storm; in Ps. XCVII, the fact that vs. 6 contains a theme occurring more often (praising Yhwh's *kbwd* among the nations, Ps. XCVI 3; Ps. LVII 6, 12; Ps. CVIII 6), in contexts which have nothing to do with a storm-theophany, pleads against considering the *kbwd* as a phenomenon of the storm.[132]

In Ps. LXIII 3, mention is made of Yhwh's *kbwd* being seen in his temple, where it might, quite concretely, designate the ark.[133] T. N. D. Mettinger[134], when speaking of the association of the *kbwd* with light and fire (Ezek., P), relates this with a theopany-ritual in the temple connected with the ark (*kbwd*). That might be so (one could point to I Kgs. VIII 10–11: when the ark was placed in the temple, a cloud filled the house of Yhwh; cp. 2 Chron. V 13–14; VII 1–3); but it does not say that the fiery clouds in descriptions of the thunder-theophany were designated with the term *kbwd* – which indeed we do not find in the extant literature.

Finally, we have the Sinai pericope (and some passages in its close proximity), which Cross adduces as evidence. Leaving aside the *ʿnn kbd* of Ex. XIX 16 (see above; the MT *kabed* must surely be retained), the

---

131 Westermann (1969).
132 Contra Weinfeld, *ThWAT* IV, 32.
133 See Lipiński (1965) 264–265, 406.
134 Mettinger (1982) Ch. IV.

relevant passages are Ex. XVI 10, where the *kbwd* appears in a cloud; Ex. XXIV 17, where it is said that the *kbwd* has the appearance of devouring fire (whilst a cloud is said to have covered the mountain when the *kbwd* rested upon it, vss. 15–16, 18); Ex. XL 34–35, where a cloud covers the tent of meeting while the *kbwd* fills it; and Dt. V 24, where it is said that Yhwh has shown his *kbwd* while his voice was heard out of the midst of the fire.

Cross concedes that the Priestly writer distinguishes between the *kbwd* and the cloud, but he is strongly inclined to believe that this distinction is secondary. In his opinion, the prose sources derived their accounts from poetic descriptions of Yhwh's theophany at the Sinai, a theophany which falls into pattern 2 (pattern 1, with which the theophany begins, is supplied by the preceding narrative, notably the event at the Reed Sea). According to Cross, these poetic descriptions derived their imagery from the traditional Canaanite language of the storm-theophany (see e.g. the thunder and lightning mentioned in Ex. XIX 16; XX 18). In the prose sources, the poetic imagery has been distorted; thus, for instance, in Ex. XIII 21–22 the fiery cloud of the theophany has become a 'column of cloud' by day and a 'column of fire' by night.

Now poetry about an event at a sea obviously did exist, apparently in early times: the 'Song of the Sea' in Ex. XV. The existence of ancient poetry about the Sinai lawgiving, however, is purely hypothetical. The only fact that could be pointed to is, that the Sinai is associated with Yhwh in Dt. XXXIII 2, Judg. V 4–5, and Ps. LXVIII 8–9, where Yhwh's terrible advance is described. To connect these passages with the Sinai lawgiving surely means stretching the evidence too far, the 'evidence' being only the word 'Sinai'. Even a relationship of these passages with the so-called 'history' of the conquest of Canaan is, to say the least, not clear.

The supposition that the distinction between the *kbwd* and the cloud is secondary, whilst originally the *kbwd* designated the fiery cloud, does, therefore, not have any foundation. Sinai-lawgiving poetry, to which the prose sources are secondary, has yet to be discovered.

Our investigation of the term *kbwd* has led to the conclusion that, although it can indicate a visible phenomenon, there is no relationship between *kbwd* and the thunder-theophany. Just as the term could not be shown to have been associated with El, it cannot be shown to have been associated with the storm-god. In my opinion, in Ps. XXIX 3 it obviously signifies a reference to vss. 1–2; *'l-hkbwd* is the god who deserves and receives the honour, the glorious god.[135]

ḥṣb lhbwt 'š

In Ps. xxix 7, we rejected the meaning 'to produce by hewing' for *ḥṣb*, whilst an *acc. instrumenti* is grammatically doubtful (see p. 39–40). Apart from 'to hew' as an activity of a stonecutter or a miner, *ḥṣb* (hi.) once occurs in a different context, notably in Is. li 9. The activity by itself is about the same as in the other occurrences, but in this case it does not refer to the human crafts. As in Ps. xxix, the subject is the deity, Yhwh. The prophet urges the arm of Yhwh to act with strength: Was it not you who slew (*ḥṣb*) Rahab, who pierced Tannin? This is the only other occurrence, where the subject is the deity (who is the 'logical subject' in Ps. xxix 7).

It seems to me to be worth considering, whether the object in Ps. xxix 7 might not also be a mythological monster, like in Is. li 9. In fact, we find something remarkably like the 'flames of fire' in an enumeration of monsters, slain by Anat, in the Ugaritic texts (*KTU* 1.3 III 38–46). The enumeration begins with Yam, and after some other monsters, among whom *tnn* (cp. Is. li 9), mentions *klbt ilm išt*, the bitch of El, Fire[136]. (In *KTU* 1.5 I 1–5, Baal acts as dragon-slayer; the attribution of the slaying to Anat is apparently a variant of the story.) The verb, used with *išt*, is *mḫṣ*, which must have a meaning resembling that of *ḥṣb*, as it occurs parallel to it four times (*KTU* 1.3 II 6–7, 19–20, 23–24, 29–30, in the passage of the massacre by Anat).

It is noteworthy, that the LXX, the Peshitta and three manuscripts of the Vulgate (Psalt. iuxt. Hebr. FKΘ) have 'flame' in the singular in Ps. xxix 7. It could be that these versions have retained an older reading. The singular 'flame of fire' is more suggestive of a mythological being than the plural 'flames of fire'.

The personified Fire, or – more probably – the pair Fire and Flame, occurs in Ps. civ 4, where the MT reads *'š lhṭ*, burning fire; but as the

---

135 I fail to see how this 'glory' can have anything to do with the 'history of salvation', as is stated by Cazelles (1961), who thinks that vs. 3b was added later to make each naturalistic explanation of the voice of Yhwh impossible. Cp. p. 41 n. 83 and p. 54 n. 125. I also fail to see why the word *kbwd* effectuates a close relationship between Ps. xxix and the call of Isaiah (Is. vi), just because there too the term *kbwd* (and the term *qdš*) is used; see Pax (1962).
136 According to *CSH*, 168, *išt* does probably not have anything to do with 'fire' because it is a name. Even so, the meaning of this name is 'fire'.

word *mšrtyw*, which refers to it, is plural, the emendation *'š wlḥṭ* has been proposed (see *BHK*). These Fire and Flame are called the ministers of Yhwh. The same psalm makes Yhwh's former enemy, Leviathan, a creature which was formed by Yhwh to play with (vs. 26).

One might make the following objection to the explanation of *lhbwt 'š* as a mythological monster in Ps. xxix 7: this verse then seems out of place in the midst of the description of the reaction of nature (which is only an onlooker). Now there is another thing that strikes us with this verse, notably that it has only one line (which is why attempts have been made to complete it). I want to suggest that it is a gloss, which would explain its being limited to one line. Only with some hesitation would I suggest what could have given rise to the gloss. The preceding verse mentions the skipping of the Lebanon like a calf, *'gl*. The list of monsters in *KTU* 1.3 III 38–46 mentions, immediately before Fire, *'gl il 'tk*, the calf of El, *'tk*. It might have happened that the glossator was reminded of the series of monsters by the word *'gl*; for it is not unreasonable to suppose that he knew his mythology.

My explanation remains, of course, hypothetical. Nevertheless, the other explanations (see p. 39–40) are not satisfying; therefore I want to propose the translation 'slays flames of fire' – being a reference to a mythological monster – as a conjecture.

Conclusions

The analysis of the main part of Ps. xxix has led to the following conclusions. Vss. 3–9b represent a thunder-theophany, which is directed against the mighty waters – with which the arch-enemy, Sea, is meant. The voice of the deity causes the fright of nature. These motifs are also found at Ugarit, where they are connected with Baal. The pair 'Lebanon-Siryon', the wilderness of Qadesh, the enclitic *–m* and the form *kmw* in vs. 6, fit in with Ugaritic usage, not or less so with OT usage. Vs. 7 might be a reminiscence of a mythological datum which is found at Ugarit.

The theophany is linked to the introduction by the words *hdrt-qdš*, the majesty of Yhwh's voice which is again mentioned in vs. 4, and by the fact that 'strength' must be given to Yhwh, which is significant if Yhwh has to subdue an enemy, but rather meaningless if this would not be the case.

The term *kbwd* could not be shown to have any connection with the storm-god (just as it has no special ties with El). The 'glorious god' is the god who has to be, and is, honoured; cp. vss. 1–2. In view of the links between the main part and the introduction it is likely, that Yhwh is also imagined to be a storm-god in the introduction. This fits in with our conclusion (p. 37), that to be honoured by the other gods was not a prerogative of El. In fact, so far as we have seen till now, it was Baal who served as a model for Yhwh in Ps. XXIX.

CONCLUSION (VSS. 9C–11)

Translation

(The glorious god thunders)
9c and in his palace all[137] cry: glory.
10 Yhwh sits enthroned on the heavenly ocean,
      Yhwh will sit enthroned as king forever.
11 Yhwh will give strength to his people,
      Yhwh will bless his people with well-being.

Interpretation

kbwd, hykl

In vs. 3b we rejected the interpretation of *kbwd* as a visible phenomenon; neither is it likely to be a visible phenomenon (a hypostatization of Yhwh) in vs. 9c, if only for the fact that this explanation would require a translation of *'mr* which lacks solid foundation.[138] A better explanation

137 The word *klw* is a crux; it may be a case of dittography, as is suggested in *BHK* (*bhyklw klw*). *KBL s.v. kl* 8 mentions Ps. XXIX 9 among the examples of *klw* meaning 'every one'. We would then have what Joüon (1923), 146 j, calls a 'vague suffix' – although Joüon does not mention Ps. XXIX 9 among his examples. This is understandable: whilst in the other instances the suffix in *klw* refers to persons who are (explicitly or implicitly) mentioned before (the literal meaning thus is: the whole of it, 'it' referring to the afore-mentioned persons considered as a group), there are no such persons mentioned in Ps. XXIX, to whom the suffix could refer; I think therefore that Ps. XXIX 9 should be struck off the list in *KBL*. In any case the interpretation of Cazelles (1961) cannot be right; he explains the suffix as referring to Yhwh, translating 'tout ce qui est à lui' (which would underline Yhwh's dominant position). If the suffix referred to Yhwh, the meaning would be: the whole of Yhwh, so that the verse would state that all parts of Yhwh were praising his own person.
138 Cross, *CMHE* 155, translates 'In his temple (his) Glory appears'; 154 n. 39: *'mr* must be vocalized *'āmōr*, in the archaic meaning 'to see', stative-passive 'to appear', cp. the Canaanite name *'amur-ba'l*, 'Baal is seen' or 'Baal appeared'. For Hebrew *'mr*, 'to see',

seems to be that the honour, which the *bny 'lym* are requested to bestow upon Yhwh in vss. 1–2, is given in vs. 9c; the psalm is thus constructed as a closed circle. In view of this, the *hykl* in vs. 9 is obviously the heavenly palace, not the earthly temple[139]: it is the abode of the *bny 'lym*, who are conferring the honour.

Again a point of contact with the Baal epic may be noted: the story of Baal and Yam culminates in Baal's acquiring a palace (*hkl*), where he is seated when he utters his 'holy voice' (*KTU* 1.4 VII 29–35; cp. above, p. 46 and the diagram on p. 49).

mbwl

Being seated in his palace, Yhwh at the same time sits enthroned on[140] the *mbwl*. With great acumen J. Begrich[141] has demonstrated, that *mbwl* originally designated the heavenly ocean, having taken on the sense of 'deluge' only in the course of time. His argument runs as follows: The term *mbwl* occurs, apart from Ps. XXIX 10, only in the flood-story and in Sir. XLIV 17, in a reference to the deluge. The first time the word occurs in P (Gen. VI 17) it is represented, by the use of the definite article, as an entity people were already acquainted with; cp. its first occurrence in J (Gen. VII 10): *my hmbwl*. Furthermore, the term is almost exclusively used to describe the *oncoming* of the *mbwl*: the *mbwl* came on earth. Evidently it concerns an entity which did not belong on earth. In J, the *mbwl* comes on through rains lasting forty days; apparently, in the vision of J, the *mbwl* belongs there where the rain comes from, ergo in the sky. If 'heavenly ocean' is assumed to be the original meaning, that explains why J and P could represent the *mbwl* as a familiar entity, this being a concept the Israelites were acquainted with (cp. Gen. I 6–7: the waters above and underneath the firmament). J always uses the expression *my hmbwl* (whilst in P we also find *mbwl* singly): these are the waters

---

Cross refers to Dahood (1963) 295–296. Dahood (1966), *ad locum*, translates *'mr kbwd* with 'a vision of the Glorious One'. Cp. De Meyer (1980), who explains *kbwd* in (i.a.) Ps. XXIX 9 as 'le Glorieux' (without comment on *'mr*). Margulis (*Bibl* 1970) combines *kbwd* with *yšb* in the following verse: 'The "Honour(-cloud)" of Yhwh is enthroned' (cp. above, p. 29–31) – a very forced translation, in my opinion.

139 Contra Loretz (1974), 191–195; 247–248. Loretz thinks that vs. 9c (according to him a gloss) stresses Yhwh's presence in the Jerusalem temple.

140 As to the preposition *l* with *yšb*, cp. Ugaritic usage; in the OT, the expression is found e.g. in Ps. IX 5 (*yšbt lks'*). Cp. Tsevat (1955) 15, 50.

141 Begrich (1928). I do not think that Loewenstamm (1984), who thinks that Begrich's argumentation is not convincing, has adduced sufficient counter-arguments.

from (i.e. coming out of) the *mbwl*; the *mbwl* itself stays where it belongs, in the sky. J's horizon is still limited as compared to that of P; accordingly, for J, forty days of rainfall suffice to inundate the earth. For P, this was not enough; therefore, instead of water from the *mbwl*, P makes the *mbwl* in its entirety come down to earth – to which are added the 'fountains of the great *thwm*', the waters under the earth. God, who had separated these waters at creation, makes them flow together in the flood-story of P, thus causing chaos to come into existence again. In P, the transition from the meaning 'heavenly ocean' to that of 'deluge' has taken place. In the course of the process of tradition, the original meaning of the term had been forgotten; that is why the gloss *mym* was added (Gen. VI 17; VII 6). In this way, *mbwl* came to signify the deluge.

The force of Begrich's argumentation has not been recognized by every one: after his publication the explanation 'deluge' for *mbwl* in Ps. XXIX is still occasionally found[142]. Yet Begrich also pointed to the difficulty which is presented by the preposition *l*, if *mbwl* is translated by 'deluge': 'above the flood' would require the preposition '*l*; a final meaning of *l* was also rejected by Begrich. To state my own arguments against the latter interpretation: 'to be seated for the flood' (i.e. in order to bring it on) is so highly elliptical as to be hardly intelligible; moreover, the two halves of vs. 10 obviously convey the same idea, that is, just as the notion *mlk* is implied in the first line, the notion *lmbwl* is implicitly present in the second; does Yhwh, then, sit enthroned to cause the flood forever?

After Ugaritic had become known, a third way has been devised to connect *l* with *mbwl* in the sense of 'deluge': the translation 'since the deluge' has been proposed, as Ugaritic *l* sometimes means 'from'.[143] When discussing *l* in Ugaritic, Gordon[144] cites Ps. XXIX 10 among the (six) OT texts, where according to him *l* means 'from' or 'since'. However, I find none of his examples convincing; in every instance *l* can also be explained in conformation with its familiar usage (provided the translation 'deluge' in Ps. XXIX is relinquished).

Finally, we meet with a compromise in the opinion of Gray, that – although 'deluge' is actually not the intended meaning in Ps. XXIX –

142 Delcor (1951) 122; Tournay (1956) 178; Cazelles (1961); Deissler (1961); see also the translations of *BdJ*, *NBG* and *NEB*.

143 Thus e.g. *NEB* ('since the flood' as an alternative for 'above the flood'). The translation 'since' is also given by Dahood (1966) *ad locum*, Freedman-Hyland (1973) and Gray (1979) 41, but these authors do not explain *mbwl* as 'deluge'; see below.

144 Gordon (1965) 10. 1; the OT texts cited by Gordon are Ps. LXXXIV 12, 2 Kgs. IV 24, Josh. III 12, 2 Kgs. XIV 28, Is. LIX 20 and Ps. XXIX 10.

'the tendency in Israel would be to see a reference to the Flood'.[145] To be sure, at some point in the history of development of the OT the original meaning of *mbwl* must have been forgotten, as the gloss *mym* in P (Gen. VI 17; VII 6) demonstrates; when this would have been, may well prove to be a fruitless debate. But we should occupy ourselves with the search for the intention of the writer of the psalm, an intention which must have been rightly understood by his contemporaries[146], rather than with later misunderstandings.

Next we have those authors who, whilst accepting the meaning 'ocean' in the present case, have taken it to refer to the hostile waters which were subdued by Yhwh. In three cases this is combined with the translation 'since' for *l*, so that *mbwl*, properly speaking, is not the enemy but must refer to the battle.[147] Having rejected this meaning of *l*, and the meaning 'above' as well[148], the only grammatically correct explanation seems to me to be that Yhwh sat directly upon his enemy (provided one accepts the interpretation of *mbwl* as a hostile power).

In a number of cases comments are made to the effect that Yhwh's victory over the *mbwl* implies his creation of the world. It is a much-debated problem whether the battle with Sea in the OT was conceived as a battle of creation or not. In a way it is not surprising to find several remarks made on creation in connection with Ps. XXIX 10: one is reminded of Yhwh's dividing of the waters, in the priestly creation-story, into waters above and underneath the firmament (Gen. I 6–7), of which Gunkel argued that it was a reminiscence of Marduk's splitting up Tiamat. Therefore, the association with creation is more readily made than if the enemy (still supposing *mbwl* is indeed the enemy) had been termed Yam.

145 Gray (1979) 42.
146 As Gray holds Ps. XXIX to be originally a Canaanite hymn to Baal, which has been adopted by Yahwism, he possibly assumes that the meaning 'deluge' attached itself to *mbwl* as soon as the psalm was taken over in Israel. The objections to this, however, are 1) the lack of evidence that Ps. XXIX had a Canaanite *Vorlage*; 2) Begrich's convincing argument that the Hebrew term *mbwl* took on the meaning 'deluge' only after a lapse of time.
147 This is explicitly stated by Dahood (1966) *ad locum*: 'since the flood' refers to the battle of Baal and Yam; less clear are the explanations of Freedman-Hyland (1973), who state that 'since the Flood' refers to the primeval flood which was conquered by Yhwh, and Gray (1979) 42: 'since the flood' refers to the unruly waters which contested the kingship with Baal.
148 Mowinckel (1922) 48 n. 1: 'hoch über der jetzt gebändigten ... "Flut" steht ... Gottes Thron'; May (1955), who mentions Ps. XXIX 10 as an example of the insurgent waters, translates 'above the flood'.

To quote some opinions: A. R. Johnson[149]: the flood signifies the chaos of waters or cosmic sea, of which Johnson remarks in his discussion of Ps. xciii, that it was in virtue of his triumph over it, that Yhwh could bring the habitable world into existence; N. H. Ridderbos[150]: Ps. xxix 10 is related to Gen. i, because there too God creates order out of chaos and directs the waters to their proper places; H. J. Kraus[151]: Yhwh has the threatening chaos lying at his feet; 'Hier klingen wohl Momente der Schöpfungstheologie an'; S. Mittmann[152] speaks of the heavenly ocean which threatens the created world, so that Yhwh's being enthroned thereon means that chaos has totally lost its power.

Given the association of *mbwl* with creation, it is also not surprising to find parallels drawn with Enuma elish. S. Mowinckel, who in his *Psalmenstudien* II writes that 'Der israelitische Schöpfungsmythus ist bekanntlich im letzten Grunde identisch mit dem babylonischen', comments in the same work on Ps. xxix 10: 'Jahwä (hat) seinen Thron – wohl im Himmel – über das gebändigte Meer aufgerichtet'; he explains *mbwl* as the 'Urmeerflut, tehom', which was beaten and split and from which the world was created.[153] Th. H. Gaster[154] does not, as a matter of fact, mention creation; but he recalls Marduk's palace Esagila, which was founded upon the nether sea (Enuma elish VI 47). R. Luyster[155], who calls Yhwh's battle with Sea 'cosmogonic', mentions Ps. xxix 10 among the examples of Yhwh's supremacy over the insurgent sea, to which he also refers as the cosmic waters, the forces of chaos, *thwm*, the Hebrew version of the Babylonian Tiamat. T. N. D. Mettinger[156], who stresses that the battle motif in the OT was linked up with creation, compares Ps. xxix 10 with the Babylonian conception, that Marduk sat upon Tiamat.[157]

It strikes us rather more when we find the opinion, that Ps. xxix represents an ancient Baal hymn or, anyway, makes use of Canaanite mythological conceptions, combined with a comment on creation. Of

149 Johnson (1955) 56, 58.
150 Ridderbos (1960).
151 Kraus (1978⁵) *ad locum*.
152 Mittmann (1978).
153 Mowinckel (1922) 46, 48, 48 n. 1.
154 Gaster (1946/47).
155 Luyster (1981).
156 Mettinger (1982) Ch. II.
157 Mettinger refers to Lambert (1963) 190: 'The Sea (Tiamat) was no doubt a small cultic structure in the Akītu house (probably a dais) and when the statue of Marduk was taken there, it was set on the dais to symbolize victory over Tiamat'.

those who consider Ps. xxix 10 to be a reminiscence of the battle between Baal and Yam I already mentioned Dahood and Gray; the first to suggest this was (as with Ps. xxix 3) J. A. Montgomery.[158] These three, however, do not associate the triumph over the *mbwl* with creation. R. J. Clifford[159], on the contrary, whilst considering Ps. xxix to be an adapted hymn to Baal, makes the following comment on vs. 10: 'Yahweh seats himself on Flood (another name for Sea), presumably the remnant of the slain monster from which he has created the cosmos'. With this he follows F. M. Cross, who translates 'Yahweh sits enthroned on the Flooddragon'; Cross too considers the battle between Baal and Yam to be a battle of creation.[160] We shall return immediately to the question of the 'cosmogonic' character of the battle at Ugarit; for the moment I only want to remark that it seems wholly unwarranted to consider the sea and the sea-monster (although it is true that they alternately function as the enemy) as one and the same thing.

Now in my opinion, the explanation of *mbwl* in Ps. xxix as a hostile power is incorrect. Apart from the sea-monsters, Yhwh's enemy is always termed *ym, nhr, thwm* (c.q. the plural of these nouns), or *mym*; we also find *(m)ṣwlh*, the deep. As I understand it, it definitely concerns an entity on earth (just like the enemy of Baal in the Ugaritic texts, who is named *zbl ym ṭpṭ nhr*). That the name *thwm* may be used for it, can be explained by the fact that according to the Israelite conception the seas are connected with the *thwm*.[161] Apparently it is assumed by those who consider the *mbwl* to be the enemy, that *thwm* and *mbwl* amount to the same thing; maybe these authors suppose that the Israelites conceived the upper and nether oceans as being connected, so that it would, in fact, be one ocean encircling the whole cosmos. There is, however, no evidence for this in the OT.[162] Moreover, also in that case a distinction was evidently made between its upper and nether parts, as appears from their different names. Therefore, if one accepts the view that the enemy was the earthly sea, we can, at the most, expect him to be termed *thwm* (which in fact he is sometimes called), but not *mbwl*.

158 Montgomery (1935) 270.
159 Clifford (1979) 141.
160 *CMHE* 155; cp. 120, on the 'cosmogonic' character of the battle with Sea at Ugarit.
161 In *KTU* 1.23 30 *gp ym* is parallelled to *gp thm*: the coast of the sea // the coast of the *thm*. Apparently it concerns the earthly sea. In the OT too *thwm* is used parallel to *ym* (e.g. Job xxviii 14; xxxviii 16). This contradicts the opinion of Snaith, who states that 'The word tehôm does not refer to the depths of any natural sea. This is the depths of the primeval ocean, of Tiamat the great sea monster'. See Snaith (1965) 397.
162 Cp. Jacobs (1975) 66–71.

If it is, nevertheless, maintained that *mbwl* designates a hostile power, the necessary implication is that the enemy was not the earthly sea, like at Ugarit, but the 'cosmic waters' which were separated at creation; we would then have a concept resembling the Mesopotamic Tiamat, not the Ugaritic Yam. That would imply, I think, that Yhwh's enemy is also regarded as such in the other texts which speak of Yhwh's enmity with the waters.

Now there have been scholars who have claimed a 'cosmogonic' character for Baal's victory over Yam. They had good reason to do so: if the presence of the 'creation through conflict' idea is assumed in the OT, and if it is assumed at the same time that the motif of Yhwh's battle with Sea was taken over by the Israelites from their Canaanite neighbours, one has to put up with a discrepancy (Baal's fight not being connected with creation) which is somewhat problematic indeed. It seems to me, therefore, that to call Baal's battle 'cosmogonic' is a device born out of necessity; it does not have, to my mind, much to be said for it.[163] The discrepancy would, of course, not exist if it is assumed (as

163 Fisher (1965) calls the series 'conflict – kingship – ordering of chaos – temple building' a 'creation of the Baal type'. Baal's kingship has many cosmic connotations, according to Fisher: it brings peace and order to the cosmos; also Baal sets the seasons, as appears from *KTU* 1.4 V 6–9. Baal's temple – thus still Fisher – is a microcosm, a fact which is illustrated by its window, which is a cleft in the clouds, and by its being built in seven days; therefore the ordering of this temple resembles the creation of the cosmos. Kapelrud (*UF* 1979) criticizes this idea: the struggle between Baal and Yam is about who is to be the ruler; the ruler has to have a temple, but the text does not say anything about the ordering of chaos or the creation of cosmos. I fully agree with Kapelrud. Cp. also Koch (1979) 469: the battle is about dominion; furthermore it is to be doubted if Baal's adversaries are conceived as chaotic powers, as the text also gives positive titles to Yam and Mot (*ṭpṭ* resp. *ǵzr*). Cross, *CMHE* 120, calls Baal's battle 'cosmogonic', stating that the tale of the establishment of a dynastic temple and its cult is a typical subtheme of the cosmogony and its ritual; it is also found in Enuma elish and in the OT. I think this is an example of carrying the comparative method too far. I may also mention Grønbaek (1984), who calls the struggle between Baal and Yam a 'cosmological myth' of which creation is the central motif, namely, creation in the sense of maintenance of the social 'cosmos'. I think, however, that the problem should not be solved by altering the definition of 'creation'. A more promising track is, in my opinion, followed by De Moor (1971), Ch. IV, who takes the possibility into consideration that two separate myths about a battle of Baal existed at Ugarit: 1) the yearly conquest of Yam in *KTU* 1.2 IV; 2) a primordial battle, connected with creation, between Baal and Anat on the one hand, and Yam and his satellites on the other, to which *KTU* 1.9 and *KTU* 1.82 and 1.83 might refer. (Cp. Loewenstamm (*ErIs* 1969), who suggests that *KTU* 1.3 III 38–46 and *KTU* 1.83 represent an older stratum of the Baal-Yam myth.) Anyway, as the second myth is hypothetical, we have, for the present, to discard the theory that Baal's battle was connected with creation.

indeed several scholars do) that Yhwh's battle did not lead up to creation; but, naturally, the reasons for this assumption would have to be independent of the consideration that it would remove the discord between the battle motif in the OT and in the Ugaritic texts. If one feels compelled to assume an essential connection between Yhwh's battle and his creation of the world (which is to be distinguished from a superficial relationship, merely consisting in the joint occurrence, in certain passages, of two actually separate motifs), one might be led to suppose that Mesopotamic not Canaanite ideas influenced the OT conception of the battle (unless one does not want to assume any external influence at all).

Thus it appears that the question of the *mbwl* in Ps. xxix 10 has brought us to a cardinal point in our investigation; for if the *mbwl* is an enemy like Tiamat, we would not have a consistent picture of the deity as Baal in this psalm – perhaps not a picture of the deity as Baal at all.

To illustrate the complications raised by the absence of the creation-motif in connection with Baal – if one wants nevertheless to assume Canaanite influence on Israel –, I want to quote some statements made by Mowinckel, after he had become acquainted with the Ugaritic texts.

Mowinckel was firmly convinced that the battle-myth in the OT was a myth of creation. When he wrote, in 1922, the comment on Ps. xxix 10 quoted by me above, the Ugaritic texts were not known; after their discovery, he had to adapt his theory regarding Babylonian influence on Israel. It is interesting to note how Mowinckel wrestled with the problem raised by the absence of the motif of creation in connection with Baal. This appears from several contradictory statements made by him.[164]

Mowinckel writes that, because the Ugaritic battle myth is not a story of creation, a direct influence of Mesopotamia on Israel must be assumed in this respect. At the same time he states that, in Israel, the Canaanite Autumn Festival was taken over, becoming the Enthronement Festival of Yhwh; that, according to a common oriental conception, creation – being conceived as a fight against the primeval ocean – was the basis of the kingship of the god; that the Israelite conception of creation as the victory of Yhwh over the primeval ocean has a Canaanite background; and that the creation myth probably came to Israel via Canaan. Then again he writes that the Ugaritic myth probably had the

---

164 The following is quoted from Mowinckel (1955) and from Mowinckel (1962) Ch. V.

Mesopotamic one as its ultimate source, and that the festival of the Canaanites was a particular version of a common oriental cultic pattern (surely the words 'particular version' must in any case also refer to the absence of the creation motif). Of course the question must be asked, how the 'creation myth' could have reached Israel via Canaan, if its basic motif (creation) was missing in Canaan. It is hardly conceivable that the battle story, having first been stripped of the creation motif, was taken over by Israel from the Canaanites, after which it was supplied by the Israelites with the creation motif, taken over directly from Mesopotamia.

The confusion becomes even greater when Mowinckel states that in Canaan the creator god was El, and that the Jebusite Autumn Festival must already have celebrated the enthronement of El Elyon. It was certainly known to Mowinckel, that El did not fight the primeval ocean. Indeed he mentions Baal's becoming king of the gods (strangely enough, after his victory over Mot – but then Mowinckel seems to identify Yam and Mot, as he writes that 'every year... Death or "Prince Sea" – *zebul yam*, as he is named in Ugaritic mythology – seeks to overthrow the land of the living'), concluding that Yhwh was El and Baal at the same time. Thus we see that Mowinckel tried to insert the creation motif into the Canaanite Autumn Festival via the mythology of El, whereas the battle (followed up by the enthronement) remained a motif connected with Baal, who was not a creator. Furthermore it does not become clear how Mowinckel rhymes the supposed Mesopotamic influence on Israel regarding the creation motif with the supposition that this motif stemmed from the mythology of the Jebusite El.

The above has given a sufficient picture of the difficulties involved. Now in my opinion, it cannot be doubted that the Canaanite conception of the battle of the deity with Sea exercised a direct influence upon Israelite belief; or, to put it better: that the Israelites shared this belief with the non-Hebrew population of Canaan (I may refer to my conclusion on p. 61, that Ps. xxix has thus far shown a consistent picture of Yhwh as a Baal). It also seems to me that an essential connection between Yhwh's battle with Sea and his creation of the world cannot be inferred from the extant texts. I think I should state my arguments for the latter conviction, in order to give a more solid foundation to the former.

First we should occupy ourselves for a moment with the current debate on the subject. As it is hardly possible to give a survey of all the authors who have discussed the question, I want to mention only a few; this may give an indication of the kind of arguments used.

Some authors have taken it for granted that the battle in the OT was a battle of creation, e.g. L. I. J. Stadelmann who, having stated that the conception of creation by division was common to all ancient Near Eastern mythologies, infers from i.a. Ps. LXXIV 12–17, LXXXIX 10–13, CIV 5–9, Job XXXVIII 8–11 and Prov. VIII 29 that 'here the separation is presented as involving a conflict'[165]; M. K. Wakeman states that the creation of the cosmos depended on the monster's defeat, remarking (with reference to the root *ḥll* in Is. LI 9, Ps. LXXXIX 11 and Job XXVI 13) that 'only when "the body" is split open does its potential for good become actual in the order of the cosmos'[166]; A. S. Kapelrud writes that the victory was not only a condition for creation, but formed part of it: 'Es ist etwas Urtiefes, das hier zum Ausdruck kommt, ein Gefühl, dass nichts erschaffen werden konnte ohne Ringen mit Schwierigkeiten und Widerständen'[167]; moreover he states that in the creation stories of the ancient Near East 'Scheidung, Trennung, ist ein Stichwort'[168], as chaos was that which does not know division; H. Gottlieb[169] speaks of the 'creation myth' as something which is self-evident.

Others have felt the need of an argument for this view, e.g. H. Ringgren, who writes that one cannot tell for sure whether, in Pss. LXXIV and LXXXIX, creation is the result of the combat, but that it is reasonable to suppose that this is implied; anyway, 'l'autorité de Yahvé sur les réalités de la nature a une relation logique avec l'issue du combat'[170]; T. N. D. Mettinger[171], who uses the expression 'creation through conflict', adduces the opinion of F. Stolz against those who have argued that in some descriptions of the battle (e.g. Ps. LXXIV 12–17) the world is represented as already existing: 'Der Mythus anerkennt kein "vorher" oder "nachher" ausser sich'[172], and 'Wieder ist nicht zu fragen, ob der

165 Stadelmann (1970) 17 n. 98.
166 Wakeman (1973) 80; cp. Wakeman (1969).
167 Kapelrud (*ZAW* 1979) 162.
168 Kapelrud (*ZAW* 1979) 165.
169 Gottlieb (1980).
170 Ringgren (1981) 391.
171 Mettinger (1982) Ch. II.
172 Stolz (1970) 39.

Kampf "vor" oder "nach" der Schöpfung stattfindet. Im Kampfmythus aktualisiert sich die Schöpfung je und je'[173]; Mettinger also refers to Ps. XXIV 1–2, Yhwh's founding of the earth on the waters.

An intermediate position between those who connect the battle with creation and those who do not is taken by those who express as their view, that various traditions have influenced the allusions to the battle in the OT. Thus O. Kaiser[174] is prepared to admit (especially on the strength of Ps. LXXXIX 10–13, XCIII 1, 3, 4, CIV 5–9 and Job XXXVIII 4–11) that Yhwh's struggle with Rahab is a battle of creation, but he infers from Job XXVI 12–13 that, in contradistinction to the battle with Rahab, the battle with Leviathan took place after creation; Leviathan is, according to Kaiser, a monster embodied by the mass of clouds, which is why Job XXVI 13 can state, parallel to the piercing of the *nḥš bryḥ* (= Leviathan; see Is. XXVII 1), that Yhwh's breath clears the sky. This image is tentatively connected by Kaiser with the Egyptian mythology of Apophis, the monster which not only tries to obstruct Re's course at night, but also threatens to take away the light by day.[175]

W. H. Schmidt[176] calls the allusions to the battle in the OT, as well as their origins, pluriform. Because the battle in Ps. CIV and Job XXVI takes place after creation, and because several texts mention the battle but not creation, we must – thus Schmidt – reckon with influence from Canaan in the first place; as Yhwh took the function of creator from El, creation and battle could be connected in the OT (see Pss. LXXIV and LXXXIX, where the battle takes place before creation – although it might be the other way round in Ps. LXXIV, because first Yhwh's deeds of salvation 'on earth' are mentioned). Moreover, Babylonian influence may have been at work in this respect (next to, possibly, Egyptian influence). A stronger term than merely 'connected' is used by Schmidt when he writes that creation and battle are to be 'identified' only when they are

173 Stolz (1970) 64.
174 Kaiser (1959) 140–152.
175 Cp. Norin (1977) Ch. II. Norin distinguishes between Egyptian influence on Israel (the monsters Leviathan, Tannin and Rahab) and Canaanite influence (Yam, Nahar). In the OT, the conflict with the monsters took place after creation, which can be compared with Egyptian mythology: Seth vanquishes Apophis every night (Book of the Dead 108); Re conquers the *snk n mw* (the crocodile of the waters, following Norin – but I may add that, according to Posener (1953), 473, these words signify 'the avarice of the waters') immediately after creation (Instruction for King Merikare, *ANET*[3] 417). Norin thinks the Israelites may have adopted these Egyptian conceptions when they were living in Egypt.
176 Schmidt (1961) 38–43.

mentioned together. However, this is not further explained by him.

Likewise J. Jeremias[177] reckons with influences from Ugarit and from Babylonia; the first must be assumed in those cases where the battle is not connected with creation. In Ps. CIV, the battle is a condition for creation; therefore the writer of this psalm must have known the Babylonian creation account. However, Jeremias also remarks that in many texts one cannot tell whether creation follows the battle or vice versa: in these texts a number of deeds of Yhwh is summed up without any chronological order. (Indeed we noted already differences of opinion as to the succession in some cases).

C. Westermann[178] points to the fact that Sumerian mythology does not know the conception of creation as a result of a battle; these two motifs were only combined in Babylon[179]; neither do the Canaanite and Egyptian traditions know this combination. This means, that the battle in the OT does not *eo ipso* imply creation. Nevertheless, Westermann speaks of a 'deutlicher Widerhall' in the OT of the concept of creation through combat, which is directly recognizable in a number of psalms. But because the OT contains only allusions to the battle – not the story as a whole – which are found in different contexts, because, moreover, there are different names for the monster, and because the battle motif is often found without the creation motif, Westermann concludes that it is a matter of 'eine Fülle verschiedener Mythen verschiedener Herkunft'; there must have been Canaanite as well as Babylonian influences, possibly also Egyptian influence. As to Gen. I, Westermann speaks of a very weak reminiscence of the battle motif in vs. 2, but on the whole he considers this account of the creation to go back to traditions older than Enuma elish, according to which the division of heaven and earth was the essence of creation, without any battle (see the Sume-

---

177 Jeremias (1965) Ch. II 2.
178 Westermann (1974) 39–48.
179 Cp. Lambert (1975). Lambert writes that Enuma elish combines two originally separate cosmologies; the one is of two levels: heaven and earth, obtained by the splitting of Tiamat (IV 135–140; V 62), the other of three levels: heaven, earth and Apsu (IV 145–146). As to the former: the idea that heaven and earth were once joined and were separated as the first act of creation is found with the Sumerians, and in the Hittite Kumarbi myth (*ANET*[3] 125), as well as in other civilizations. Presumably it was very old, and taken over in Mesopotamia from prehistoric tradition. However, the author of Enuma elish has not been too faithful to this tradition in that he has inserted the three-decker version between his statements about the two halves of Tiamat. Also the body thus sundered is not elsewhere a mass of water, so probably the author, or a lost source on which he depended, has joined the old myth on to the story of the defeat of Tiamat.

rian myth of Gilgamesh, Enkidu and the Netherworld, and the Sumerian poem of the Pickaxe[180]). In Egypt too, the conception of creation through division of heaven and earth is found.[181]

Finally we arrive at those authors who deny any connection of the battle with creation in the OT.

D. J. McCarthy[182] settles the question by stating that the so-called 'creation motifs' in the OT are merely figures of speech; they symbolize salvation.

L. Vosberg[183] uses the same arguments that we have met already, namely the fact that in Canaan the creator and the divine warrior are two different gods; that we find the battle without creation in the OT, and reversely creation without the battle; and that the battle takes place after creation in Ps. CIV. In addition, Vosberg counters the opinion that the battle leads up to creation in Pss. LXXIV and LXXXIX by drawing attention to the nominal clauses in Ps. LXXIV 16, LXXXIX 12, which according to him disconnect the battle in the preceding verses from creation in the following.

H. W. F. Saggs[184] argues, that neither in Ps. LXXIV nor in Ps. LXXXIX is there any causal connection between the battle and creation. In Ps. LXXIV, beasts already existed to whom Leviathan could be given as food; besides, there were rivers which could be dried up. Saggs does not think it likely that these were primordially existent waters; if so, they are here fully demythologized and thus from quite a different stratum of belief from Tannin and Leviathan, which would be against the conclusion that the passage (vss. 12–17) is the relic of a single consecutive myth. In Job XXVI, if the verses preceding the mention of the defeat of the monster(s) do refer to cosmic creation (and they could equally refer to God currently and constantly maintaining the universe), they do not make cosmic creation the culmination of a *Chaoskampf*, but either antecedent or parallel to it. Moreover, Enuma elish is not a paradigm for ancient Near Eastern creation myths; it is a conflation of originally separate elements, with as central theme the assertion and justification of the supremacy of Marduk and Babylon. Divine combat is known from several Mesopotamian myths, but these do not mention creation; on the

---

180 Kramer 37 and 52.
181 Referring to Dantinne (1961), Westermann suggests that *br'* (Gen. I 1) might signify 'to separate'; Dantinne bases this on Josh. XVII 15, 18 and Ezek. XXIII 47.
182 McCarthy (1967).
183 Vosberg (1975) 10, 46–48.
184 Saggs (1978) 30–63.

other hand, in a number of early Mesopotamic myth fragments creation occurred without combat. 'In view of these facts, it appears difficult to maintain the view taken by Gunkel, and most recently stated
explicitly by M. K. Wakeman, that there was one all-embracing myth
in which cosmic creation was necessarily linked with a divine combat,
and on the basis of this hypothesis to create a synthesis in which Old
Testament allusions to God's control of a monster and Old Testament
references to cosmic creation fall together as examples of the postulated
myth occurring in the Israelite tradition.'[185]

On Gen. I I – II 4a, Saggs holds that it contains a reaction against
Babylonian ideas, rather than a demythologization of earlier Israelite
concepts or a direct adaptation of Mesopotamic ideas (see for instance
the function of sun and moon, which seems to be minimized, as the light
was created first; the purpose was to combat the idea that the heavenly
bodies were divine beings).

Thus we see that, apart from arguments based on the state of affairs
outside Israel, the arguments roughly amount to these: it is (im)possible
to assume a causal relationship between battle and creation in those OT
passages where they occur jointly, because 1) creation is mentioned
before/after the battle; 2) it can(not) be inferred from the texts that
during the battle the earth already existed. Now in my opinion, the
order in which the two are mentioned is a doubtful criterion in lyrical
poetry (cp. Jeremias); in fact now the one, then the other is mentioned
first. (Only I am not able to grasp the meaning of the remark – Mettinger, Stolz –, that the sequence is irrelevant as it concerns a myth.)

The mention which is made of existing things together with a reference to the battle (he beasts in Ps. LXXIV 14; note also the mountains in
Ps. CIV 6) could be the final argument; but then one might counter that
those beasts were only created at the time of the conflict, or that the
mountains were *in statu nascendi*.

Therefore I propose that we set about it via another road. Knowing
the way creation, through a battle with Sea, was accomplished in
Enuma elish, we might expect it to have been pictured in the same
manner in Israel – always assuming that the battle with Sea in the OT
was a battle of creation. Indeed those who assume this (at least partly) to
be the case, are reckoning with Babylonian influence as a matter of
course. In Enuma elish, Tiamat was split into two halves, an image

---

185 Saggs (1978) 60.

which we also find in Gen. 1 6–7.[186] The question is, whether the OT poetry about a conflict with Sea also knows this conception.

Accordingly, we have to inquire into the exact manner in which Yhwh deals with the sea in the poetical passages. I want to divide the texts into 1) those which mention creation in the immediate vicinity of a reference to the sea (or other terms for the waters), and 2) those which mention only a conflict with the waters. Although as a matter of fact mythological imagery is used in descriptions of the event at the Reed Sea, those texts in which 'the sea' (etc.) indicates the waters in which the enemy was drowned or through which the Israelites passed will be left out, as these events form a complication when it is a matter of finding out Yhwh's dealings with the sea as his primeval enemy. The event at the Reed Sea will occupy us in another chapter of the present study.

1 Yhwh is the author of the following actions:

	with regard to the water	explicit reference to creation
	a *to make*	
Ps. XCV	5 to make (*'śh*) the sea.	5 idem + to form (*yṣr*) the dry land.
Ps. CXLVIII	4–6 to create (*br'*) and to establish (*'md*) the waters above the heavens.	4–6 idem; creation of the heaven of heavens is implied.
	b *to use as a foundation*	
Ps. XXIV	2 to found (*ysd*) the earth upon the seas and to establish (*kwn*) it upon the rivers.	2 idem
Ps. CIV	3 to build (*qrh*) upper chambers on the waters.	2 to spread out (*nṭh*) the heavens; 5 to found (*ysd*) the earth; 8 mountains rise, valleys sink into their places.[187]
Ps. CXXXVI	6 to spread out (*rq'*) the earth upon the waters.	6 idem; 5 to make (*'śh*) the heavens.

186 One should note, however, that Gen. 1 6–7 differ from Enuma elish in that the waters are turned into the upper and nether oceans, whereas Tiamat is made into heaven and earth.

187 Sutcliffe (1952) takes the waters as subject of this sentence: 'They go up to the mountains, they go down to the valleys, to the place thou hast established for them'. Indeed this gives a better connection with vs. 9, which has the waters as subject; but I find the matter difficult to decide, as vs. 8 may have been put in between the statements about the waters in rather an off-hand way.

Job XXVI 10 to draw a circle (*ḥqq ḥg*) upon the waters at the boundary between light and darkness.

7 to spread out (*nṭh*) the north over the void and to hang (*tlh*) the earth upon nothing.

Prov. VIII 27 to draw a circle (*ḥqq ḥwg*) upon the *thwm*.

27 to establish (*kwn*) the heavens; 29 to mark out (*ḥqq*) the foundations of the earth.

d *to establish a border, to set bars and doors*

Ps. CIV 9 to establish a border (*śym gbwl*), not to be passed, for the *thwm* which covered the earth – the waters standing above the mountains – (6, *l.* *ksth*) but which was driven away (7); the waters will not cover the earth any more.

2 to spread out (*nṭh*) the heavens; 5 to found (*ysd*) the earth; 8 mountains rise, valleys sink into their places.[188]

Ps. CXLVIII 6 to establish a border (*ntn ḥq*) for the waters above the heavens.

4–6 to create (*br'*) and to establish these waters; creation of heaven of heavens implied.

Job XXXVIII 8–11 to shut up (*skk*) the sea with doors (*dltym*) at its coming from the womb; to establish (*śbr* †, LXX *tithesthai*) a border (*ḥq*) for it, to set up a bar (*bryḥ*) and doors (*dltym*), calling a halt to its proud waves.

4–6 to found (*ysd*) the earth, measuring it and putting up its pillars and corner-stone.

Prov. VIII 29 to assign to the sea its border (*śwm ḥq*), so that waters will not transgress command.

27 to establish (*kwn*) the heavens; 29 to mark out (*ḥqq*) the foundations of the earth.

Or. Man. 3 to fetter (*pedan*) the sea, to shut up (*kleiein*) the deep (*abussos*) and to seal it (*sphragizesthai*).

2 to make (*poiein*) heaven and earth.

e *to cleave*

Ps. LXXIV 15 to cleave open (*bq'*) spring (*m'yn*) and brook (*nḥl*).

16–17 to establish (*kwn*) moon and sun, to fix (*nṣb*) the boundaries of the earth, to create (*yṣr*) summer and winter.

Prov. III 20 to cleave open (*bq'*) the *thmwt*, whilst the clouds drop dew.

19 to found (*ysd*) the earth, to establish (*kwn*) the heavens.

f *to gather, to gather in clouds*

Ps. XXXIII 7 to gather (*kns*) the waters of the sea as a dam (*nd*; *l. cum vrs. n'd:* as – in – a skinbottle), to put (*ntn*) the *thmwt* in storehouses.

6 to make (*'śh*) the heavens and their host.

188 See p. 75 n. 187.

Job XXVI	8 to bind (ṣrr) the waters in the clouds; the clouds are not rent (bqʿ) under them.	7 to spread out (nṭh) the north over the void and to hang (tlh) the earth upon nothing.
Job XXXVIII	9 (at the coming of the sea from the womb, 8) to make clouds its garment (lbš) and darkness its swaddling-band (ḥtlh).	4–6 to found (ysd) the earth, measuring it and putting up its pillars and corner-stone.
Cp. Prov. VIII	28 to make the clouds firm (ʾmṣ) whilst the springs (ʿynwt) of the thwm are strong (ʿzz).	27 to establish (kwn) the heavens; 29 to mark out (ḥqq) the foundations of the earth.

g *to summon and pour out*

Am. V	8 to summon (qrʾ l) the waters of the sea and to pour them out (špk) over the earth.	8 to make (ʿśh) constellations.
Am. IX	6 to summon (qrʾ l) the waters of the sea and to pour them out (špk) over the earth.	6 to build (bnh) upper chambers in the heavens and to found (ysd) a vault upon the earth.

h *to rebuke*

Ps. CIV	7 waters of thwm flee at rebuke (gʿr), at sound of thunder.	2 to spread out (nṭh) the heavens; 5 to found (ysd) the earth; 8 mountains rise, valleys sink into their places.[189]
Job XXVI	11 to scold (gʿr) so that the pillars of heaven tremble (as appears from 12, the object of the rebuke is the sea).	7 to spread out (nṭh) the north over the void and to hang (tlh) the earth upon nothing.

i *to stir*

Is. LI	15 to stir (rgʿ) the sea so that its waves roar.	13 to spread out (nṭh) the heavens, to found (ysd) the earth; 16 to plant (nṭʿ; Pesh. nṭh) the heavens, to found (ysd) the earth.
Jer. XXXI	35 to stir (rgʿ) the sea so that its waves roar.	35 to give (ntn) sun, moon and stars.
Ps. LXXIV	13 to stir (prr; or: break?) the sea.	16–17 to establish (kwn) moon and sun, to fix (nṣb) the boundaries of the earth, to create (yṣr) summer and winter.
Job XXVI	12 to stir (rgʿ) the sea.	7 to spread out (nṭh) the north over the void and to hang (tlh) the earth upon nothing.

j *to still*

Ps. LXV	8 to still (šbḥ) the roaring of the seas and of their waves.	7 to establish (kwn) the mountains.

189 See p. 75 n. 187.

Ps. LXXXIX	10 to still (*šbḥ*) the waves of the sea.	12 to found (*ysd*) the world; 13 to create (*brʾ*) the north and the south.
Sir. XLIII	23 to still (*kopazein*) the deep (*abussos*).	23 to plant (*phuteuein*) islands in it.

k *to dry up*

Is. XLIV	27 to say to the deep (*ṣwlh*): be dry (*ḥrb*), I will dry up (*ybš*) your rivers.	24 to make (*ʿśh*) all things, to spread out (*nṭh*) the heavens and to spread out (*rqʿ*) the earth.
Ps. LXXIV	15 to dry up (*ybš*) ever-flowing rivers.	16–17 to establish (*kwn*) moon and sun, to fix (*nṣb*) the boundaries of the earth, to create (*yṣr*) summer and winter.

l *to rule, to be mightier than, to tread upon*

Ps. LXXXIX	10 to rule (*mšl b*) the surging sea (or: the arrogance of the sea).	12 to found (*ysd*) the world; 13 to create (*brʾ*) the north and the south.
Ps. XCIII	3–4 to be mightier than (*ʾdyr mn*) rivers, mighty waters (*mym rbym*) and the breakers of the sea.	1 the world is firmly established (*kwn*).
Job IX	8 to tread upon the heights (*drk ʿl-bmty*) of the sea.	8 to spread out (*nṭh*) the heavens; 9 to make (*ʿśh*) constellations.

m *to fight the monsters*

Ps. LXXIV	13–14 to shatter (*šbr*) the heads of the Tanninim on the waters; to crush (*rṣṣ*) the heads of Leviathan, giving him as food to the beasts of the desert.	16–17 to establish (*kwn*) moon and sun, to fix (*nṣb*) the boundaries of the earth, to create (*yṣr*) summer and winter.
Ps. LXXXIX	11 to crush (*dkʾ*) Rahab like one slain (pierced with the sword, *ḥll*); to scatter (*pzr*) the enemies.	12 to found (*ysd*) the world; 13 to create (*brʾ*) the north and the south.
Job IX	13 to be angry with the helpers of Rahab, who are crouching (*šḥḥ*).	8 to spread out (*nṭh*) the heavens; 9 to make (*ʿśh*) constellations.
Job XXVI	12–13 to smite (break to pieces, *mḥṣ*) Rahab and to pierce (*ḥll*) the fleeing serpent, clearing the heavens.	7 to spread out (*nṭh*) the north over the void and to hang (*tlh*) the earth upon nothing.

The following combinations occur:

Ps. LXXIV 13–15 to stir (to break?) the sea; to shatter the heads of the Tanninim and of Leviathan; to cleave open spring and brook; to dry up rivers.

Ps. LXXXIX to rule the sea; to still the waves; to crush Rahab; to scatter
10–11   the enemies.
Ps. CIV   to build the upper chambers on the waters; to rebuke the
3, 7, 9   waters of the *thwm* so that they flee; to establish a border
           for them.
Ps. CXLVIII to create and to establish the waters above the heavens; to
4–6   establish a border for them.
Job IX   to tread upon the heights of the sea; to be angry with the
8, 13   helpers of Rahab.
Job XXVI   to gather the waters in the clouds; to draw a circle upon
8, 10–13   the waters; to scold; to stir the sea; to smite Rahab and to
           pierce the serpent.
Job XXXVIII to shut up the sea with doors; to gather it in the clouds; to
8–11   establish a border for it; to set up a bar and doors.
Prov. VIII to draw a circle upon the *thwm*; to make the clouds firm
27–29   whilst the springs of the *thwm* are strong; to establish a
           border for the sea.

The verbs used for the activity of creation in those passages where no
water is mentioned are about the same as those we met in the right-hand
column above; we find, with heaven or earth as object (with very few
exceptions, such as the mountains or the wind): to make, to create (*'śh,
br', yṣr*); to spread out (*nṭh, mṭh, ṭpḥ, rq'*); to found, to establish (*ysd, kwn*).

Although we still have to consider the texts of group 2, it is possible
already to draw some conclusions. Our question was, whether the
waters – according to the OT poetry – were split at creation into two
halves or not. There are only two verbs in the passages we have seen
which might let us suppose that they were, notably *bq'* (Ps. LXXIV 15;
Prov. III 20) and *prr* (Ps. LXXIV 13). I do not think, however, that
anything like the splitting of Tiamat is meant by these verses.

As to *bq'*, we may start from Prov. III 20. Here, the cleaving of the
thmwt is parallelled by the dripping of dew (*ṭl*) from the clouds. (That
one form of dew was produced by the clouds is an idea which we also
meet in the Ugaritic texts; see *KTU* 1.3 II 39 *ṭl šmm*, dew of heaven).

This suggests, that the *thmwt* are cleft in order to give beneficent
moisture on earth (cp. Vulg. Prov. III 20 *eruperunt abyssi*). This explanation is confirmed by *KTU* 1.19 I 42–46, where a drought (the absence of
the sweet voice of Baal) is described by there being 'no dew' (*bl ṭl*) and
'no surging of the two oceans' (*bl šr' thmtm*); as for the OT, a confirmation is found in Dt. XXXIII 13 *mbrkt yhwh 'rṣw mmgd šmym mṭl wmthwm*

rbṣt tḥt: his land be blessed by Yhwh with the choicest gift of heaven, the dew, and with the *thwm* which couches below (*mṭl* should not be emendated into *m'l*, as *BHK* advises).

In view of this, it seems to me that Ps. LXXIV 15 signifies that Yhwh causes springs and brooks to flow ('to cleave springs and brooks' is a proleptic construction); the first half of the verse is thus antithetic to the second half: it is also in Yhwh's power to dry up ever-flowing rivers. (Consequently, I disagree with J. A. Emerton, who writes: The whole of Ps. LXXIV 15 describes the removal of the primeval waters from the earth. God cleft open springs, so that the water might descend through them.[190])

The verb *prr* in Ps. LXXIV 13 presents a difficulty. Some translations have 'to divide' (e.g. *RSV*); cp. the dictionary of Gesenius, who assumes as the original meaning of the root *pr* 'to split'; next 'to rip', 'to break open' etc.; out of this the meaning of a 'jumping movement' (which the root has in Arabic) would have developed. *KBL*, on the contrary, assumes two different roots: I *prr* 'to break', II *prr* 'to stir, rouse'; the latter occurs according to *KBL* in Ps. LXXIV 13, Is. XXIV 19 and Job XVI 12. Unfortunately the last two passages do not clear the matter up, as they allow both meanings; Is. XXIV 19: the earth is convulsed or the earth cracks; Job XVI 12: he shook me or he broke me.

The use of *prr* is almost exclusively figurative. If we follow *KBL* in assuming two different roots, we have two occurrences of *prr* II which are not figurative (Ps. LXXIV 13 and Is. XXIV 19), and one instance of *prr* I, notably Koh. XII 5: *wtpr h'bywnh*; according to *KBL* this refers to the bursting of the fruit. The ancient versions render these three texts as follows: Ps. LXXIV 13 LXX *su ekrataioosas tèn thalassèn*; Pesh. *pršt ym'*; Vulg. iuxt. Hebr. *dissipasti mare*. Is. XXIV 19 LXX *aporiai aporèthèsetai hè gè*; Pesh. *mdl tdwl 'r'*; Vulg. *contritione conteretur terra*. Koh. XII 5 LXX *diaskedasthèi hè kapparis*; Vulg. *dissipabitur capparis*. We have thus: to prevail against, to separate, to scatter, to be at a loss, to be stirred, to be shattered, to be dispersed, to be scattered. I think we may conclude from these translations, that the verb refers to a 'destruction', with the connotation of 'breaking to pieces'. The Peshitta rendering 'to separate' in Ps. LXXIV 13 seems to be based on this connotation; but it is to be noted that the Peshitta has neglected it in Is. XXIV 19. What we do not have unambiguously, is 'to split into two halves'. I think it most likely that the 'routing' of the sea is meant in Ps. LXXIV, or the 'breaking of its might'.

190 Emerton (1966) 129–130.

One might remark that, although the waters are not said to have been split, it is different with the monsters: in Ps. LXXXIX 11 and Job XXVI 13 we find the root *ḥll*. However, *ḥll* refers to the slaying of an enemy with the sword – which does not necessarily mean that the enemy is cut in two. In Ps. LXXXIX Rahab is crushed like one pierced (with the sword), which shows that *ḥll* has taken on the general meaning of 'to slay'. Nowhere is it explicitly stated that the monsters were split into two halves.

Before examining further how far the verbs summed up above refer to a battle, we will consider group 2: the texts which mention a conflict with the waters but not creation.

Sometimes the references to a punishment of the sea(monster) pertain to the future; in a number of cases these threats are directed at the sea of a particular people. There is, however, no reason to exclude these passages, as they are clearly based on the concept of Sea as a dangerous enemy; the connection of the sea with a special people, as well as the transfer of the punishment to the future, is only a further development of this mythological image. On the other hand, passages in which it is stated that, in the future, people will pass through the sea, will be left out, for the same reason as those about the exodus are omitted here (cp. p. 75).

2 Yhwh is the author of the following actions:

	a *to establish a border, to set a guard*
Jer. v	22 to establish the sand as a border (*śym gbwl*), not to be passed, for the sea.
Job VII	12 to set a guard (*śym mšmr*) over the sea and Tannin.
	b *to rebuke, to be angry*
Is. L	2 to rebuke (*gʿr*) the sea and the rivers.
Nah. I	4 to rebuke (*gʿr*) the sea and the rivers.
Hab. III	8 to be angry, furious (*ḥrh ʾp, ʿbrh*) with the rivers and the sea.
Ps. XVIII = 2 Sam. XXII	16 to rebuke (*gʿr*) the waters (Ps. XVIII)/the sea (2 Sam. XXII).
Ps. XXIX	3 to rebuke (*qwl ʿl*) the waters.
Aeth. Hen. CI	7 rebuke (*embrimèsis*) of the sea.

	c *to wield a bow and arrows*
Hab. III	9 The text is not clear; a bow (*qšt*) and arrows (*mṭwt*) are mentioned (apparently to be used against the rivers and the sea; see vs. 8); the verse goes on with the words *nhrwt tbq' – 'rṣ*, you split the earth into rivers (?). Presumably this is the effect of the arrows.

	d *to dry up*
Is. XIX	5 the water of the sea and the river (of Egypt) dry up (*nšt, ḥrb, ybš*).
Is. L	2 to dry up (*ḥrb*) the sea and to turn rivers into desert (*śym mdbr*).
Jer. L	38 the waters (of Babel) dry up (*ḥrb, ybš*).
Jer. LI	36 to dry up (*ḥrb, ybš*) the sea and the well (of Babel).
Ezek. XXX	12 to make the streams of the Nile dry land (*ntn ḥrbh*).
Nah. I	4 to dry up (*ḥrb, ybš*) the sea and all the rivers.
Ps. XVIII = 2 Sam. XXII	16 the beds of the waters (Ps. XVIII)/ of the sea (2 Sam. XXII) become visible (*r'h*).
Job XII	15 the waters are held back (*'ṣr*) and dry up (*ybš*).
Or. Sib. V	447 the sea dries up (*xèros einai*).
Aeth. Hen. CI	7 the sea is afraid (*phobeisthai*) and dries up (*xèrainesthai*).

	e *to tread upon*
Hab. III	15 to tread upon (*drk b*) the sea and the mighty waters (*mym rbym*).

	f *to make disappear*
Rev. XXI	1 the sea exists no more (*ouk estin eti*).

	g *to fight the monsters*
Is. XXVII	1 to punish Leviathan with the sword (*pqd bḥrb*) and to kill (*hrg*) Tannin.

The following combinations occur:

Is. L 2	to rebuke the sea; to dry up the sea and to turn rivers into desert.
Nah. I 4	to rebuke the sea; to dry up the sea and all the rivers.
Hab. III 8, 9, 15	to be angry with the rivers and the sea; to wield a bow and arrows; to tread upon the sea and the mighty waters.

Ps. XVIII 16 =   to rebuke the waters/sea, of which the beds become
2 Sam. XXII 16   visible.
Aeth. Hen. CI   to rebuke the sea so that it dries up.
7

I think we may draw the following conclusions concerning the conception of the sea (and other waters) in Israel.

The sea is considered a continuous danger in present times, as it was in the beginning, when the world was created. As appears from the texts of group I, at the time of creation the waters (the seas, the *thwm* and the *mbwl*), of which it is said twice that they were made by Yhwh, were confined to their proper places. Part of the waters was shut in beneath the earth; it is said that the earth was spread out upon them, and as the earth has, according to one text (Is. XL 22), the shape of a disc, mention is made of the corresponding disc of the *thwm*. Likewise a border was established for the heavenly ocean, upon which Yhwh built his palace. Apertures were made in the soil, through which the water of the *thwm* could pass on (from the 'store-houses') to the earth, in springs and brooks. As to the sea, it was shut up behind a bar and doors (not a very clear picture) and confined within borders (cp. the texts under 2a); moreover its waters appear to be used to fill the clouds, from which they are finally poured out as rain.[191] The confinement of the waters does not seem to have been altogether a peaceful event: they are called 'proud', which is why they had to be 'rebuked' and 'stilled'. Be that as it may, Yhwh's rule over the waters (which is so firm that he can be said to tread upon their heights) also enables him to stir the sea, which appears to be powerless even when its waves roar.

Clearly we do not have a picture like in Mesopotamia, where Marduk split Tiamat in order to create heaven and earth out of her. However, up till now we have passed over those statements of group I which are stronger indicators of a battle, notably:

– Ps. XXIV: the founding of the earth upon the seas and rivers; this recalls the title of the Ugaritic Yam (*zbl ym ṯpṭ nhr*), against whom a battle was delivered.
– Ps. CIV: the *thwm* covered the earth but fled before Yhwh's rebuke, after which its border was established.
– Ps. LXXIV; LXXXIX; Job IX; XXVI: the fight with the monsters.
– Is. XLIV; Ps. LXXIV: the drying up of the waters; cp. the punishment of the waters according to the texts of group 2d.

191 Cp. Hillmann (1965) Part B Ch. II d.

The expression in Ps. xxiv is indeed suggestive; only the reference is not explicit as to what happened before the earth was founded.[192] Ps. civ is more explicit. According to this psalm the earth – being already in existence – was covered with the *thwm*; there were already mountains above which the waters were standing. When it is said that these mountains 'rise up' and valleys 'sink down' after the disappearance of the waters, this must mean that the profile of the earth becomes visible. Apparently the inundation is represented as having taken place at the time of creation, as the founding of the earth is mentioned immediately before. The fight with the monsters too seems to have taken place at the time of creation, according to the above-mentioned texts (at least three of them; Job ix is not so very clear on this). The 'drying up' of the waters must be considered together with the texts of group 2.

In this group, the time of creation could very well be referred to by the texts under a. The passages under f and g, and the passage in the Sibylline Oracles, contain visions of the future. As for the other texts (apart from those about Egypt and Babel, which are of course not pertinent to the question): these are definitely referring to an existent world. Nah. i, Hab. iii, Ps. xviii = 2 Sam. xxii and Ps. xxix mention the reaction of nature when Yhwh advances against the waters: the trembling of the earth and the mountains, the withering of the green. According to Is. l and Aeth. Hen. ci, the drying up of the water results in the dying of the fish. Job xii does not only mention Yhwh's ability to dry up the waters, but also (in the same verse) his power to make them destroy the land.

Except for Hab. iii, where it is only a question of shooting and treading upon the waters (which means invading their domain) the punishment implies every time that the waters are dried up. It is clear from Ps. xviii, where it is said that their beds become visible, and from the 'turning into desert' of the rivers and the dying of the fish in Is. l (cp. Aeth. Hen. ci), that the drying up does not merely refer to chasing the waters from places where they do not belong (in the right order of creation). The punishment involves something unnatural; that is why it can serve as an image for the ruin of Egypt and Babel.

Bearing this in mind, we will return to the two texts of group i which speak of 'drying up'. Is. xliv 27 was included in group i on the formal criterion of having creation mentioned in its immediate vicinity;

192 It would seem as if the pair *ym – nhr* had become such a common element of poetical speech, that it could also be used without the connotation of a battle with Sea; cp. below, p. 156.

but, to be exact, two verses of quite a different content separate the reference to creation (vs. 24) from that to the drying up of the deep. In the light of what was said above, vs. 27 must refer to Yhwh's power to act with the deep and its rivers as he likes, not to an act of creation. In Ps. LXXIV 15, the drying up of ever-flowing rivers is mentioned after the cleaving open of spring and brook. Although it cannot be proved with absolute certainty, I am inclined to believe that here the same antithesis is meant as in Job XII 15: Yhwh makes the waters flow and he makes them cease as he likes.

Our investigation has shown that the sea was regarded as a perennial enemy, of whom it can be said even in a late text as Rev. XXI 1 that, in the new creation, he will exist no more. This does not mean to deny that the sea was considered an enemy from the beginning of the world – which is why the conflict with the waters can be mentioned in one breath with creation. But, if it were a 'battle of creation' in the true sense of the word, one would not expect any conflict at the time when the created world was already in existence, as several texts in group 2 represent it. Moreover, one would not expect unnatural things to happen: rivers turning into desert and beds of streams drying up.

This, combined with the fact that we do not hear of any splitting of the sea or creating heaven and earth out of it, must lead to the conclusion that the battle with Sea in the OT was not a battle of creation. We can only say that according to the OT the sea was given its proper place at creation; but the same holds true for heaven, earth and the mountains.

The image of Gen. 1 6–7, where the *thwm* is divided by the firmament into two parts, stands wholly by itself in the OT; it may very well be a piece of learning which was picked up in Babylon by the Jewish religious leaders.

Our argument has taken the following steps. According to a number of authors the *mbwl* in Ps. XXIX 10 signifies the hostile water which was subdued by Yhwh. This is often combined with the opinion, that vs. 10 refers to Yhwh's creation of the world. According to some, this creation-motif is related to Babylonian conceptions (Tiamat); others relate it to the Ugaritic mythology of Yam, who would have been defeated in a 'cosmogonic' battle. A few authors are of the opinion that the term *mbwl* indicates the Canaanite Yam (Ps. XXIX being an ancient Baal hymn) without there being any question of creation.

I have argued that Yhwh's enemy is an entity on earth (*ym*, *nhr*, just like at Ugarit), whereas the *mbwl* is found in heaven. If one wants to maintain that the *mbwl* is one part of the split enemy, this would imply that the Babylonian concept of Tiamat had found its way into Israelite poetry; anyway, Yhwh's battle would then differ considerably from that of Baal, which was not a battle of creation (although some have called it so). With some statements of Mowinckel I illustrated the difficulties which arise, if one tries to combine the theory of Yhwh's enemy being something like Tiamat (the battle being a battle of creation) with the theory of Canaanite influence on Israel.

Being convinced of the similarity of the Israelite and the Canaanite ideas about the battle with Sea, I have tried to substantiate this by demonstrating that Yhwh's conflict with the waters was not conceived of as a battle of creation. As the current debate on this question seemed to have come to a dead end (in so far as neither of the two parties has apparently been able to convince the other), I have tried to throw light on the matter by an analysis of the terminology.

If I am right in my conclusion, that according to the OT Yhwh did not create heaven and earth as a result of his combat with the waters, we have removed an obstacle standing in the way of the assumption of a shared Canaanite-Israelite belief.

Similarity of Israelite and Canaanite ideas

Now there is one further item which points to a common Canaanite-Israelite belief. We have seen that the ever-recurring punishment of the waters in the OT is, that they dry up. After Baal has slain Yam, in *KTU* 1.2 IV, the text reads (l. 27): *w yšt.ym*. It is highly interesting to read J. A. Montgomery's explanation[193]: Montgomery suggests that we have here the root *nšt*, which occurs in Is. XIX 5 – a verse which I will quote in full (see also above, 2d):

wnštw-mym mhym wnhr yḥrb wybš

and the water of the sea will dry up, and the river will dry up and be dry.

The correspondence of this verse with the Baal text – as Montgomery also pointed out – is striking: in both texts it concerns *ym* and *nhr* (the line in the Ugaritic text goes on with: (Baal) made an end of judge *nhr*). Montgomery translates the Ugaritic text with: (Baal) dries up the Sea. J. Hoftijzer[194] takes the g-stem of Ugaritic *nšt* to be intransitive: the sea fell dry. This would be in accordance with Hebrew usage, where the qal

193 Montgomery (1935) 276.
194 Hoftijzer (1981) 166 n. 539.

of nšt has an intransitive meaning (Is. XLI 17; Jer. LI 30; in Is. XIX 5, however, a nifal is used). On the other hand, Montgomery's translation is syntactically preferable, as Baal is the subject of the two other verbs in the sentence.

E. L. Greenstein[195] writes that wyšt cannot be derived from nšt 'to dry up', because the qal of this verb is intransitive in Hebrew. He thinks that, if the meaning had been 'Baal dried up Yam', Ugaritic would have used a d-stem (*ynšt) or a shafel (*yššt). Greenstein argues that Hebrew (which knows a nifal of nšt) regularly employs the nifal as the passive form of transitive verbs in the piel or the hifil when the qal is intransitive.

However, I do not think that the possibility of the existence of a g-stem of Ugaritic nšt with a transitive meaning is to be excluded on the ground of the intransitive qal of the verb in Hebrew. Nšt occurs only twice in the qal. Though it is used intransitively in both cases, it is not at all impossible that the qal was also used with a transitive meaning. There are several instances of a transitive use of the qal next to an intransitive use[196]; e.g. ṭbl, which has the meanings 'to dip' and 'to dive' in the qal (whilst it is moreover employed in the nifal with a passive meaning).

Moreover, the translation of the Ugaritic line as proposed by Greenstein is unsatisfactory. Greenstein derives yšt from šyt, translating yqt b'l. w yšt.ym with 'Ba'lu ensnares and places Yammu (in the snare)'. Although he admits that this is syntactically 'unusual', he adduces some cases in Hebrew of a verb implying an object within itself, whilst the noun that is implied in the verb serves as the unexpressed object of the following verb. The best examples are Ps. CXIX 106 nšb'ty w'qymh, I have sworn (i.e. taken an oath) and I will uphold (sc. the oath), and Ex. XXI 22 'nwš y'nš k'šr yšyt 'lyw b'l h'šh, he shall be fined (i.e. pay a fine) as the husband may exact from him (sc. a fine). In the Ugaritic line, the noun 'snare', which is implied in yqt, has thus to be supplied, so that one may read yqt b'l.w yšt.ym.*mqt (a double accusative).

I think, however, that the line cannot be interpreted in this way. In the case of an ellipse, it is self-evident which word must be supplied, as in the Hebrew examples. If one were to say 'I have framed the picture and put it', it would surely not be understood as 'I have put it in a frame'; instead, it would be asked 'where did you put it?'. The same holds true for 'he ensnared Yam and placed him'. The absence of any word ex-

---

195 Greenstein (1982).
196 Joüon (1923) 41 a; GK 117 u, v.

pressing where Yam was placed, makes a derivation from *šyt* highly improbable.[197]

Moreover, it is uncertain whether *yqt* must be derived from the root *yqt̠*, 'to ensnare'. De Moor's objection[198], that Ugaritic knows the word *yqšm*, meaning 'fowlers', seems to be valid. Contrary to Greenstein's opinion, there are no instances of the ensnaring of Yam in the OT (Greenstein's translation of Job XXVI 13 is based upon a conjecture). It seems safest to translate *yqt* with 'he uprooted'; cp. Arab. *qatta*.

F. M. Cross[199] and E. Th. Mullen[200] derive *yšt* from the root *šty*: Baal drank Sea. Although this is grammatically correct, it is not, in my opinion, a very likely alternative.

Many authors connect *yšt* with the Arabic verb *šatta*, to which they attribute the meaning 'to disperse', 'to scatter', or the like. De Moor[201] however points out, that the meaning of this verb is 'to become dissolved' and only in the d-stem 'to dissolve'; accordingly, we should expect a d-stem in the Ugaritic text (**yštt*), unless we assume a g-stem with a causative meaning.

If we assume a causative g-stem in the case of *nšt*, however, we should not reject this possibility in the case of *štt*. Nevertheless, I would maintain that the translation 'to dry up' has the most to be said for it, because of the congruence with Is. XIX 5, quoted above.

If 'to dry up' is the meaning of the Ugaritic verb, there is not only a correspondence between Ugarit and the OT as to the names of the enemy, but also a correspondence as to the punishment.

The absence of the conception of a 'battle of creation' with the waters in the OT, together with the verbal conformity with Ugarit (*ym*, *nhr*, *nšt*; also, as is well-known, several names of the monsters) must lead to the conclusion that Yhwh's enemy and Baal's enemy were one and the same, that is: the earthly sea. This disqualifies the *mbwl* in Ps. XXIX 10 as the hostile power.

The mbwl *as reservoir of rain*

In my opinion, the statement in Ps. XXIX 10 that Yhwh is seated upon

---

197 For the same reason, De Moor's translation 'he put Yammu down' (sc. on the shore) has to be rejected, the addition 'on the shore' being De Moor's own invention. See De Moor (1971) 139.
198 De Moor (1971) 138.
199 *CMHE* 115.
200 Mullen (1980) 57.
201 De Moor (1971) 138.

the *mbwl* is not made without reason. The *mbwl* is the reservoir where the rain comes from; that Yhwh sits enthroned thereon, means that he is able to give the rain. This completes the picture of a Baal which, as we have argued, is presented by Ps. xxix: after his victory over Yam, Baal becomes king; his dominion brings on the fertilizing rains. It should moreover be noted that there is a verbal congruence between Ps. xxix 10 and the Baal epic, in that Yhwh is called king 'forever' (*l'wlm*), whereas Baal is said to have won his 'everlasting kingship' (*mlk 'lmk*, *KTU* 1.2 IV 10) by his victory over Yam.

In support of my explanation of the *mbwl* in Ps. xxix, I want to adduce a further argument. First I must mention some other authors, who are of the opinion that the rain is referred to in the concluding verses of the psalm. E. J. Kissane, A. R. Johnson and J. Schildenberger see a reference to the rain in vs. 11.[202] With Johnson, this forms part of his general theory concerning the Israelite Autumn Festival. Yhwh gives the rain in virtue of his triumph over the cosmic sea (called *mbwl* in Ps. xxix; cp. above, p. 65), a triumph which was celebrated on this occasion. An important witness is Zech. xiv 16–17, where it is said that whoever does not go up to worship the king, the Lord of Hosts, at the Feast of Booths, will get no rain. Furthermore Johnson calls attention to the concept of the 'windows of heaven' (Gen. vii 11; viii 2; 2 Kgs. vii 2, 19; Is. xxiv 18; Mal. iii 10), through which the water of the heavenly ocean comes down as rain.

R. Hillmann[203] associates (by way of hypothesis) the picture of the deity sitting enthroned on the *mbwl* with Baal Shamem. A fundamental characteristic of each type of Baal is the gift of rain, for which the window in the palace of the Ugaritic Baal served as an aperture. Hillmann furthermore adduces Ps. civ 3 (Yhwh's upper chambers are built upon the waters) + Ps. civ 13 (Yhwh drenches the mountains from out of his upper chambers). Ps. xxix 11 is not considered by Hillmann.

J. L. Cunchillos[204] also connects Yhwh's *hykl* with Baal's palace and its window, through which the rain comes down when Baal utters his voice; this explanation would accord well with Ps. xxix 7–9 where, in

---

202 Kissane (1953) *ad locum*: 'Here the words of the angels are a promise of rain, which will ensure a rich harvest.' Johnson (1955) 56: '... a guarantee that He can be relied upon to ensure the seasonal rains and the consequent prosperity of His people'; see also the foregoing pages. Schildenberger (1960) 685: 'Vielleicht spricht V. 11b vom Segen des Gewitterregens.'
203 Hillmann (1965) Part B Ch. II b.
204 Cunchillos (1976) Chs. I, IV.

the opinion of Cunchillos, the fertilizing effect of Yhwh's voice is depicted (vs. 7 cp. above, p. 39 n. 79; vs. 8: Yhwh causes the wilderness to bring forth; vs. 9: Yhwh causes the hinds to calve and drenches the forests). Vs. 11 also refers to fertility, but in addition it is a reminiscence of the history of salvation; therefore it is impossible to understand Ps. xxix as an ancient Baal hymn.

It seems to me that the one really strong argument can be furnished by Ps. xxix 11; if this verse actually refers to fertility, this would support the idea that the mention of the *mbwl* is meant as an implicit reference to the rain. (Vss. 7–9 on the contrary do not, in my opinion, refer to fertility; cp. above, p. 38–42.) According to several scholars vs. 11 is typically Israelite in character. This implies that, if one holds Ps. xxix to be an ancient Baal hymn, vs. 11 is regarded as a later addition. Thus H. L. Ginsberg[205]: vs. 11 is a nationalistic addition; W. H. Schmidt[206]: vs. 11 is typically Israelite, because the gods of Canaan do not know personal care for the people or the individual; F. C. Fensham[207]: 'This unique link between Yahweh and his people is a pure Israelite feature which does not occur in the Canaanite world'; H. Strauss[208]: vs. 11 is about the god who intervenes in history; it contains 'die Wunschbitte..., Jahwe möge diese eindrucksvolle, kosmisch-naturhaft erscheinende Macht seinem Volke in der Verleihung von *šlwm*, also geschichtlich, zuwenden'; F. M. Cross[209]: 'The final bicolon appears to be an Israelite addition'; J. Gray[210]: The gift of *šlwm*, especially if taken as 'well-being' in the material sense, may belong in the original hymn to Baal; the gift of strength too rather suggests a renewal of the blessings of nature, to which the Baal cult was directed; 'But the addition "to His people" (*le'ammo*), which is regularly used of the sacral community as constituted by the Covenant, probably indicates an Israelite addition'.

We meet here with two presuppositions: 1) care for 'his people' is not a characteristic of Baal; 2) *šlwm* is a concept bound up with history (which is the typical domain of Yhwh).

Although I do not hold Ps. xxix to be an ancient Baal hymn, I do think that Yhwh is pictured as Baal in this psalm from beginning to end. In order to show that vs. 11 expresses the consequence of Yhwh's being

205 Ginsberg (1938).
206 Schmidt (1961) 49, 74.
207 Fensham (1963) 93.
208 Strauss (1970) 97.
209 *CMHE* 155 n. 44.
210 Gray (1979) 42.

seated on the *mbwl* (namely, fertility), it must not only be demonstrated that the blessings mentioned in this verse are not necessarily bound up with history (although even if they were, vs. 11 would not be incompatible with Canaanite ideas; cp. above, p. 29) but may indicate 'well-being' in a general sense, involving not least the fertility of the land – but also that the care for 'his people' does not preclude the deity's functioning as Baal.

To demonstrate the latter, two texts may suffice:

– *KTU* 1.5 VI 23–25 (= 1.6 I 6–7) *b'l.mt.my.lim.bn dgn.my.hmlt. at̲r b'l*: Baal is dead. What will become of the people of the son of Dagan, what of the multitudes behind[211] Baal?

– *KTU* 1.119 26–36, containing a prayer, to be directed to Baal when enemies are attacking the city of Ugarit; Baal is asked in this prayer to drive them away.

To demonstrate the former, I first want to quote a Ugaritic formula, also adduced in *RSP*[212] as a parallel to Ps. xxix 11. The formula occurs in two letters: *KTU* 2.4 5–6 *tšlm⟨k.tġ⟩rk t'zz⟨k⟩[ ]lm*, may the gods grant you well-being, may they guard you and grant you strength; *KTU* 5.9 I 2–4 *ilm tġrk.tšlmk t'zzk*, may the gods guard you, may they grant you well-being and strength. It is thus a greeting-formula, referring to one's well-being in general. The 'strength' does not have anything to do with military activity: the first letter is addressed to a priest (the *rb khnm*); the second one is a writing exercise, in which the pupil has written at random the words which came into his head, including the greeting-formula.

If we are justified in seeing a reminiscence of this Ugaritic formula in Ps. xxix 11, this would plead against the assumption that *'z* and *šlwm* must have a 'historical' connotation in this verse. (It is somewhat surprising to read that M. Dahood, who adduces the formula as a parallel to Ps. xxix 11 in *RSP*, translates *'z* in this verse with 'victory' in his commentary on the psalms.) Moreover it would contradict the 'typically Israelite' character of vs. 11.

---

211 Probably, we have to do with the preposition *at̲r*. Other possibilities (see De Moor (1971) 194–195): the multitudes of those following Baal (part. of *at̲r*, to follow), or: the multitudes of the place of Baal (cp. Acc. *ašru*), or: to end the sentence with 'multitudes', taking *at̲r b'l* as the first words of the following sentence. Del Olmo Lete (1981), 222–223, takes *bn dgn* as subject of *mt*, parallel to 'Baal': Baal is dead, what will become of the people? The son of Dagan, what will become of the multitude? But, whatever the translation, it concerns Baal's people in any case.

212 *RSP* I II 545.

In the OT, '*z* can be used for many different things; it is not especially a term out of the military sphere. *Šlwm* is according to G. Gerleman[213] the condition of being amply satisfied, outwardly as well as inwardly; 'peace' is in his opinion only an accessory meaning of the term. That it may refer to fertility, can be based upon Ps. CXLVII 14 *hśm-gbwlk šlwm ḥlb ḥtym yśbyʿk*: who brings prosperity to your realm; he satisfies you with the choicest wheat.

The root *brk* is often used in relation to fertility.[214] Gen. XLIX 25 parallels the blessings of heaven to those of the *thwm*; cp. Dt. XXXIII 13: his land be blessed with the choicest gift of heaven, the dew, and with the *thwm*. In Dt. XXVIII 12 the promise that Yhwh will give the rain is followed by the words, that he will 'bless all the work of your hands'. Ezek. XXXIV 26 speaks of the rain as 'showers of blessing'.

Lastly, we must pay attention to Mal. III 10b *'m-l' 'ptḥ lkm 't 'rbwt hšmym whryqty lkm brkh ʿd-bly-dy*: (put me to the test) if I will not open the windows of heaven and pour forth blessing in abundance for you.

Here, the word 'rain' is replaced by the word 'blessing'. But another interesting thing is, that here the 'windows of heaven' are mentioned, which according to Gen. VII 11 were opened (*'rbwt hšmym npthw*) so that the *mbwl* could pour down its waters. Of course I am not the first to remark that we find the same expression in the passage *KTU* 1.4 VII 25–31, where Baal opens a window (*yptḥ urbt*) in his palace and utters his holy voice; but – to my knowledge – a comparison has not yet been made between all four texts: *KTU* 1.4 VII 25–31, Ps. XXIX 9–11, Gen. VII 10–11 and Mal. III 10. This comparison shows a remarkable congruity.

Baal	Ps. XXIX	Gen. VII	Mal.
yptḥ urbt		*'rbwt npthw*	*'ptḥ 'rbwt*
hkl	*hykl*		
	mbwl	*mbwl*	
	brk		*brkh*

213 Gerleman, *ThHAT* II.
214 See Keller-Wehmeier, *ThHAT* I. Toll (1982), 116, thinks the meaning 'potency' is present in expressions like *gśmy brkh* (Ezek. XXXIV 26), the fructifying rains.

Conclusions

I think therefore that we are justified in interpreting the conclusion of Ps. xxix as follows: Yhwh is seated in his palace upon the *mbwl*, which enables him to send down the fructifying rains, whereby he blesses his people with prosperity. Far from being a secondary addition, vs. 11 thus forms the logical consequence of the foregoing; indeed this verse could be called the culmination of the whole psalm.

RÉSUMÉ

The following conclusions were drawn from the analysis of the three parts of Ps. xxix. The honour, to be conferred upon Yhwh by the gods, does not imply that Yhwh is represented as El. The main part of the psalm depicts Yhwh as a storm-god, who raises his thundering voice against the waters, so that all nature trembles with fear. This is followed up by the statement that Yhwh sits as king in his palace, where he receives honour. The encompassing verses are not to be seen apart from the main part: the deity sits enthroned as king in virtue of his being triumphant over the hostile sea, and as such he is honoured. As this ending takes up the motif of the introduction, it must be for the same reason that the gods are invited to pay homage in the opening verses; we definitely do not have a picture of El here. This conclusion is supported by the fact that the introduction has two internal links with the main part: the 'strength' is given to Yhwh because he has to exercise his power against the waters; the 'holy majesty' occurs again in the main part: the 'majesty' of Yhwh's voice.

The consequence of Yhwh's triumph is that he sits enthroned as king 'till eternity' upon the heavenly ocean; this does not signify that he has created the world, but that he is able to bless his people with the rain, which ensures their welfare.

When we insert Ps. xxix into the diagram on p. 50, the motifs 'battle with Sea', 'thunder', 'anxiety of nature', 'kingship' and 'fertility' may be marked in.

The correspondence with the Baal epic is almost total: Baal triumphs over Yam and wins thereby his 'eternal kingship'. After he has got his palace, he opens a window and utters his 'holy voice', whereat nature trembles with fear. Baal's dominion ensures the fertilizing rains for the 'people of the son of Dagan'.

My conclusion is, that Ps. xxix depicts Yhwh as Baal from beginning to end.

II

PSALM XXIX AND ISRAELITE RELIGION

The Baal characteristics ascribed to the deity in Ps. xxix demand an explanation of their presence, as the deity is not named Baal but Yhwh. When examining the interpretations which have been given of the psalm as a whole, we meet with various explanations of its 'Canaanite' character. Of course it makes a difference whether one considers Yhwh to be totally depicted as Baal in the psalm or only partially so: in the case of the former, the presence of a complete text with a Baal character in Yahwistic literature has to be explained; but also in the case of the latter, the Baal traits have to be accounted for. We will now examine the various opinions.

Literary imagery – polemics

In an article of which the title indicates its purport, T. Worden expounds a view which is also taken by a number of other investigators; it deserves to be quoted in full[1]: 'There are many echoes in the Old Testament of the Ugaritic literature; it seems beyond doubt that the Israelites borrowed freely from Canaanite sources. But it is a gross error to conclude, from this fact alone, that the Israelites borrowed also their religious notions and rites. This distinction is an important one: it is easy to exaggerate the connection between Canaanite fertility rites and Old Testament ritual: all the easier because the *literary* dependence is often striking. ... If, therefore, we show that many of the expressions used of Yahweh have been borrowed from Ugaritic literature concerning Baal, we do not thereby imply that the Israelite notion of Yahweh was derived from, and in all things resembled the Canaanite idea of Baal. We know that the religious leaders of Israel constantly fought against this danger of syncretism, and many of the evil practices they denounced are now more clearly understood in the light of the Ugaritic texts. The people often succumbed to the attractions of the Canaanite fertility cult, but this is ever regarded as an evil, as an 'adultery' against Yahweh:

---

1 Worden (1953) 276–277.

the Ugaritic texts give us a clearer understanding of the Israelites' sins, but at the same time they display by contrast, the perfection of the religion of Israel: "Every new analogy enhances our respect for the quality of the sacred poetry of Israel, which inherited the best of Canaanite literary art and poetic imagery, but used it in the construction of an edifice which surpassed it immeasurably from the literary point of view alone".'[2]

Thus, Ps. xxix is regarded by some as an example of Canaanite influence in the literary sphere – not as evidence of shared religious ideas. To quote a few statements: H. Cazelles[3]: The original version of Ps. xxix (dating from the time of David) glorifies Yhwh's control of nature, with expressions derived from the language of Canaan; E. Pax[4]: The Ugaritic hymn which served as a model for Ps. xxix is only a skeleton which has been filled with a new spirit by the psalmist; B. Margulis[5]: The Yahwistic author of Ps. xxix has been influenced by Canaanite poetry, but the imagery is only Baal-*like* (note emphasis); H. Strauss[6]: The faith of God's people erects a testimony within history (as Ps. xxix 11 speaks of the god who intervenes in history), using the forms current in its environment.

It is only one step from here to the opinion, that Ps. xxix conveys some definitely anti-Canaanite ideas. This theory does not ignore the fact that some qualities of Baal were indeed ascribed to Yhwh; only the reason why Yhwh was credited with them is not found in any spontaneous belief of his worshippers, but in the wish to derogate from Baal. Thus F. C. Fensham[7] thinks that Ps. xxix may have been intended as a missionary poem, to convert Canaanites to Yahwism by using their idiom[8]: R. Hillmann[9] speaks of the 'dethronement' of Baal by Yhwh, who claimed Baal's qualities for himself; L. Bronner[10]: Ps. xxix contains a polemic against Canaanite mythological beliefs, in that the psalm shows the god of Israel possessing the qualities which were ascribed to Baal by the Canaanites; P. C. Craigie[11] detects in Ps. xxix (according to

---

2 Quotation taken from W. F. Albright, *BASOR* 83 (1941), 42.
3 Cazelles (1961).
4 Pax (1962).
5 Margulis (*Bibl* 1970).
6 Strauss (1970).
7 Fensham (1963).
8 Cp. above, p. 21.
9 Hillmann (1965) 197–198.
10 Bronner (1968) 62.
11 Craigie (1972) 145.

him a victory song 'a deliberate use of Canaanite language in a sarcastic taunt against the defeated Canaanite foe'; H. J. Kraus[12] speaks of a 'polemical-antithetic component' in Ps. xxix, directed against the worship of Canaanite deities; cp. A. H. W. Curtis[13], according to whom the OT motif of Yhwh's subjugation of the waters originally served to express the idea that Baal did not in point of fact control the waters; F. Gradl[14]: Ps. xxix celebrates the victory of the Israelites over the Canaanites and their gods.

As we have seen above (p. 20–22), one reason to see polemics expressed in Ps. xxix, against Baal or against the gods of Canaan in general, is the honour bestowed upon Yhwh by the *bny 'lym*. As to this argument, I have tried to show above that it does not hold. Another argument is, that the character of the psalm is typically Yahwistic (and consequently incompatible with the religious beliefs of Canaan). Especially vs. 11 is credited with this character, either because of a supposed reference to history, or because mention is made of Yhwh's people, or both. However, I have tried above to refute these suppositions (p. 90–91; cp. also p. 29). Other 'Yahwistic' notions in the psalm are discovered in vs. 3b (cp. p. 59 n. 135), in the term *mdbr qdš* (cp. p. 41 n. 83), and in the term *mbwl* which is thought to signify the deluge (cp. p. 63–64). For my own opinion, I may refer to my comments on these verses.

However, all has not been said with this. Even where Yhwh is pictured in the same way as Baal, commentators have found occasion to speak of a difference in character: Yhwh's holiness is not comparable with that of Baal, because pagan religions know 'the holy' only as a neutral concept, the antipole of the biblical *vis dynamica*[15]; Yhwh is an all-powerful deity, revealing himself through nature as well as giving strength and peace to his people, whereas Baal is the very thunder and lightning, being a god solely in the rainy season and resting in his grave in summer[16]; between Yhwh and Baal exists an unbridgeable gap: the gap between transcendence and immanence[17]; 'For the God of Israel has nothing in common with the mythological beliefs of the people of

12 Kraus (1978⁵) 384.
13 Curtis (1978).
14 Gradl (1979).
15 Pax (1962), with reference to Von Rad (1957) 205.
16 Fensham (1963), with reference to Kapelrud (1952) 94.
17 Hillmann (1965) 197–198, with reference to Eissfeldt (1914).

Canaan. ... He is above nature and controls it, but is never part of it.'[18]; Yhwh is not a thunder-god: the thunder-storm is only a mode of his manifestation, out of which he comes forward 'in voller Personhaftigkeit'[19].

It is far from easy to follow this argumentation, not to mention the unproved contention that the same concepts (holiness; manifestation of the god in a thunder-storm) have a different meaning in Israel and in its environment. Of course there are differences of character between Baal and Yhwh – although a full comparison is impossible because of the scantiness of the evidence, especially as regards Baal in the first millennium B.C.. Anyway, when we consider the whole of the OT, we meet qualities of Yhwh which are not found with Baal; reversely, there is a surplus on Baal's side. Now the argumentation (apart from the homage paid by the *bny 'lym*, an argument which we rejected) apparently turns on these extra qualities: either typically Yahwistic traits are thought to be explicitly present in Ps. xxix (but we rejected this idea too), or the Baal traits in the psalm are thought to have a 'Yahwistic flavour' because of a general difference between the two deities, from which it would follow that the Baal characteristics were attributed to Yhwh as literary ornaments or by way of polemic.

The logic of this reasoning is questionable. If the surplus qualities on Yhwh's side were incompatible with his having fought the sea, there would have been reason to doubt the seriousness of this belief: it could have been 'literary imagery' in that case, although another explanation might be found in the circumstance that the OT texts date from different periods. But as a matter of fact, I cannot see any incompatibility between Yhwh's fight with the sea and his other qualities. So far the 'literary imagery'; but the case for 'polemics' is even harder to defend. We are asked to vizualize the Israelites having purposely attributed Baal traits to Yhwh in order to minimize the importance of Baal, on the ground of the dissimilarity of the two gods. This appears to me to be a rather illogical theory.

However, there is one more argument in defense of the supposed polemics, notably the antagonism between Yahwism and the Baal cult which finds expression in a number of OT passages; I may recall the words of T. Worden, quoted on p. 94, that there was a constant fight against the 'danger of syncretism'. R. Hillmann writes in his otherwise

18 Bronner (1968) 6.
19 Kraus (1978⁵) 384.

very illuminating study[20]: 'Jahwe Zebaoth, Inbegriff alles kriegeri-schen,... duldet Baals Autoritätsanspruch neben sich nicht'. Apparently Hillmann was aware of the difficulty indicated by me at the end of the last alinea, as he speaks of the 'contradiction' involved in the adoption of Baal traits by Yhwh, who was radically different from Baal; but the competition between the two deities is considered by Hillmann to be a satisfactory explanation of this phenomenon. A. H. W. Curtis[21] even states that polemic was necessary at the time when Yhwh and Baal competed for the favour of the people.

My answer to this is based on a methodological consideration. As the OT is a compilation of texts from different periods, we cannot take it for granted that the religio-historical circumstances which we meet in one text also apply to another. Obviously a certain amount of polemics against the Baal cult is present in the OT; but when we find functions of Baal ascribed to Yhwh in a text which does not express any polemical attitude, the logical conclusion seems to be that the text in question does not stem from times or circles which were polemically inclined.

In other words, we must not conceive of the OT as a closed system. Although this seems to be a truism, it is remarkable how some interpre-tations of Ps. xxix are based on precisely that supposition. Thus, po-lemics are detected in words which do not express them[22].

An ancient Baal hymn

We now have to consider another explanation of Yhwh's Baal charac-ter in Ps. xxix, namely H. L. Ginsberg's theory that Ps. xxix was originally a Canaanite hymn to Baal, which was adopted by Yah-wism.[23] Ginsberg suggested that the adoption of the hymn by Israel might have been due to the fact, that David and Solomon were on good terms with Phoenicia. It is interesting to compare this with the 'pole-

---

20 Hillmann (1965) 197.
21 Curtis (1978).
22 To which lengths commentators may go in imposing meanings upon the text in order to be able to interpret it as un- (i.e. anti-) Canaanite, may be shown by two more examples. Kraus (1978⁵), 384, admits that Yhwh's *qwl* in Ps. xxix is 'Naturhaft', but suggests that, at the same time, Yhwh's *dbr* is indicated by it: 'Aber kann man denn in Israel unter *qwl-yhwh* eine andere Stimme verstehen als ebendie Stimme des Gottes, der sich seinem erwählten Volk kundgetan hat?'. Gradl (1979) states that no other psalm is so Yahwistic (meaning nationalistic), as the name Yhwh occurs in it no less than 18 times.
23 Cp. above, p. 54.

mics' theory, which reckons with bad terms throughout, between the two religions anyway.

The theory was further explored by Th. H. Gaster.[24] According to Gaster Ps. xxix shows a general Near Eastern pattern, which involved the storm-god's slaying his enemy, thereby acquiring dominion and being installed in a new palace. Thus we see that Cross, according to whom the theophany descriptions follow certain patterns, of which Ps. xxix offers an example[25], was not suggesting something altogether new. Nevertheless, the interpretations of Ps. xxix by Gaster and by Cross are differently accentuated. Whereas Cross lays stress on the reaction of nature as a regular feature of the theophany, this point does not get special attention from Gaster; Gaster, on the other hand, stresses the point that Ps. xxix is a typical 'hymn of laudation', which is also found in the final section of Enuma elish, where the gods recite the honorific names of Marduk, and in the Baal epic, where Kotar honours Baal with a paean (*KTU* 1.4 VII 23–37). As to Ps. xxix, the hymn of laudation would more precisely consist in vss. 3–9b, which Gaster takes to be the recital by the *bny 'lym*. Now I do not think Gaster is right in this, as the text of Ps. xxix does not indicate such a recital; neither is a paean by Kotar indicated in the Baal epic, so that the hymn of laudation is less 'typical' than Gaster thinks. However, I fully agree with Gaster as to the pattern in Ps. xxix; as I have tried to demonstrate in the previous chapter, there is even more reason to speak of a pattern than was seen by Gaster, because *mym rbym* can be explained as Yhwh's enemy, Yam.

Gaster, however, did not go so far as to suggest that a general Near Eastern pattern of myth and ritual obtained in the official cult of Yhwh. His opinion can best be shown by a literal quotation[26]: 'All that we are here suggesting is that certain hymnodic patterns, derived from these earlier usages[27], survived in literary convention... At the same time, we would not deny that the survival often involved more than a mere persistence of forms... It can scarcely be doubted... that beside the official cult of Yahweh in Jerusalem there existed a more primitive folk-religion throughout the length and breadth of Palestine. This may have taken the form of mere folkloristic and unmeaning customs rather than of formal religion, but it must certainly have had its influence upon the cult of Yahweh; and it is not unreasonable to suppose that the zealous

24 Gaster (1946/47); Gaster (1961) 443–446.
25 Cp. above, p. 43–51.
26 Gaster (1946/47) 64–65.
27 This refers to the ritual of the New Year Festival.

propagandists of the latter may frequently have tried to "fetch the public" by adopting and adapting the songs and airs current in the former'.

We may contrast Gaster's opinion with the 'Myth and Ritual' theory, according to which the official cult of Yhwh at Jerusalem comprised a festival, celebrating the enthronement of Yhwh after his triumph over chaos. Although we regularly find the view expressed that this festival stemmed from the cult of El Elyon, we also meet with the opinion that its basic ideas originated in the cult of Baal. Thus J. Gray, who elaborates Mowinckel's thesis stated in *Psalmenstudien* II, writes: 'In the Enthronement Psalms we believe that we penetrate behind the doctrine of the Reign of God to the sacramental experience of it, insofar as we believe that there we have evidence of the ultimate cultic *Sitz im Leben* of the assurance that in the conflict of the forces of disorder to disrupt the order, or government, of the Divine King, God is experienced as effective to vindicate His rule'[28]; this is according to Gray a 'direct development of the leading motifs as well as the imagery of the epiphany of Baal as King in its cultic *Sitz im Leben* in the autumn festival'.[29] Ps. xxix is called by Gray 'one of the earliest adaptations of a hymn to Baal from the liturgy of the Canaanite autumn festival in the corresponding Israelite "festival of Yahweh"'.[30]

Thus, we have been confronted with several possibilities, between which we must try to decide. Either Ps. xxix was composed outside Israel as a hymn to Baal, which was subsequently taken over by the Israelites, or it was an original Israelite composition. In the case of the former, it was either adopted because the notions expressed in it were in accord with the Yahwistic creed, or for some other reason (apart from polemics: this idea was already rejected by us on the previous pages), like for instance the reason suggested by Gaster. If it concerned true Yahwistic notions, there are again two possibilities: there may or may not have been a yearly festival, celebrating Yhwh's battle, his triumph and his ensuing kingship, which brought fertility to the land. On the other hand, if we assume such a festival to have existed, this need not imply that Ps. xxix had been a hymn to Baal. That is only one of three possibilities, the other two being that it was a cult hymn composed in Hebrew without a Canaanite model, or – if one assumes the Israelite festival to stem from the cult of El Elyon – that it had been a hymn to El.

28 Gray (1979) 1.
29 Gray (1979) 3–4.
30 Gray (1979) 42.

Let us consider first which arguments we have got for or against Ps. xxix being an ancient Baal hymn. Partly, this question is bound up with the analysis of the text which I have presented in the previous chapter. It stands to reason that, if my conclusion (viz that Yhwh is depicted as Baal from beginning to end) is not accepted, the possibility of the psalm having been a hymn to Baal is ruled out; at the most, this could hold true for part of the hymn, but the adaptations made in Israel would still give us cause to speak of an 'original Israelite composition'. If, on the contrary, my conclusion is accepted, it does not necessarily follow that the psalm was originally Canaanite. Although I have tried to put forward a stronger case for Yhwh's Baal character in the psalm than any of its adherents up till now, in that I have proffered a rather extensive argumentation against such as think otherwise, I would not jump to the conclusion that the hymn was originally dedicated to Baal as readily as has been done by some.[31]

As it would seem to me, this conclusion has at least partly sprung from the notion, perhaps hardly consciously felt, that Yahwism could not by any means have produced these Baal-like conceptions: it *must* therefore have been a matter of adoption of foreign material. Instead, I suggest that we set about it with an open mind: as long as we do not have any pointer in the direction of a Canaanite original, we have to assume a Yahwistic origin of the psalm.

We shall now discuss some opinions on a possible Canaanite *Vorlage* of Ps. xxix. On the one hand, A. Fitzgerald[32] has tried to make plausible that Ps. xxix was translated into Hebrew from a Canaanite original dedicated to Baal, by making use of a stylistic argument. Alliteration, Fitzgerald writes, is a typical feature of Ugaritic poetry, and often the names of deities fit into the alliterative pattern. If the name *b'l* is substituted for *yhwh* in Ps. xxix, a distinct alliterative pattern emerges. 'There is not a single line where the name "Yahweh" fits better,.and in most lines it does not fit at all.' Original as this argument is, it is of course highly speculative. I think one could argue for the name *yhwh* equally well, by pointing to the assonance in vss. 1–2 if *yhwh* is pronounced *yahu*: *habu leyahu*.

On the other hand, some scholars have tried to refute the hypothesis of a Canaanite *Vorlage* of Ps. xxix. There are two authors whose theories I want to discuss now, namely P. C. Craigie and J. L. Cunchillos.

31 E.g. Gaster and Cross.
32 Fitzgerald (1974).

Craigie has disputed the idea of a Canaanite origin of Ps. xxix more than once.[33] His reasoning in the article in *VT* runs as follows: There is a continuous line of development in Hebrew poetry, beginning with the Song of the Sea, and ending up with the Enthronement Psalms. Ps. xxix represents an intermediate stage in this development; the psalm is directly dependent upon the Song of the Sea. In the Song of the Sea – a victory song –, Canaanite motifs were used for the first time, as a poetical expression of the religious interpretation of the victory. Ps. xxix is also a victory song, because the storm-theophany was traditionally used to describe the support of the deity in battle (a confirmation of this characterization of the hymn is found by Craigie in its 'short staccato lines'); but the Canaanite motifs, which form a continuation of those used in the Song of the Sea, are beginning to be transformed in this hymn. Whilst the historical element is reduced in Ps. xxix, the mythological motifs are expanded (see e.g. vs. 10 *lmbwl yšb*, as compared to the impersonal use of *ym* in Ex. xv); thus, Yhwh's power received a cosmological expression. In addition, the psalm employs elements of the Canaanite language in order to mock the enemy, as a 'sarcastic taunt against the defeated Canaanite foe' (cp. above, p. 96). Especially the stress laid upon the 'voice' of Yhwh is thought by Craigie to serve this purpose, as Baal's voice played an important rôle in warfare (see the texts in which the battle-cry of the pharao is compared with the voice of Baal (*EA* 147 – cp. above, p. 45 – and *ANET*³ 249[34]). Finally, in the Enthronement Psalms, the military character has receded into the background an the Canaanite motifs have undergone a more radical transformation; they are now a 'rich theological expression of Israelite religion'.

The continuity between Ex. xv 1–18 and Ps. xxix is further substantiated by Craigie as follows: 1) In Ex. xv as well as in Ps. xxix the word '*z* has been used with two different meanings: 'strength' (Ex. xv 13; Ps. xxix 1) and 'refuge, protection' (Ex. xv 2; Ps. xxix 11). 2) *yhwh šmw* (Ex. xv 3), a battle-cry, recurs in Ps. xxix 2, where Yhwh's *šm* is honoured because of his strength. 3) Ex. xv 11 mentions the gods; the concept of a 'council of gods' has been further elaborated in Ps. xxix 1 (cp. above, p. 22).

Now first of all I want to observe that there is not a single line in Ps.

---

33 Craigie (1972); Craigie (1979). Craigie has also discussed Ps. xxix in 'The Poetry of Ugarit and Israel', *Tyndale Bulletin* 22 (1971), 3–31, but this has not been available to me.
34 'His battle-cry is like (that of) Baal in the heavens.'

xxix which marks the psalm as a song of triumph, celebrating the defeat of the Canaanites. It is an offence to logic to suppose that, if element x sometimes occurs in combination with element y (i.c. the thunder-theophany in combination with the deity's aid in battle), every occurrence of element x must necessarily imply the presence of element y. As to the supposed sarcasm, we have seen above that the adherents of the 'polemics' theory are apt to impose meanings upon the text which the unbiassed eye is unable to detect.

The exact relationship between the Song of the Sea and Canaanite mythology will be discussed in the next chapter; but it cannot be doubted that a relationship of a kind existed. Now to explain the Canaanite motifs in Ps. xxix by a supposed influence from the mythological elements in the Song of the Sea, means to deny the possibility that this mythology could have become known in Israel in any other way than via that particular hymn. Hard arguments indeed would be needed to maintain such a position; at the very least, it would be necessary to make a strong case for the literary dependency of the psalm on the Song of the Sea. I am not able to discover any argument by which this dependency is made plausible in Craigie's article. A frequently occurring word like 'z (which, by the way, does not mean 'refuge' in Ps. xxix 11 in my opinion[35]), the mentioning of Yhwh's šm (yhwh šmw is, moreover, no battle-cry in Am. iv 13, v 8, ix 6 and Jer. xxxi 35) and of the gods, are not exclusive enough to suggest a direct borrowing – let alone the difficulty of making out which of the two texts is the receiving one.

In his article in UF 11 Craigie approaches the problem by considering the stylistic aspect. In RSP[36], M. Dahood sums up a number of word pairs which occur in Ugaritic as well as in Ps. xxix, concluding that the psalm must have had a Canaanite *Vorlage*. On close examination however, Craigie argues, these word pairs do not prove anything at all; we must take it, therefore, that Ps. xxix is Hebrew poetry, reflecting a Canaanite theme.

It will be necessary to go a little further into the question of the poetic form of Ps. xxix, as it may throw some light on the problem of the origins of the psalm. There are two things to which we must pay attention: the word pairs, and the so-called 'expanded colon'. I want to begin with the latter.

---

35 I would prefer to reserve this meaning for the expressions with the verb 'to be': Yhwh *is* somebody's refuge.
36 *RSP* I II and II I.

The term 'expanded colon' was coined by S. E. Loewenstamm.[37] The expanded colon is a type of verse in which the sentence is interrupted, and then, in the second colon, resumed and completed; we often find a third colon added in synonymous parallelism with the expanded colon. We need not go into details as to the different types of expanded colon; for these I may refer to Loewenstamm's article. I merely want to give one example in Ugaritic: *ht.ibk b'lm/ht.ibk.tmḫṣ./ht.tṣmt ṣrtk (KTU* 1.2 IV 8–9), Lo, your enemies, o Baal/lo, your enemies you will shatter/ lo, you will destroy your oppressors. We note here an intervening formula, namely the address 'o Baal', by which the sentence is interrupted. The intervening formula may also have another syntactical function, or it may be completely missing.

In the OT, there are more patterns of the expanded colon than in Ugaritic. The Ugaritic pattern in the example quoted above is, for instance, found in Ps. xcii 10 *ky hnh 'ybyk yhwh/ky hnh 'ybyk y'bdw/ytprdw kl p'ly 'wn*, For lo, your enemies, o Yhwh/for lo, your enemies will perish/scattered will be all evildoers. However, the OT knows a great variety of forms; these deviations from the ancient patterns cause Loewenstamm to write that 'the Bible constitutes a developed stage in the history of Canaanite literature'.[38]

In Ps. xxix, we find several examples of the expanded colon. Vss. 1–2 'Give to Yhwh, sons of El/give to Yhwh honour and strength/give to Yhwh the honour of his name/bow down to Yhwh before the holy majesty' are analyzed by Loewenstamm in the following way: 'The third colon is concatenated with the expanded colon itself by tripling the repetitive formula *hbw lyhwh* and this concatenation is reinforced even more by repetition of the noun *kbwd*. The three cola thus combine into a tricolic unit which is paralleled by the fourth colon *hšthww lyhwh bhdrt qdš'*.[39] Loewenstamm furthermore calls attention to vss. 5 and 8 (to which I may add vs. 3 a, c – if one assumes vs. 3 b to be an interpolation –). Take for instance vs. 5 (the other instances are constructed in a like manner) *qwl yhwh šbr 'rzym/wyšbr yhwh 'rzy hlbnwn*, The voice of Yhwh smashes cedars/Yhwh smashes the cedars of the Lebanon. Loewenstamm: 'The clear meaning of this verse is that the voice of the Lord breaks the cedars of Lebanon. *Lbnwn* thus serves as a complementary formula coming at the end, and in the repetitive formula that precedes

---

37 Loewenstamm (JSS 1969); cp. Loewenstamm (1975), which is not a withdrawal of the original viewpoint of the author – as the title might suggest.
38 Loewenstamm (JSS 1969) 196.
39 Loewenstamm (JSS 1969) 189.

the complementary formula there occur changes'.[40] So far Loewen-stamm. – Two conclusions may be drawn from the above: 1) Ps. xxix makes use of ancient literary traditions; 2) Ps. xxix shows a considerable liberty in handling these traditions. It is to be noted, that Ugaritic also shows some variety in the use of the expanded colon. I may especially refer to an article by Y. Avishur[41], from which I quote an example, in Ugaritic, of the 'missing intervening formula': *grš ym/grš ym.l ksih/⟨n⟩hr l kht.drkth* (*KTU* 1.2 IV 12–13; cp. lines 19–20), Chase away Yam/chase away Yam from his throne/ Nahar from the seat of his dominion. Ps. xxix 3, 5, 8 too are cases of a 'missing intervening formula'.

However, the Ugaritic texts we know are generally less free than Hebrew in their variations of this literary device. As Ps. xxix shows a considerable freedom, this seems to me to plead against a direct Ugaritic *Vorlage* of the psalm. I therefore disagree with Albright who, after analyzing the style of Ps. xxix, concludes that the psalm was a 'relatively little changed adaptation of a Baal hymn to the cult of Yahweh'[42], which he dates 'probably in or about the tenth century B.C.'. As Loewenstamm has noted, Albright indiscriminately throws examples of what he calls 'repetitive parallelism' on a heap, without distinguishing properly between mere parallelism and the 'expanded colon'. Accordingly, he does not analyze the style of Ps. xxix correctly (he mentions vss. 4 and 5a, and vss. 7 and 8 together as examples of 'repetitive parallelism' of the kind of vss. 1–2a) and he does not notice the differences between the style of Ps. xxix and the Ugaritic use of the expanded colon.

As to the dating of the psalm, I think that a consideration of its style is a valuable complement of D. A. Robertson's grammatical approach[43]; as 'linguistic' Robertson takes 'morphology and syntax only'. Robertson does not find any positive linguistic evidence of Ps. xxix being 'early' (that is, before the 8th century B.C.); but he recognizes the

---

40 Loewenstamm (*JSS* 1969) 194. Compare Loewenstamm's analysis of this verse with that of Mittmann (1978), who is of the opinion that vs. 5a contains 'eine Wesensaussage über die Stimme Jahwes', while vs. 5b, as appears from the wayyiqtol-form, pictures the act which is the concrete result of the 'wesenhafte Eigenart' of Yhwh's voice. Consequently, the object in vs. 5a (cedars) is of a general character, and is specified in vs. 5b (cedars of the Lebanon). Mittmann's view seems to me to be totally wide of the mark.
41 Avishur (1972).
42 Albright (1946) 6.
43 Robertson (1972).

hypothetical character of his conclusions. 'No positive evidence' does not mean that Ps. xxix might not have to be dated early.

The style of Ps. xxix indicates a certain lapse of time since the 14th century (the Ugaritic texts) – but not too great a lapse for the style having changed altogether. Of course, the moot point is how tenacious literary traditions are.

The stylistic feature of the expanded colon, which is found in Ps. xxix, sheds some light upon the question of the word pairs. The controversy between Dahood and Craigie as stated in Craigie's article in *UF* 11 (see above, p. 103), has been formulated by Craigie in a more general way in another article[44], where he writes: Dahood's aim is to recover from the Ugaritic and Hebrew texts 'the Canaanite thesaurus from whose resources the Ugaritic and Hebrew poets alike drew' (*RSP* I p. 74). The object of this paper is to examine the theoretical basis of the hypothesis concerning parallel word pairs in Ugaritic and Hebrew poetry, and then to inquire whether the hypothesis is as valuable for biblical scholarship as has been claimed. Craigie then goes on to expound the conclusions drawn by him from a test: examples of Accadian and Arabic poetry were examined to determine what kind of parallel word pairs were employed. The tests have indicated strongly that any poetry, insofar as it employs parallelism, will make use of similar word pairs. All that has been clearly established so far is the common use of parallelism in both Hebrew and Ugaritic poetry, which necessitates *ipso facto* the use of many common parallel word pairs to convey the poetic parallelism of thought. – This, then, is the background of the article in *UF* 11 which deals especially with Ps. xxix.

Now before turning to details, I want to remark the following: there is a difference between the assumption that Ps. xxix had a Canaanite *Vorlage*, and the assumption of a common 'Canaanite thesaurus from whose resources the Ugaritic and Hebrew poets alike drew'. To dispute the former need not necessarily imply a rejection of the latter possibility.

The evidence in favour of a Canaanite *Vorlage*, as it is stated by Dahood in *RSP*, needs indeed to be viewed with a critical eye. I do not intend to sum up all the word pairs which are adduced by Dahood as evidence; Craigie is certainly right in saying that a number of them do not have any significance with respect to the supposition of a Canaanite origin of the psalm. However, to some of Dahood's word pairs I would attribute significance. I mentioned already in my analysis of the text the

44 Craigie (1977).

formula *ḥwy-kbd* (see p. 31, above), the pair Lebanon // Siryon (above, p. 39) and the combination *mlk – 'lm* (above, p. 89). Craigie remarks that *hšthww* and *kbwd* are not strictly parallel in Ps. xxix, whilst *ḥwy* and *kbd* form part of a longer formula in Ugaritic; as to the pair Lebanon // Siryon, this occurs also in the Accadian literature; and the combination *mlk – '(w)lm* is found in Egyptian poetry.

I would answer to the first objection, 1) that *hbw kbwd* and *hšthww* do stand in parallelism; 2) that it is not of importance whether the words are strictly parallel, but only that they occur together in a fixed formula; 3) that indeed the Ugaritic formula has been changed in Hebrew, but this does not plead against it being the same formula. As to Lebanon // Siryon and *mlk – '(w)lm*: their occurrence elsewhere does not impair the significance of their common occurrence in the Ugaritic literature and the OT, whilst moreover *mlk 'lmk* occurs precisely in the context of Baal's battle with Yam – which we concluded to be a central point in Ps. xxix. Furthermore, of the 12 word pairs mentioned by Dahood, 11 are discussed by Craigie, but he omits to mention the pair *šl(w)m // 'z(z)*, which I think undoubtedly points to a common stock of formulas.[45] As I remarked above, we must also take the common feature of the expanded colon into account: this reinforces, in my opinion, the conclusion which is to be drawn from the word pairs. Now with *šl(w)m // 'z(z)* we notice a reversal of the Ugaritic pair in Hebrew; moreover, the Ugaritic verbs have been substituted in Hebrew by nouns plus the verbs 'to give', 'to bless with'. In the same way, the sequence of *ḥwy* and *kbd* in the Ugaritic formula has been reversed in Ps. xxix and the verb *kbd* is circumscribed by a noun plus the verb 'to give' (cp. above, p. 31). It is as with the expanded colon: Hebrew poets have taken a certain liberty with the traditional forms (but I must add that also in Ugaritic the normal sequence of fixed pairs is sometimes reversed[46]).

I therefore agree with Cassuto[47], who stresses the fact that the OT formed a continuation of Canaanite literature (which is not the same thing as imitation): Ugarit and Israel were heirs to the same Canaanite literary tradition. Cassuto discusses a number of these literary conventions.

In view of the above, I am inclined to regard Ps. xxix as an original Hebrew composition, not as a mere slavish translation of a Ugaritic

45 See above, p. 91. The pair *šlm – 'z* is also found in *KAI* 26 A III 3–4; C III 17–18.
46 See Loewenstamm (1971) 94; Watson (1981).
47 Cassuto (1971) Ch. II, 'The Relationship between Ugaritic Literature and the Bible'.

hymn, but at the same time to recognize its dependency on Canaanite literary forms – just as its contents show common religious conceptions.

However, we still have to consider the extensive study of J. L. Cunchillos.[48]

Cunchillos notices the following contra-indications against a Canaanite *Vorlage* of Ps. xxix (apart from the 'typically Yahwistic' character of vs. 11, which we discussed already in the previous chapter): the name Baal does not occur in the psalm, and the psalm contains several terms which are not known in Ugaritic (such as *mbwl*). In reply to this I may say that of course we do not expect the name Baal to occur if the hymn has been 'Yahwized'; and as to the Hebrew terms: that the Israelites used their own language does not prove that the concepts were typically Israelite (the heavenly ocean, for instance, was called at Ugarit one of the two *thmtm*). Furthermore, Cunchillos tries to undermine the position of a prominent supporter of the 'Baal hypothesis', namely Gaster, whose methods are severely criticized by him. Gaster would draw parallels in an indiscriminate way, and moreover, parallelism is not identity, Cunchillos remarks, just as superfluously as when he says with respect to the Canaanite style of the psalm that Canaanism need not imply Baalism.

I admit that Gaster's methods were not always strict enough; but in Ps. xxix he has spotted the pattern all right, as I hope to have made clear above. Not a single counter-argument against this is brought forward by Cunchillos. Of course, Cunchillos's vision is hindered by his not recognizing a reference to the hostile waters in vs. 3, which is an important factor in the pattern. To be sure, Gaster himself did not notice this point, but Mowinckel, who did, nevertheless did not serve as an eye-opener for Cunchillos (so as to enable him to perceive the pattern); for Mowinckel's explanation of 'the waters' finds no favour either in the eyes of Cunchillos. Cunchillos's criticism of Mowinckel is that, in order to arrive at his explanation, he has been forced to alter the text of vss. 3, 4 and 10. Let us consider this criticism. In vs. 3, Mowinckel adds: *wyr'm* (hereby changing nothing in the content of the verse) while he deletes *'l hkbwd* as a gloss; the nominal clause of vs. 4 (which verse, by the way, does not have anything to do with the subject in hand) is supplied by Mowinckel with the verb 'to be'; in vs. 10 Mowinckel adds *m'l*: Yhwh sits enthroned high above the flood. Indeed I think Mowinckel is wrong in his interpretation of vs. 10, where he supposes the *mbwl* to be the

48 See Cunchillos (1976) 145, 151, 168, 177–184, 187.

equivalent of the *thwm* = Tiamat – just as I believe that Mowinckel's explanation of vs. 3 as a reference to creation is not correct. But how the deletion of *'l hkbwd* in vs. 3 by Mowinckel could make any difference to the sense (so as to enable him to see in *mym rbym* the hostile waters) escapes me – unless Cunchillos means to say that *'l* is here the proper name El, which would make it impossible to see in *mym rbym* an allusion to the hostile waters (because El did not fight them).[49] Taking it that that is indeed what Cunchillos means to say, we may well be surprised, for Cunchillos also grants the possibility of explaining *'l* in vs. 3 as the appellative 'god'; what is more, he uses this as an argument against Stolz's opinion that, because of this term (taken by Stolz as a proper name), the psalm was originally dedicated to El.[50] Cunchillos, in fact, wants to have it both ways.

That is also shown by his digression on the Ugaritic proper names *yrǵm il* and *yrǵm bʻl*.[51] These names, thus Cunchillos, might point to a mixing of traditions at Ugarit (both El and Baal having been regarded as thunder-gods). If so, Stolz's contention that the hymn must have been dedicated to El (not to Baal) because it would be illogical if the adapter had replaced the name Baal by the name El in vs. 3 (whilst in the rest of the psalm replacing it by the name Yhwh), is of no avail (indeed Cunchillos wants to refute an original dedication of the hymn to El); for if El and Baal traditions were mixed at Ugarit, the Ugaritic *Vorlage* of the psalm might already have contained the name El in a hymn to Baal (perhaps in an attempt to identify the two gods). However, when it is a matter of refuting the hypothesis that Ps. xxix had been dedicated to Baal, Cunchillos (like Stolz assuming that we have the proper name El in vs. 3, and thinking that it could only have been a Baal hymn if El and Baal motifs were already mixed at Ugarit) remarks that the evidence of

49 It does not make much difference to this argument whether vs. 3b is placed between vss. 3a and 3c (close to *mym rbym*) or before vs. 9c – as I would prefer.

50 See above, p. 18. I have countered Stolz's opinion on p. 55, n. 127.

51 *KTU* 1.102 19, 26. Dahood (1968), 368, translates 'may El/Baal thunder'; he is followed in this by Rainey (1974), 192, and by Dietrich-Loretz-Sanmartín (1975). According to De Moor (1970), 326–327, the names mean 'may Ilu/Baʻlu have compassion'; cp. Arab. *rǵm* 'to be humble', Hebr. *rʻm* II 'to be disconcerted', Syr. *rʻm* 'to have compassion'. Stamm (1979) follows Dahood as to the meaning of the verb, but translates 'El/Baal has thundered'; he compares this with the Accadian name *Išgum-Irra*, 'Irra has roared'. Stamm thinks the names might refer to a thunder-storm during the birth of the bearers – an explanation which cannot be right, however, if it concerns names of divine statues (cp. Xella (1981) 328–331). See Cunchillos (1976) 78, 144–147.

these names does not amount to much (as they may mean 'may El/Baal have compassion').

In reply to these intricate reasonings I only want to repeat what I have said above: Baal was also called *il*, that is, god, just like the OT knows this appellative. What should turn the scale in the matter of 'proper name versus appellative' is the text of the psalm as a whole, which – as I have tried to demonstrate – presents a coherent picture of Yhwh as a Baal. This makes the translation 'the god who is honoured' (instead of reading the proper name El in the expression '*l hkbwd*) rather obvious. Needless to say that, if I am right, Mowinckel's deletion of '*l hkbwd* cannot make any difference to the interpretation.

As I have mentioned, Cunchillos believes in an original dedication of the hymn to El no more than he believes in an original dedication of the hymn to Baal. Nevertheless, he detects a number of 'Elistic data' in the psalm.[52] Accordingly, he suggests the solution that Ps. xxix must have originated in Israel, because it is a known fact that the Israelites wanted to assimilate Yhwh to El.[53] As I have contested the idea that the psalm represents Yhwh partly as El, I naturally disagree with this conclusion – that is to say, the psalm may perfectly well have originated in Israel, but this cannot be based on Cunchillos's argumentation.

We are left with the question, how does Cunchillos explain the Baal characteristics in the psalm? As to this, he poses two alternatives: either Yhwh possessed these characteristics already before he was confronted with Baal, or he took them over from the Baal religion. This is a very interesting question indeed – although we do not know (as Cunchillos

52 Cunchillos (1976) 143–144. As 'Elistic data' Cunchillos regards not only the honour paid by the assembly of gods and the occurrence of the proper name El (but see above for my refutation of the opinion that Yhwh is represented as El in the introduction), but also the mention of the Siryon, because it was regarded as the mountain of El and the gods; see Lipiński (1965), 119, who infers this from the fragment of the Gilgamesh epic discovered by Bauer. Rev. l. 13 reads *Sa-ri-a ù La-ab-na-an*; these are the domicile of the Anunnaki, as appears from rev. l. 20. Lipiński thinks this idea must be due to West-Semitic influence, and that especially the Siryon was regarded as such. (It is stated in rev. l. 13 that the Siryon and the Lebanon trembled before the word of Ḥuwawa; this parallel to Ps. xxix 6 is thought so striking by Stolz (1970), 155 n. 29, that he even suggests that the notions of the psalm ultimately went back to a 'god of the Lebanon', perhaps called Ḥuwawa-Humbaba.)
53 Cunchillos (1976) 148–152; cp. 187–196 and Appendix II, 'Relaciones entre 'El-Baal-Yhwh en Israel'. A comparable argument for an origin of the psalm in Israel is given by Schmidt (1961), 47 n. 159, namely that Yhwh is pictured partly as Baal, partly as El – which is not to be expected in a Canaanite hymn. Cp. above, p. 23.

pretends to know) if there ever was a time before Yhwh was confronted with the Baal religion.

Cunchillos solves the question in favour of Yhwh's independency from Baal. Already before the arrival of the Israelites in Canaan Yhwh possessed the characteristics attributed to him in Ps. xxix: he dominated nature and he was called king. In order to defend this viewpoint, Cunchillos adduces a number of texts about the pre-Canaanite or the early Canaanite period of Israelite history.

Refraining from a discussion of each separate text, I want to remark the following:

It is an error to take the so-called 'historical' texts at face-value. This has been aptly demonstrated by B. Zuber[54], who points to the great lapse of time between the events which are described and the writing down of these texts. We do not even know if the Israelites ever were in Egypt – not to mention 'the character of Yhwh before the arrival of the Israelites in Canaan'. All that we do know, is a Yahwism which is indigenous in Canaan. But apart from that, Cunchillos's catalogue of Yhwh's qualities 'before his confrontation with Baal' does not comprise typical Baal characteristics, or for that matter, the special characteristics of the deity in Ps. xxix. Therefore, his exposition does not touch upon the problem of Ps. xxix. It may be true that Yhwh, according to the story, guaranteed the proper sequence of the seasons after the deluge, made the land of the patriarchs fertile, acted as a storm-god at Sinai, may be supposed to have acted as a king when he concluded the covenant at Sinai with his vassals, and was actually called king by the prophetizing Bileam – but what we are discussing with respect to Ps. xxix is a well-defined mythology, consisting of the sequence 'battle with Sea – thunder and anxiety of nature – kingship – gift of fertility'. The examples adduced by Cunchillos offer nothing of the sort. Therefore, I do not think he has put up anything remotely resembling a defense of Yhwh's possessing Baal features independently of Baal.

Thus, Cunchillos has not offered proper counter-arguments against a Canaanite *Vorlage* which was dedicated to Baal; neither has he solved the problem of the Baal characteristics in Ps. xxix.

As regards the question: 'was Ps. xxix originally a hymn to Baal?' I would draw the following conclusions:

Neither Fitzgerald, nor Craigie nor Cunchillos have offered conclusive arguments. Methodologically, an Israelite origin has to be assumed

---

54 Zuber (1976); see esp. Ch. III, 'Die mündliche Tradition'.

if there are no positive indications for a Canaanite origin. The style of the psalm seems to support the idea that it originated in Israel.

If we assume the Israelite origin of the psalm, it is reasonable to suppose that its conceptions 'belonged to Yahwism'. The distinction made by Gaster between 'folk religion' and 'official Yahwism' seems to me to be somewhat forced. Of course, Gaster suggested this in the context of his theory that Ps. xxix was adopted from a foreign religion; but also when we assume Ps. xxix to be originally Israelite we may ask ourselves whether Gaster's distinction is valid. I think that 'official Yahwism' is a product of much later times.[55]

We will now pass on to the question of the Enthronement Festival.

An Enthronement Festival

The question whether an Enthronement Festival existed in Israel is closely bound up with the question of what motifs were connected with it. When Mowinckel enumerates a quantity of motifs which occur in the OT in connection with the festival, regardless of their time of origin, one is bound to feel reserve. Let us consider it this way: we have concluded that Yahwism was acquainted with the conception of the deity becoming king after his battle with Sea; we have met this picture in a fragmentary form in a number of poetical passages (see the diagram on p. 50), and in a rather less fragmentary form in Ps. xxix, where the whole series 'thundering against the waters – anxiety of nature – kingship – gift of fertility' is present. It might then not be too hazardous to postulate the existence of a festival where Yhwh's triumph was celebrated, probably in the autumn when the rainy season returned.

I have mentioned the LXX heading of Ps. xxix: 'on the last day of the Festival of Booths', saying that of course this does not tell us anything about the pre-exilic period. But I am inclined to attach some weight to this evidence combined with that of another late passage, which has often been adduced in defense of the Enthronement Festival, namely Zech. xiv 16–17: the nations shall go up yearly to Jerusalem to worship the King, the Lord of Hosts, and to celebrate the Festival of Booths; but whoever shall not go up, on him shall fall no rain. If these ideas were connected with the Festival of Booths after the exile, and if Ps. xxix was sung at this festival – whilst we may further assume that Ps. xxix was an old hymn and the ideas expressed in it were known in

55 See e.g. Ringgren (1963) 276–277.

early times, then we might infer from this that the same ideas were connected with a pre-exilic Autumn Festival. Although this means subscribing to Gray's opinion (see p. 100) that the mythology of the Israelite Autumn Festival was similar to the mythology of Baal, it need not imply the adoption of Gray's opinion that Ps. xxix was originally a hymn to Baal. Indeed, as I hope to have made clear, there is no reason to regard it as such.

However, we still have to consider the theory that the Israelite Enthronement Festival, and the ideas connected with it, stemmed from the cult of El Elyon. My rejection of the opinion that (part of) the conceptions found in Ps. xxix had to do with El does not bear upon this question, because we were discussing the Ugaritic El – whilst El Elyon, in the view of the adherents of the said theory, was different from the high god El who is known from the Ugaritic texts. Notably, El Elyon would have functioned as a combattant of chaos, which means that he had got some characteristics of the Ugaritic Baal. If this would be correct, we would perhaps have to revise our theory that Yhwh is pictured as Baal in Ps. xxix.

We have seen[56] that Mowinckel assumed influence from the cult of the Jebusite El on the Israelite Enthronement Festival, because he was convinced that Yhwh's battle was a battle of creation. As is well-known, El bore the epithet qn 'rs[57], and according to Gen. xiv 19 the Jebusite El Elyon was called the creator of heaven and earth.[58]

It must be the supposed element of 'creation' in the Enthronement Festival, which has caused the persistence of the theory that this festival was a continuation of the (hypothetical) Enthronement Festival of El Elyon at Jebus. On may note, for instance, the opinion of A. R. Johnson[59], that Ps. xxix may originally have been a Jebusite hymn belonging to the Autumn Festival in honour of El Elyon; we saw that, according to Johnson, Yhwh's triumph over the cosmic sea (the $mbwl$) implied his creation of the world. H. Gottlieb[60] calls the concept of Yhwh as lord and creator of the world the kernel of the Jerusalem New Year Festival

56 Above, p. 68–69.
57 Recently, Miller (1980) has discussed a new occurrence of the epithet, namely in an inscription from Jerusalem (Avigad 195–196, Pl. 42B, late 8th or early 7th century B.C.), which contains the words r/l qn 'rs; the reading l instead of r is indeed attractive.
58 We cannot be absolutely sure that these epithets refer to creation, however; cp. p. 28 n. 42.
59 Johnson (1955) 54–58; cp. above, p. 65.
60 Gottlieb (1980) 67–69; cp. above, p. 70.

which originated in the cult of El Elyon; sometimes the creation is described as a battle against the sea. To mention yet another recent study: T. N. D. Mettinger[61] states that the battle with chaos was introduced in the Israelite theophanic tradition under the influence of the Jerusalem cult tradition; the battle with chaos was, according to Mettinger, a battle of creation.[62]

Now if the fact that Baal was not a creator god, whilst El Elyon was, were the only argument for the supposed influence from the cult of El Elyon on the Israelite Autumn Festival, it would suffice to refer to my conclusion[63] that the battle with Sea in the OT was not a battle of creation. However, there are other arguments too, which we will have to discuss now.

The theory that the Jebusite El Elyon possessed some characteristics which, at Ugarit, belonged to Baal, has been extensively defended by F. Stolz.[64] According to Stolz El had, in Jerusalem, adopted the characteristics of a 'naher Gott' (as contrasted with a 'ferner Gott'). Notably he would have functioned as a combattant of chaos c.q. the hostile nations (which are the manifestation of the powers of chaos in history). Stolz's argumentation is based on the occurrence of *'l*, *'lywn* and *šdy* – the latter two being epithets of El – in the OT, in contexts which point to these functions.

The uncertain factor in this theory (of which Stolz also is aware) is the fact that these names were applied to Yhwh by the OT writers as a matter of course; we cannot tell for certain, when we meet them, whether their occurrence actually implies an El tradition cropping up in the OT (of which the writer himself need not have been conscious) or not. Therefore, I am not convinced of El's having functioned as a combattant of chaos, a god who ever anew had to gain his kingship in battle – which was celebrated at the Jebusite Enthronement Festival, as Stolz supposes.

Moreover, Stolz adduces only a few examples of *'l* c.q. *'lywn* in a context which mentions the hostile waters, namely Ps. XVIII 14 = 2 Sam. XXII 14, Ps. XXIX 3 and – a less clear example – Ps. XLVI 5. Thus,

---

61 Mettinger (1982) 33, 71; cp. above, p. 70–71.

62 Mettinger is, however, not very clear on this subject, as he also writes that maybe the battle motif was originally not a cosmological motif in Israel (70). But he states explicitly that the Jebusite El had Baal characteristics (35).

63 Above, p. 85.

64 Stolz (1970) 149–180.

even if it is granted that the occurrence of *'l*, *'lywn* or *šdy* in the OT may point to an original El-tradition in some cases, there is still not much to go upon if it comes to proving a combat of El with Sea. A great many texts are quoted by Stolz; but how much weight he attaches to the respective passages is not always clear to me. I have, therefore, made a selection (as true as possible to Stolz's intentions); I want to arrange these texts under three headings:

1 The thundering voice of the deity.
 – 1 Sam. II 10 *'lywn (text. emend.) yr'm*.
 – Ezek. I 24; X 5 *qwl ('l)-šdy*.
 – Ps. XVIII 14 = 2 Sam. XXII 14 *w'lywn ytn qlw*, par. *wyr'm yhwh* (as appears from the context, this is directed against the waters).
 – Ps. XXIX 3 *'l-hkbwd hr'ym* (the same verse mentions the hostile waters).
2 The gift of fertility.
 – Gen. XLIX 25 *'l šdy* blesses with blessings from heaven and from the *thwm*.
3 The battle with the nations.
 – Gen. XIV 20 *'l 'lywn* has given the enemies into Abram's hand.
 – Is. VIII 10 *'mnw 'l* (in the context of the triumph over the hostile nations); cp. Is. VII 14; VIII 8. Cp. also 2 Sam. XXIII 5: the house of David is *'m-'l*. Stolz thinks that, also in Ps. XLVI, which is about the victory over the nations, *'l* must be read instead of *yhwh ṣb'wt* in the refrain; the MT reads: *yhwh ṣb'wt 'mnw*.
 – Is. XIII 6; Joel I 15 the day of Yhwh comes like a destruction by *šdy*.
 – Ps. XLVI 5 the city of God is the most holy among the dwellings of *'lywn* (the psalm is about God's protection against the hostile nations; but vss. 3–4 mention the insurgent waters).
 – Ps. XLVII 3 *yhwh 'lywn* is a redoubtable king over the whole earth (vs. 4 mentions the triumph over the nations).
 – Ps. LXVIII 15 *šdy* disperses kings.
   The motif of the judgment of the nations (thus Stolz) must be considered as a variant of the 'Völkerkampf'.
 – 1 Sam. II 10 (see ad 1) goes on to mention this judgment (but in this part of the verse the deity is called *yhwh*).
 – Ps. LXXXII (called by Stolz a 'Bruchstück des Jerusalemer Chaoskampfmythus'): judgment is passed on the unjust gods (i.e. the nations); although the deity who acts as judge is called *'lhym*, who is pictured standing in the council of *'l*, Stolz assumes that in point of fact the judge was thought to be El.

Now I think that we cannot infer from isolated references to the thunder or to the gift of fertility that the deity was a 'Chaoskämpfer'. Turning, therefore, to the texts which mention a hostile element, we find that it concerns human adversaries in the majority of cases. Now it cannot be doubted, that the inimical nations which are overthrown or judged according to the OT, are sometimes depicted as a power of chaos; they can also be compared with the hostile waters (see e.g. Is. XVII 12). Mowinckel counted a 'Völkerkampfmythus' among the themes of the Enthronement Festival of Yhwh; but others too have noticed the mythical character of the theme of the hostile nations. (This is, for instance, aptly formulated by W. Staerk[65], who calls Hab. I 5–11 a 'typische, nach einem bestimmten Schema geformte mythische Darstellung der widergöttlichen Weltmacht'). Only, it does not follow that the Jebusite god who conquered the foreign nations was also the god who conquered Sea.

As the connection between these two motifs is one of the main themes of Stolz's study as a whole, we must make a further digression in order to be able to weigh his argument properly. Stolz argues that the cosmos which is created in Enuma elish has two aspects: the natural order and the social order. This is concluded by him from the fact that Enuma elish was recited at the Akitu Festival, at which these two aspects played a rôle: the *hieros gamos* rite aimed at fertility, thus at order in nature (moreover the ordering of the astral world is explicitly mentioned in Enuma elish), and the ritual of the abasement of the king was an atonement which aimed at the renewal of the social order. This meaning of Enuma elish is confirmed, according to Stolz, by other Mesopotamic myths about a 'Chaoskampf'. Especially the Sumerian myth called Lugal-e could be compared with Enuma elish, in that the conquered demon can be explained as a symbol of chaos in nature (violent inundations) as well as in society (the human enemies of the nation).

Because of the similarity of the 'Chaosmacht' in the Baal-Yam myth and in Enuma elish – thus still Stolz –, we must assume that the purport of these two myths is the same. That means, that Baal is represented in the Baal-Yam myth as a creator of order in the cosmos and in society. Indeed Baal was the state god of Ugarit who supposedly functioned as conqueror of the foreign nations.

The fact that the foreign nations are not explicitly mentioned in the Mesopotamic chaos-myths, is explained by Stolz as follows:

65 Staerk (1933) 6.

Myth is about a 'timeless reality'; the reality of the 'Chaoskampfmythus' is, that the hostile power is conquered. Now the mentioning of the hostile nations would not fit in with the mythical reality because, as history teaches, the enemy may be the victor. Accordingly, the form in which to express the victory over the hostile nations is the hymn: the hymn expresses the experience by which the reality of the myth is confirmed. (On the other hand, the lament is the literary form to express the reverse.) In fact, we find the deity praised as conqueror of the foreign nations in Mesopotamic hymns.

The Baal-Yam myth contains a passage in which Anat slays human enemies (*KTU* 1.3 II); this is, according to Stolz's theory, not to be expected in a myth; but it can be explained in his opinion by the circumstance that the text is not a proper myth, but a reflection on mythical material.

The motif of the hostile nations occurs in the OT in psalms and prophetic texts; in Israel too, its original form must have been the hymn. Stolz assumes that the motif was inherited from the Jebusite religion; here, too, it must have been expressed in hymns. But there has been a development from Jebusite to Israelite religion: in the former, the myth of the battle with chaos must have taken an important place, whereas in the latter the myth was superseded by the hymn – which shows that Israel attached greater value to experience. Anyway – to round off Stolz's argumentation – it concerned the experience of the reality which was originally expressed in the myth: that the power of chaos had been worsted.

In this way, then, Stolz can argue that the OT passages about the foreign nations, in which the deity is designated as '*l* (etc.), point to a Jebusite 'Chaoskampfmythus' in which El conquered the sea. In my opinion, however, the nations and the sea are not interchangeable. In my view, Stolz's theory is based on a faulty interpretation of the texts he adduces as evidence. Stolz's basic assumption is, that there was one 'Chaoskampfmythus' in the ancient Near East; this myth – as he concedes – existed only in different concrete versions, but all versions are believed by him to be expressions of 'das gemeinsame Grundmuster des Chaoskampf-Erlebens'.[66] Indeed Stolz declares himself to be an adherent of the phenomenological approach to religion, although he is also aware of its pitfalls. I think, however, that he has not sufficiently avoided

---

66 Stolz elucidates 'das Chaoskampf-Erleben' by Freud's theory of 'das Ich' and 'das Es': 'Wo Es war, soll Ich werden', that is, chaos must become cosmos.

the pitfalls. When Stolz states that 'die Inland-Ausland-Beziehung' is a central theme of the 'Chaoskampfmythus', he is transferring the theme of one myth to another without textual evidence: fur Lugal-e, it may hold true, but in Enuma elish one looks in vain for hostile nations. Moreover, to derive the meaning of Enuma elish from the Akitu Festival (which, to be precise, has not to do with hostile nations either), is, in my opinion, a misjudgment of the status of this text. That it was recited at some point in the celebrations (which covered 12 days) does not imply that its meaning was determined by that of the festival. I think Stolz's supposition rests upon a too narrow definition of myth, which he takes to be indissolubly connected with the cult.[67]

Furthermore – even supposing that Enuma elish had to do with the 'Inland-Ausland-Beziehung' – I cannot find that Enuma elish and the Baal-Yam myth have the same purport, seeing that the one is about the creation of the world and the other is not. However, we must ask whether the Baal epic contains the motif of the hostile nations. There is indeed the passage about the massacre by Anat; but the difficulty is, that its meaning is not clear.

Anat slays enemies in west and east (that is, everywhere), continuing the massacre in her own temple. Typical features are, that she perfumes herself before and after the massacre, and that she gets into a state of ecstasy. This suggests some ritual; indeed Stolz, following Kaiser[68], thinks it may be the ritual killing of prisoners of war. H. Gese[69] thinks it is an offering, notably by Anat to herself, in order to strengthen herself with the blood. Gese does not think the enemies in west and east were people who offered resitance to the Baal cult, as the second massacre is in Anat's own temple. J. Gray[70] thinks of imitative magic to promote fertility; he also writes that, if there is a relationship between this passage and the fight with Yam, it might concern worshippers of Yam. However that may be, I think that it is taking it too far to connect the passage with the OT passages about a 'Völkersturm' and the annihilation or total subjugation of the foreign nations. Moreover, it is hard to tell if the

---

67 Stolz writes that 'der Mythus ist magisch wirkendes Wort' (12), that 'jeder Mythus ist ... Bestandteil eines Rituals' (13), and that 'Das Ritual ... findet Gestalt in einem Fest. Nur jetzt darf der Mythus gesagt werden' (14). Lately, however, he has apparently changed his opinion, as he writes (1982) that myths can be classified, among other things, by the criterion whether they are connected with the cult or not.
68 Kaiser (1959) 71 n. 289.
69 Gese (1970) 66–67.
70 Gray (UF 1979).

passage bears any relation to the battle with Yam, to the effect that the people killed by Anat would constitute a variant of Baal's enemy.

There is therefore, in my opinion, no foundation in the non-Israelite texts for the supposition that the god who conquers the foreign nations is, as a 'Chaoskämpfer', also the conqueror of Sea. That means, that the OT texts about the hostile nations quoted above cannot be used as evidence of El's battle with Sea. The evidence in support of such a battle is thus reduced to Ps. XVIII 14 = 2 Sam. XXII 14, Ps. XXIX 3 and Ps. XLVI 5.

The evidence of Ps. XLVI however is questionable. For the largest part, the psalm is about God's protection against the hostile nations; the deity is called *yhwh* or *'lhym* (as it concerns the Elohistic psalter, the original reading may have been *yhwh* in every instance), and only in vs. 5 *'lywn* is used, to indicate the god of the holy city. The insurgent waters of the sea are only mentioned in passing (vss. 3–4; notably, not in the verse where *'lywn* is mentioned). Supposedly, the use of the name *'lywn* was prompted by ancient tradition, Jerusalem having been the place where El Elyon was worshipped (Gen. XIV 18). But the evidence is surely stretched too far if it is supposed, that all elements of the psalm (including vss. 3–4) originate in ancient traditions about El Elyon.

It is another matter with Ps. XVIII 14 = 2 Sam. XXII 14 and Ps. XXIX 3: here, we have an immediate connection between *'lywn* resp. *'l* and the hostile waters. Thus, we have got two passages on which to base the hypothetical battle of El with Sea. Ps. XVIII 8–16 = 2 Sam. XXII 8–16 use the name Yhwh twice against once *'lywn*; Ps. XXIX uses (apart from *'l* in vs. 3b) the name Yhwh throughout. Therefore, we have not got a single text in which *'l* or *'lywn* is *exclusively* used in connection with the battle with Sea.

This situation, combined with the element of uncertainty mentioned by me above, namely that the OT writers were in the habit of using *'l* and *'lywn* to indicate Yhwh, leads to the conclusion that Stolz has not adduced sufficient arguments for his thesis, that the Jebusite El possessed characteristics which belonged to Baal at Ugarit.

When H. Gottlieb[71] expounds the view that the Jerusalem New Year Festival, at which Yhwh was worshipped as creator of the world, originated in the cult of El Elyon, he supports his argumentation with references to Stolz's study (which he calls 'exciting'). Now there is an argument against a derivation of the festival from the Baal cult to be found in

---

71 Gottlieb (1980) 76–78.

Gottlieb's article, which is also based on a suggestion made by Stolz, but which did not yet come up for discussion on the foregoing pages. Stolz remarks[72], that the Baal cult seems to have been introduced into Jerusalem at a comparatively late stage. He deduces this from the fact that hardly any names with the element *b'l* occur which can with any certainty be traced back to the region of Jerusalem[73], and that polemics against the Baal cult are not found with the 8th century prophets from the southern kingdom. As an additional argument, Gottlieb refers to the statements in the books of Kings about the institution of a Baal cult by Athalia and by Manasse (2 Kgs. VIII 18, 27, cp. 2 Kgs. XI 18; 2 Kgs. XXI 3, cp. 2 Kgs. XXIII 5).

Stolz's argumentation – although it is an *argumentum e silentio* – seems to carry more weight than Gottlieb's, as the passages in Kings could also refer to old practices which received a new stimulus. Only it could be argued against Stolz, that the occurrence of one theophoric name with the element *b'l* at Jerusalem suffices to prove that Baal was known in that region. Oesterley and Robinson have already called attention to the name *b'lyd'* (1 Chron. XIV 7), a son of David who was born to him in Jerusalem.[74] (It is interesting, by the way, to read their conclusion: as David was devoted to Yhwh, they infer from this name that 'This can mean only that Yahweh Himself was intended and, in fact, He was probably indistinguishable from the older *Ba'als* save by His name'.[75]) Stolz, it is true, also mentions this name; but he attaches more value, than is apparently done by Oesterley and Robinson, to the fact that the name also occurs as *'lyd'* (2 Sam. V 16; 1 Chron. III 8).

Now a possible explanation of this alternative form of the name is given by A. S. Kapelrud.[76] Kapelrud mentions the name *mryb'l*, a son of Jonathan (1 Chron. VIII 34; IX 40) with its alternative form *mpybšt* (i.a. 2 Sam. IV 4), and the name *'šb'l*, a son of Saul (1 Chron. VIII 33; IX 39) with its alternative form *'yšbšt* (i.a. 2 Sam. II 8). Apparently these names have been changed intentionally. From this, Kapelrud draws the conclusion that the author of the books of Samuel avoided names with the element *b'l*; this is also the reason, in the view of Kapelrud, why *b'lyd'* was changed into *'lyd'* by the author of Samuel. Only, Kapelrud's explanation does not account for the fact that the form *'lyd'* also occurs in 1

72 Stolz (1970) 154.
73 Stolz refers to Mulder (1962) 169–173.
74 Oesterley-Robinson (1937²) 199.
75 Oesterley-Robinson (1937²) 199–200.
76 Kapelrud (1965) 33.

Chron. III 8. We should therefore take it that there is not sufficient proof of Baal worship at Jerusalem in early times.

However, this does not imply — still supposing that there was indeed an Enthronement Festival of Yhwh — that notions which were derived from the Baal cult could not have belonged to it. The worshippers of Yhwh may have come into contact with the Baal religion at many places[77]; indeed it is likely that they knew it well, judging by Ps. xxix alone. Therefore I cannot see any problem in the assumption that the conception of Yhwh in the supposed Enthronement Festival was influenced by beliefs about Baal, even though Baal was not worshipped at Jerusalem or elsewhere in the south.[78] The festival might for instance have originated in Silo, and it might have been brought to Jerusalem from there.[79] The decision ought to depend on the question, whether the concepts which supposedly belonged to the festival resemble the beliefs about Baal or not. If they do, this might even explain the absence of names with the element *b'l* in Jerusalem or the southern region in general: if Yhwh exercised functions of Baal, Baal himself may as a consequence have receded into the background.

Gottlieb however adduces yet another argument, which concerns precisely the functions of Yhwh: the absence of the elements of the *hieros gamos* and the death and resurrection of the deity in the Jerusalem cult of Yhwh would be understandable, if influence from the cult of El Elyon rather than from the Baal cult is assumed (provided we take it that the cult of El Elyon did not comprise these elements).

In reply to this, I want to remark the following.

As to the *hieros gamos* rite, we do not even know for certain if it belonged to the Baal cult at Ugarit. K. Koch[80] draws attention to the fact that a sexual function of Baal is not particularly emphasized in the Ugaritic texts. The picture of the Baal cult which is given in the OT is

---

77 Cp. Schmidt (1961) 77. Against the opinion 'dass Jahwe durch Verschmelzung mit El Eljon zum König geworden sei' it is argued by Schmidt that Yhwh's kingship is not only derived from the kingship of El, but also from that of Baal; he adds: 'Damit entfällt der Hauptgrund, den Anfang von Jahwes Königtum erst in Jerusalem anzusetzen.' (on p. 76 he has suggested Silo).

78 Stolz (1970), 154 n. 23, also mentions the fact that, on the ostraca from Arad from the time of the kings, the element *b'l* is lacking in theophoric names, in contradistinction to the ostraca from Samaria.

79 On Canaanite elements in the Israelite cult at Silo see E. Otto (1976), who supposes that there was a continuity between the cults of Silo and Jerusalem, due to the religious policy of David.

80 Koch (1979) 467.

certainly different; but then, the cult of Baal may have changed in the course of time. The emphasis laid by the OT on the sexual practices belonging to the Baal cult need not occupy us now: if the official cult of Yhwh comprised an Enthronement Festival which was influenced by the Baal religion, this must surely date from an earlier time, before the prophetical denouncements of Baalism.[81]

As to the death and resurrection: it has to be admitted that this is a major difference between Baal and Yhwh. However, this need not invalidate the assumption that the 'battle with Sea – kingship' mythology was attributed to Yhwh because the Israelites were acquainted with it from the Baal religion. We do not know if this mythology was connected with El Elyon, but we know for a fact that it was connected with Baal. The conclusion can hardly be avoided that, in view of the contacts which the Israelites must have had with the Baal religion, they did not arrive independently at this belief. Now if such an independency from the Baal religion is defended on the basis of the absence of a conflict with Mot in Yahwism, one has to make plausible that the two motifs (Baal-Yam and Baal-Mot) were connected in such a way as to be virtually inseparable. Otherwise, it is not understandable why the one could not have been taken over without the other.

Perhaps, we have got here a new argument for the Israelite origin of Ps. XXIX: if Israel had autonomy in religious beliefs (not having adopted the conflict of the deity with Mot), then it surely was autonomous with regard to its hymns.

81 Although the OT pictures Yhwh without a consort, other ideas seem to have been current too. The words *lyhwh.šmrn.w l'šrth* in an inscription on a jar from Kuntillet 'Ajrud (Meshel Inscriptions E, 8th cent. B.C.) may refer to Yhwh and his Ashera (meaning the goddess); alternatively, *l'šrth* could refer to a wooden cult object (a symbol of the goddess). See Meshel-Meyers (1976); Gilula (1978/79); Fritz (1979); Meshel (1979); Stolz (1980) 168–171; Emerton (1982). The words 'Yhwh and his Ashera' are also found in inscription no. 3 from Khirbet el-Qōm (IDAM 72–169, ± 750 B.C.), be it that they are separated by an intervening word. The text reads (2) *brk.'ryhw.lyhwh. (3) wmṣryh.l'šrth.hwš'lh.* Lemaire (1977) proposes to reverse the word order of the first two words of line 3 (not including *w*); accordingly he translates 'blessed be Uryahu by Yhwh and by his Ashera; from his enemies he saved him'. Jaroš (1982) keeps the actual word order and translates 'blessed be Uryahu by Yhwh; because from his enemies he has, through his Ashera, saved him'. See also Stolz (1980) 172–173; Mittmann (1981); Angerstorfer (1982); Dever (1982). These inscriptions support the theory of De Boer (Leiden 1974), 46–47, that the plural forms in Gen. I 26 ('let *us* make man in *our* image') point to a mythical *Vorlage* in which Yhwh addressed a goddess. Anyway, if Yhwh was pictured with a consort, a radical difference from Baal in this respect can no longer be maintained.

Concluding, we may say, that there are no convincing arguments for a derivation of the Israelite traditions concerning Yhwh's battle with Sea from traditions connected with the Jebusite El.[82] Moreover, such a derivation seems to have no point if it is accepted, that Yhwh's battle with Sea cannot properly be called a battle of creation.

Conclusions

An answer should now be formulated to the question we put to ourselves at the beginning of this chapter: how can the consistent picture of the deity as Baal in Ps. xxix be explained?

We have rejected the explanation 'polemics'; neither does 'literary imagery' seem to be a solution, as it is hardly conceivable that a hymn would have been composed, consisting solely of literary imagery. The existence of a Canaanite *Vorlage* dedicated to Baal could not be proved. We have assumed therefore that the psalm originated in Israel, and that its notions formed part of the Yahwistic creed. There may have been a festival to which this psalm belonged. The assumption that such a festival stemmed from the cult of El Elyon had to be rejected.

Thus, if Ps. xxix expressed Yahwistic beliefs, Yhwh was, at the time when Ps. xxix was composed, credited with the same properties as Baal in the Ugaritic Baal-Yam myth. Of course this does not preclude his having possessed other qualities as well in the eyes of his worshippers.

It is not my intention to go into the question of the relationship between Yhwh's Baal traits and his other characteristics; I merely want to investigate the Baal component of Yhwh's character. The thesis of W. H. Schmidt[83] for instance, that the notion of the kingship of Yhwh underwent influence from El as well as from Baal, does not contradict what I have said above. Only I think it likely that the El characteristics were acquired by Yhwh at a later stage. In my opinion, the Israelites are certain to have venerated El in the first stage of their history, whilst Yhwh formed part of the pantheon headed by El. Gradually, Yhwh must have replaced El, thereby acquiring his properties. To mention

---

82 An article by E. Otto (1980) should also be mentioned; but I cannot find new arguments in it for the opinion that the Jebusite El possessed Baal characteristics. What is new in Otto's article is, that he tries to explain *why* this should have been the case. According to Otto, the 'ferner Gott' adopts traits of the 'naher Gott' in times of distress, because the 'nahe Götter' do not seem able to help any more. Jebus suffered from attacks on its territory in the time of the Amarna letters.

83 Schmidt (1961) 71.

one more study, that of Lipiński[84]: Lipiński's main conclusions need not invalidate my assumption either. Lipiński concludes that Yhwh's kingship has several aspects: apart from being the 'great king of the country', like El and like the feudal suzerains, Yhwh was also called king in his function of leader of the military operations; the latter quality, thus Lipiński, 'shows a certain parallelism' to the kingship of Baal[85], because Yhwh too was hailed as king after having triumphed over his enemies. Now it may be true that this military aspect also played a rôle, but that need not keep us from assuming that there was a time when the 'battle with Sea – kingship' mythology was taken seriously (as Ps. xxix testifies).[86] It is not a question of 'either – or'. We must be careful not to try and force the beliefs of the Israelites during a great span of centuries into one logical system.

As I have rejected the idea, that the attribution of Baal qualities to Yhwh resulted from a hostile attitude towards Baalism, I do not believe that Yhwh acquired his Baal traits after the prophets started their denouncements of the Baal religion. This particular conception of Yhwh must surely date from earlier times. It could be possible (that is, if we assume that Yahwism originated in a region where Baal was known[87]), that Yhwh possessed his Baal traits from the beginning. That would mean that the Israelites, seeing that Baal could satisfy a fundamental need by sending the rain, wanted to possess 'a Baal of their own'.

If we take it that Yhwh functioned at one time as an Israelite Baal, we would like to see this confirmed by other texts. The passages mentioned by me on p. 50 (see diagram) do not add much to the evidence, as they do not present the pattern of Baal motifs as completely as Ps. xxix. There is, however, another text which pleads for my assumption: the so-called Song of the Sea. This text also demonstrates the independency of the Israelite population, in that the Baal motifs are transformed in it in quite a remarkable way. It remains to be shown that, essentially, the deity of the Song of the Sea was just as much a Baal as the deity of Ps. xxix. If I succeed in showing this, a text which represents an important OT tradition would betray Yhwh's Baal character – which might suggest that Yhwh's Baal traits were not accidental.

84 Lipiński (1965).
85 Lipiński (1965) 463.
86 Lipiński (1965), 130–135, is of the opinion that the Israelites must have told stories about Yhwh's battle with Sea, but he does not think that these formed part of the living creed of Israel at the time when the OT was written.
87 Cp. below, p. 209.

PART TWO

THE TALE OF THE SEA

I

THE SONG OF THE SEA

Translation

Ex. xv 1b I will sing to Yhwh, for he rose in triumph;
the horse and his rider he hurled into the sea.

2 Yah is my strength and my protection; he came to my succour.
He is my god, and I will praise him,
the god of my father, and I will exalt him.

3 Yhwh is a warrior; Yhwh is his name.

4 The chariots of Pharao and his army he threw into the sea,
the choice of his combatants was submerged in the Reed Sea.

5 The deeps covered them,
they sank into the depths like a stone.

6 Your right hand, Yhwh, powerful in strength,
your right hand, Yhwh, crushed the enemy.

7 In your great triumph you smote your adversaries;
you let loose your blazing anger, it consumed them like stubble.

8 By the blast of your nostrils the waters were heaped up,
the floods stood like a mound,
the deeps congealed in the heart of the sea.

9 The enemy said: I will pursue, I will overtake, I will divide the spoil;
my throat will be satiated with them;
I will draw my sword, my hand will exterminate them.

10 You blew with your breath, the sea covered them;
they sank like lead in the mighty waters.

11 Who is like you among the gods, Yhwh,
who is like you, powerful among the holy ones,
awesome in glorious deeds, worker of wonders.

12 You stretched out your right hand, the earth swallowed them.

13 You led in your faithfulness the people which you rescued,
    you guided them by your strength to your holy dwelling-
    place.
14 Peoples heard of it, they were perturbed;
    trembling seized the inhabitants of Philistia.
15 Then the chiefs of Edom were terrified;
    the leaders of Moab, shuddering seized them;
    all the inhabitants of Canaan melted away.
16 Terror and dread fell upon them;
    because of the might of your arm they stiffened like a stone,
    while your people passed through, Yhwh,
    while the people which you acquired passed through.
17 You brought them and you planted them on the mountain
    which fell to your share,
    the place you made into your residence, Yhwh,
    the sanctuary, Lord, which your hands established.
18 Yhwh will be king forever and ever.

21b Sing to Yhwh, for he rose in triumph;
    the horse and his rider he hurled into the sea.

Notes on the translation

1 Unless it is assumed that the song was composed after the custom of
riding on horse-back was introduced, one has to interpret the expression *sws wrkbw* as 'the horse and his chariot-driver'. If this meaning has
indeed been intended, the wording seems to be a little awkward; but we
meet with the same phenomenon in the Qadesh inscriptions of Ramses
II, where it is said that Ramses mounted on his horse (B 88, R 18; cp. P
267) whilst he obviously (as is seen from the reliefs) drove in a chariot. I
think therefore that we may keep to the less forced translation 'the horse
and his rider', an expression which was actually meant to refer to chario-
try.
2 The meaning 'protection' for *zmrh* was first suggested by
Th. H. Gaster[1], and has been convincingly defended by S. B. Parker.[2]
Apart from the parallelism in the Hebrew formula in vs. 2a (a synony-

1 Gaster (1936/37), with reference to the Arabic root *ḏmr*. Cp. *Thesaurus* III 1363
'victor'; I. Zolli, *GSAI* (1935), 290 'strength', with reference to the same Arabic root.
Cp. also *HAL s.v. zmr* III and *zmrh* II.
2 Parker (1971).

mous pair of words joined by *w* in one colon with a further synonym in the parallel colon), Parker bases his argumentation on the Ugaritic text *KTU* I.108 24, where *ḏmrk* (your protective force) occurs directly after '*zk* (your strength), as a quality of the god Rapiu. (In contradistinction to S. E. Loewenstamm[3], Parker does not think that the translation of *ḏmrk* should be made to depend on the translation of the verb *ḏmr* on this same tablet, l. 3, namely 'to play on the lyre'.)

The reading *zmrty* can be defended in two ways: Loewenstamm[4] points to the theological tendency (already noted by A. Geiger) to absorb the name *yh* into the preceding word, a tendency which was later reversed and the divine name restored (*zmrtyh* becoming *zmrt yh*); E. M. Good[5] quotes I. O. Lehman[6], who observed that one consonant (in this case the *y* of *yh*) may occasionally do duty for two, either at the end or at the beginning of a word.

8   The expression *blb-ym* by itself need not imply depth. 'In the heart of' (*i-na libbi*[bi]) the sea is an expression used in the Amarna letters (*EA* 114 19; 288 33), where it refers to sailing 'on the sea'. Cp. also Ezek. XXVII 4, 25, 26; XXVIII 2, 8 (*blb ymym*), where the depth is not meant either. Prov. XXIII 34 (*blb-ym*) is not clear. In Jon. II 4 however, *lbb ymym* is parallel to *mṣwlh*, the depth; cp. also Ps. XLVI 3 (*lb ymym*, the place where the roots of the mountains are anchored). This seems to be the meaning in Ex. XV 8, as *thmt* probably refers to 'the fountains which, in the mythology, connected the sea with the primeval waters under it'.[7] When these fountains 'congealed', the sea was no longer fed by the subterranean ocean.

9   G. Schmitt[8] observes that *yrš* (hi.), which is used with the Canaanites as object in Deuteronomy and Joshua, is commonly translated with 'to drive away', but that it must have the same meaning as the other verbs referring to the Canaanites in Deuteronomistic literature, that is: to exterminate. It is used parallel to verbs meaning 'to destroy' e.g. in Dt. IX 3.

11   The LXX and the Syrohexapla have the plural 'holy ones'. E. Lipiński[9] remarks that the scribes must have suppressed the plural ending

---

3   Loewenstamm (*VT* 1969).
4   Loewenstamm (*VT* 1969).
5   Good (1970).
6   Lehman (1967).
7   Stalker (1962) *ad locum*.
8   Schmitt (1970) Ch. I 1.
9   Lipiński (1965) 283 n. 2.

–*m* of *qdšm*, for theological reasons. That seems a likely explanation – although the word *'lm* which has been kept in the MT must have been just as offensive.

Qdšym also occurs in Ps. LXXXIX 6 and 8; they are called *bny 'lym* in vs. 7. At Ugarit, *ilm* is paralleled by *bn qdš* (*KTU* 1.2 I 20–21, 37–38; 1.17 I 1–22 five times[10]).

12 'Earth' is here more or less identical with 'underworld'; Acc. *erṣetu* and Ugaritic *arṣ* may also take on this meaning.[11]

Date of composition

Scholars have held the most widely divergent views on the date of composition of the Song of the Sea. In my opinion, this controversy can now be regarded as settled, due to the study of D. A. Robertson.[12] Robertson's method is as follows. First it is determined what OT poetry can be dated on non-linguistic evidence. Poetry which is datable in this way is found to stem from the middle of the 8th century and after; it is termed 'standard poetic Hebrew' by Robertson, and the grammatical forms characteristic of it are called 'standard forms'. Not a single poem can be dated on non-linguistic evidence to the early period. The nature of early poetic Hebrew must therefore be determined on the basis of a reconstruction. The linguistic characteristics of early poetry are established by correlating Ugaritic poetry and the so-called 'Canaanite glosses' in the Amarna letters on the one hand, with rare grammatical features of OT poetry as a whole on the other.

Similarity between a poem of unknown date and the reconstructed early poetry constitutes evidence in favour of an early date; similarity between a poem of unknown date and standard poetry constitutes evidence in favour of a date in the 8th century or thereafter. A clustering of early forms is regarded as a precondition for their use as evidence of an early date. The clustering may be of two kinds: either a sizable number of examples of one form must occur in a given poem, or a sizable number of different forms, each of which may occur only once.

A methodological problem is the possibility of archaizing. If a poem of unknown date, which displays early forms, also contains grammatical forms characteristic of standard poetic Hebrew, it may be an indica-

---

10 Partly reconstructed.
11 See Schmid, *ThHAT* I, 230, by whom more instances of this use of *'rṣ* are cited.
12 See Robertson (1972) *passim*.

tion of archaizing. On the other hand, it is theoretically possible that standard forms were already in use in the early period (the 'early forms' would then already have been archaisms by that time). Still, one would expect a greater clustering of archaic forms in early poetry than in poems of much later date. Indeed we meet in standard poetry only an isolated archaic form here and there.

The results of the linguistic approach have to retain a hypothetical character, because we do not know whether the presence of standard forms is evidence of archaizing or not. However, one conclusion seems to be firmly grounded, and that concerns the Song of the Sea. This poem displays a great concentration of archaic forms whilst lacking standard forms, so that there is strong evidence for an early date.

The archaic forms by which early poetic Hebrew is characterized are the following:
- the preservation of the y/w of a final y/w-root when it opens a syllable;
- the use of zw/zh as relative pronouns;
- the use of the affix $-nhw$;
- the use of the 3 masc. plur. pronominal suffix $-mw$ with verbs and nouns;
- the use of the affixes $-y$ and $-w$;
- the use of the enclitic $-m$;
- the distribution of the two finite verbal forms in past narrative.

The Song of the Sea presents the following picture:
- preservation of y vs. 5;
- zw as relative pronoun vss. 13, 16 (NB '$\check{s}r$ does not occur in the song);
- affix $-nhw$ vs. 2;
- suffix $-mw$ with verb vss. 5, 7, 9 (twice), 10, 12, 15, 17 (twice) (NB the standard form $-m$ does not occur in the song);
- affixed $-y$ vs. 6 (this morpheme, affixed to a noun or participle to denote the appositional state, occurs in the Amarna glosses);
- enclitic $-m$ (with k) vss. 5, 8.
- As to the use of the verbal forms, Ugaritic employs the suffix and prefix conjugations indiscriminately for narrating past events.[13] W-prefix is seldom found at the beginning of the line in the Ugaritic texts (if so, it is mostly found in the formula 'and x answered'); its position is generally medial, so that its use appears to be based on the appropriateness of the w. Standard poetic Hebrew uses the suffix and

---

13 See Held (1962).

w-prefix conjugations for narrating past events; they are repeatedly in parallelism and there is no indication that they differ syntactically. W-prefix is frequently initial. In this respect, standard poetry resembles Hebrew prose. The prefix conjugation without w is in prose almost exclusively used as a past frequentative. In standard poetry, where it occurs occasionally, it is either a frequentative or a preterit.

Now in Ex. xv 1–18 we find 11 prefix forms for narrating past events; they are paralleled by suffix forms in vss. 12, 14 and 15. (Robertson does not count *yrh* in vs. 4 and *yrdw* in vs. 5, as initial w/y-verbs do not show the difference between the suffix and prefix conjugations in 3 masc. sing. and plur. except by their vocalization).

Robertson raises the question whether vss. 6 and 7 must be regarded as past narrative or as a general statement. In the case of the latter, we would not have 11 but 7 prefix forms for narrating past events. But the most natural interpretation seems to me, to take these verses as referring to the event at the sea. One must of course take *ḥrn* metaphorically; it does not refer to 'fire' in the literal sense.

For the rest, the suffix conjugation is used to narrate past events, apart from one w-prefix form, notably in a medial position (vs. 17). It is clear that Ex. xv 1–18 exhibits a significant clustering of early forms. There is no evidence of archaizing, and in this respect the poem is unique, as every other poem in the OT contains a smaller or larger number of standard forms. Therefore, we have good reason to regard the Song of the Sea as the oldest piece of Hebrew poetry which has been handed down to us. Robertson proposes the 12th century B.C. as its date, but he admits that attempts to arrive at an absolute chronology are precarious. I want to add that to take the 8th century as the fixed point for an absolute chronology (as the oldest 'standard poetry' is thought by Robertson to stem from that time) might be a mistake. The oracles of Amos, Hosea, Micah and Isaiah could represent a later stage of Hebrew in their extant form. But as to the relative chronology, I think that Robertson's conclusion is fully justified.

Moreover, the archaic forms are evenly distributed throughout the poem (vss. 2, 5, 6, 7, 8, 9, 10, 12, 13, 14, 16, 17), so that theories according to which the song consists of an older and a younger part are in my opinion erroneous.[14]

14 Lately, for instance, Zenger (1981) has argued that the song consisted originally of vss. 1b, 5, 6, 7, 11, 12; vss. 8a, 10, 13, 15a, 16, 17, 18 would have been added in the time of the exile. The remaining verses stem from a redactor who inserted the song in the Pentateuch, according to Zenger.

As to the poetic style, we may note that the expanded colon[15] occurs three times, in vss. 6, 11 and 16. Loewenstamm[16] remarks the following about these verses.

Ad vs. 6: The repetitive formula and the intervening formula deviate from the normal. As a rule, it is the address that intervenes between the repetitive formulas. Here, however, the address proper is part of the repetitive formula, and the intervening formula *n'dry bkḥ* is in apposition to the address (in my opinion: in apposition to the subject).

Ad vs. 16: If the verse had read 'until *the* people pass by, O Lord, until the people pass by whom thou hast purchased', we would have had an expanded colon in which the complementary formula *'m zw qnyt* would have served as the determination of the subject. But the subject of the repetitive formula is determined by the personal pronoun (*'mk* – thy people), thus turning the expanded colon into a verse of two parallel cola, each of which is complete and comprehensible in itself, even if the origin of this verse from the expanded colon is quite obvious.

Vs. 11 is called by Loewenstamm 'still further removed from the pattern of the expanded colon'. We must note, however, that Loewenstamm translates *qdš* by 'holiness'. With the interpretation of *qdš* as 'holy ones', we are not so very far removed from the original pattern of the expanded colon. The word 'gods' is substituted by a synonym in the parallel colon, and the complementary formula (*n'dr*) is not found at the end but within the repetitive formula.

Thus we see that, just like Ps. xxix, the Song of the Sea depends on Canaanite literary traditions, but evinces freedom in developing these ancient patterns.

In addition, we may note some word pairs which are also found in Ugaritic literature[17]:

– vs. 2 *'z – zmrh* (cp. *KTU* 1.108 21–22, 24 *'z – dmr*);
– vss. 6–7 *'wyb – qm* (cp. *KTU* 1.10 II 24–25 *ib – qm*);
– vs. 9 *ḥrb – yd* (cp. *KTU* 1.15 IV 24–25, V 7–8 *yd – ḥrb*);
– vs. 11 *'lm – qdš⟨m⟩* (cp. *KTU* 1.2 I 20–21, 37–38; 1.17 I 1–22 five times *ilm – bn qdš*);
– vs. 17 *hr nḥlh – mkwn lšbt* (cp. *KTU* 1.1 III 1; 1.3 VI 15–16; 1.4 VIII 12–14; 1.5 II 15–16 *ksu tbt – arṣ nḥlt*);
– vs. 17 *hr nḥlh – mqdš* (cp. *KTU* 1.3 III 30, IV 20 *qdš – ǵr nḥlt*).

---

15 Cp. above, p. 104–105.
16 Loewenstamm (*JSS* 1969) 186–187.
17 In a few cases, it concerns a partial reconstruction.

Thus, we have found stylistic features (expanded colon, word pairs) which resemble Ugaritic literature in vss. 2, 6, 6–7, 9, 11 (twice), 16, 17 (twice). Obviously, the Song of the Sea is heir to the Canaanite literary tradition; this corroborates Robertson's conclusion, as it suggests a date of composition which is early rather than late in Israelite history.

Attempts have been made to gather some information about the date of composition of the song from 'historical' allusions which it is thought to contain. Thus, the mentioning of Philistia in vs. 14 occasions B. W. Anderson to write in his comment *ad locum* in the *RSV*: Philistia was settled by the Philistines about 1175 B.C.; hence the poem was written after that event (Anderson must mean: after that date). S. I. L. Norin[18] believes vs. 14 to be secondary because the tradition does not know of a conflict with the Philistines before the conquest – to which the second part of the song is generally thought to refer. (I may note in passing that a conflict with the Philistines is not implied by vs. 14; only their settlement in Palestine is presupposed by this verse.) F. M. Cross[19], who also believes this part of the song to refer to the conquest and who dates the song about 1100 B.C., considers the following problem: if the Philistines were not there at the time of the conquest, the reference to them would be anachronistic; in that case the song can hardly have been composed about 1100 B.C., because sufficient time would have to have passed for the precise time of the coming of the Philistines to have been forgotten. However, new evidence concerning the fall of the Hittite empire, the conquests of Ugarit and Cyprus, and the southern sweep of the Sea Peoples requires that the date of the first Philistine settlements be placed a good deal earlier, in the reigns of Ramses II (1304–1237) and Merneptah (1237–1225). Thus, there is no anachronism in the poem according to Cross.

In the same way, vs. 15 has elicited speculation; according to Cross the titles of the chieftains of Edom and the nobles of Moab are used correctly, which would point to an early date of the song; according to Norin, the reference to Edom is secondary because Israel did not have a conflict with Edom at the time of the conquest. (But see my remark on Norin's comment about the Philistines.)

In reply, I want to remark that we do not possess the necessary information to justify these speculations. The stories about a journey in the wilderness and a conquest of Canaan are of a much later date. We do

18 Norin (1977) Ch. III.
19 *CMHE* Ch. VI.

not know whether these events did actually occur, let alone when and in which manner.

The only fact which may be deduced from vss. 14 and 15 is, that the Song of the Sea was composed at the time when Israel was living in Canaan – that is, not in the circumstances related by the prose account in Exodus.

Another 'historical' allusion which has been used to date the song is found in the 'mountain' in vs. 17. If this refers to Sion, the temple in Jerusalem must have existed; this would exclude a date of composition before the time of Solomon. In my opinion however, the mentioning of 'the mountain' has been occasioned first and foremost by the mythological structure of the song; of course it is likely that it referred to an actual mountain at the same time, but there is no way of identifying this mountain – except by first establishing the date and place of composition of the song. Therefore, 'the mountain' will not bring us any further in the question of dating.

Content

In the context of the prose account in Exodus, the picture which is presented by the Song of the Sea is clear enough. A road through the sea is made for the Israelites fleeing out of Egypt, whilst the pursuing Egyptians are drowned in the returning floods. In the second part of the song, the settlement in the promised land Canaan is referred to. But we may rightly ask, whether the song has always been part of the account in the book of Exodus. There is every reason to doubt this: given the result of the linguistic analysis, the prose account is obviously younger than the song. It will therefore be best to analyze the song independently of its present context.

Several scholars have remarked, that the song does not speak of Israel's crossing of the sea. Thus, for instance, N. Lohfink[20] observes that vss. 8–10 describe how Yhwh creates a path through the sea by causing the water to congeal and how the enemy takes that path, whereupon Yhwh makes the water fluid again so that the enemy is drowned; but the crossing of the Israelites is not explicitly described. In vs. 16, the verb 'br refers, according to Lohfink, to Israel's passage through the hostile nations. Others have interpreted vs. 16 as a reference to the crossing of the Jordan, for instance G. W. Coats[21], who considers the 'sea-river

---

20 Lohfink (1963).
21 Coats (1969).

parallel' an important element in the structure of the song. In the opinion of F. M. Cross[22], the song does not even implicitly relate Israel's crossing of the sea: 'There is no suggestion in the poem of a splitting of the sea or of an east wind blowing the waters back so that the Israelites can cross on a dry sea bottom or of the waters "returning" to overwhelm the Egyptians mired in the mud. Rather it is a storm-tossed sea that is directed against the Egyptians by the breath of the Deity'. As to vs. 16, Cross joins those who see in '*br* a reference to the crossing of the Jordan. The other verse which is crucial in this respect is vs. 8.

According to Cross, vs. 8b should be translated 'the deeps foamed in the heart of the sea', instead of 'congealed'. As everything appears to turn on the meaning of the verb *qp'*, we have to look more closely at this verb. Cross remarks the following. In the OT, there are only three occurrences of the root other than in Ex. xv 8: Zech. xiv 6, where the meaning is wholly obscure; Zeph. i 12, of the dregs of wine; and Job x 10, used of the curdling of cheese (parallel to the pouring of milk). Apparently, the action common to wine dregs and curdled milk is the precipitation of sediment or solids. In Mishnaic Hebrew and the Aramaic of the Talmud, the basic meaning is 'to precipitate' of solids in liquid, hence 'to rise to surface', 'form scum, froth or foam', 'to curdle'; in the d-stem and causative stem, 'to skim', 'remove foam from wine', and 'to make float', 'to coagulate blood (by boiling)', 'to foam over', and 'to flood'. The derivative *qippuy* means most often 'froth' or 'spume', and is used specifically of the froth on the surface of fermenting wine (e.g. Aboda zara 56a). In Syriac the verb means 'to skim off', 'to collect', 'to float (of scum or froth)'. Cp. *qepaya*, 'flotsam', 'scum', and *qupaya*, 'spume', 'foam', 'floatage', 'scum (of broth)'. In the Aramaic text of Aḥiqar, *qp'* occurs in association with the sea and has been translated 'flood', and 'foam'.[23] The latter reading is preferable. These data require that we take *qape'u tehomot* to mean 'the deeps foamed', or 'the deeps churned into foam', or the like, probably under the figure of wine.

In my opinion, this reasoning is incorrect. In the first place, it is safest to deduce the meaning of a root occurring in the OT from other OT passages where the root is found; not until this method fails should we have recourse to other Semitic languages or younger Hebrew. Now Zech. xiv 6 and Zeph. i 12 are not wholly clear (Cross does not add an

---

22 *CMHE* 131.
23 Aḥiqar 117.

explanation to his remark on Zeph. 1 12)[24]; but Job X 10 clearly refers to the curdling of milk in the process of making cheese.[25] As to the occurrences of the root outside the OT, we meet first of all the 'basic meaning' 'to precipitate' of solids in liquid – as is stated by Cross himself. What this meaning and the other meanings of the verb have in common, seems to be the appearance of something non-liquid out of the liquid, like froth, which can be removed with a skimmer. In this way (the appearance of something non-liquid out of the liquid) the meaning 'flotsam' can also be explained. Moreover, the liquid as a whole turns into a non-liquid in the case of 'curdling' and 'coagulating' (of blood) – two meanings which are attested in the Mishnah and the Talmud. But as I remarked, the text in Job should be regarded as our primary witness; thus, we have to conclude that in the Song of the Sea too, it is a matter of liquid adopting the solid state. This is confirmed by the LXX, where we find the translation *epagè* in Ex. XV 8b.[26]

Moreover, the statement that the floods 'stood' like a mound (Cross translates rather inaccurately 'mounted up' as a hill) suggests that they are immobile; contrast the description of a storm-tossed sea in Ps. CVII 25–26, where it is said that the wind 'lifts up' the waves, so that the seafarers 'mount up' to heaven and 'descend' to the depths.

Furthermore, Cross's interpretation makes it difficult to explain how the enemies happened to be in a position to be drowned at all. According to Cross, they were at sea in barges. But then, why were they? They were pursuing the Israelites; vss. 9–10 tell us that that was just what they were doing when the sea covered them. Accordingly, the route of the Israelites must have taken them across this sea. If it is denied, as is done most emphatically by Cross[27], that the song refers to their crossing, it remains unexplained why the enemy ventured out to sea. (At the most, one could argue that the Israelites did not go on dry ground but were in barges too, and perhaps that is what Cross means to say; but the fact of their crossing cannot be overlooked.)

If I am right in my interpretation of vs. 8, the Israelites did cross the sea on dry ground according to the song.

24 In Zech. XIV 6, the LXX reads *kai pagos* (*wqp'wn*). As to Zeph. 1 12: a comparison with Jer. XLVIII 11 (*šqṭ 'l-šmryw*) suggests, that *hqp'ym 'l-šmryhm* means 'those who sit still upon their dregs'.
25 Cp. LXX A *epèxas*; Vulg. *coagulasti*.
26 Cp. also *HAL s.v. qp'*.
27 Apart from what was quoted above, Cross writes (*CMHE* 132): 'Most extraordinary, there is no mention of Israel's crossing the sea'.

The defeat of the enemy is told over and over again, in vss. 1, 4, 5, 6, 7, 10 and 12. The enemy is 'hurled into the sea', 'thrown into the sea', 'submerged in the sea', 'covered by the deeps', 'sinking into the depth', 'crushed by Yhwh's hand', 'smitten by Yhwh', 'consumed by Yhwh's anger', 'covered by the sea', 'sinking in the waters', and 'swallowed by the earth', that is, the underworld. This happens during their pursuit of the Israelites (vs. 9), and Yhwh causes it to happen by 'blowing with his breath' (vs. 10). The only other fact which we learn until vs. 13 is, that Yhwh congeals the water with his breath. Furthermore, this part of the song contains praises of Yhwh. The contents of vss. 1–12 can be rendered schematically as follows:

– praise of Yhwh;
– defeat of the enemy;
– praise of Yhwh;
– defeat of the enemy;
– congealing of the waters;
– the enemy pursues;
– defeat of the enemy;
– praise of Yhwh;
– defeat of the enemy.

After that, attention is focussed on Yhwh's people, which is 'led', 'rescued' and 'guided to Yhwh's dwelling-place' (vs. 13), to the amazement and awe of the peoples which hear of it (vss. 14–16a). We are told how these peoples are 'perturbed', 'seized by trembling', 'terrified', 'seized by shuddering', 'melting away', 'befallen by terror and dread' and 'stiffening like a stone', while Yhwh's people 'passes through' (vs. 16b).

According to Cross, the song describes 'the dread which overwhelmed the enemy in the land as Israel was poised for Holy War'. As far as I can see, it describes nothing of the sort.

As we decided to analyze the song apart from its present context, we must consider solely what is stated in the poem. It will be useful to repeat the schematic presentation of it contents, now up to and including vs. 16:

– praise of Yhwh and defeat of the enemy alternate; about half-way the congealing of the waters and the pursuit of the enemy is mentioned;
– guidance of the rescued people to Yhwh's dwelling-place;
– terror of the peoples which hear of it,
– while Yhwh's people passes through.

What do these peoples hear? That Israel's enemy has been defeated in the sea, that the waters congealed, and that the rescued people is guided to the dwelling-place of their god. Nowhere is it stated that the peoples are threatened by Israel. Surely it must be the miraculous rescue of the Israelites, and the guidance they receive from their god, which causes all this shuddering and trembling.

This guidance stretches from the happening in the sea to the arrival at Yhwh's dwelling-place. Therefore, the verb '*br* in vs. 16b may either refer to the passage through the sea, or to the march from the sea to Yhwh's dwelling-place (in which case it means, as Lohfink suggested, to pass 'through the nations'), or possibly to both. One thing is certain: there is no indication that the passage through the river Jordan is meant by this verb.

The Song of the Sea ends with the arrival of Yhwh's people at Yhwh's dwelling-place, that is: the mountain he acquires. On this mountain, Yhwh builds his palace (which is his temple), where he will reside as king. No indication is given of the exact site of this mountain.

The so-called 'song of Mirjam' repeats the content of the opening line of the Song of the Sea. I do not see any point in the discussion, whether the Song of Mirjam is the refrain or title of the poem of vss. 1b–18, or whether it is the nucleus from which the longer poem originated.

Mythological elements in the Song of the Sea

Studies, in which the relationship between the tale of the Reed Sea and mythology is discussed, generally take other OT texts into account besides the Song of the Sea. Some of these will therefore be briefly mentioned in the following survey of opinions; later on, these passages will be more fully dealt with.

As we know, Mowinckel regards the 'creation myth' – in which creation is effected via a battle with chaos – as the basic cult myth of the Enthronement Festival. But in Mowinckel's view, other myths belonged to the festival as well:

'Zu dieser, nach unseren Begriffen rein mythischen, Begründung des Königtums Jahwä's ist... eine nach moderner Auffassung geschichtliche getreten. Im Mittelpunkt der Welt steht Israel. "Land" und "Erde" sind eins. Höhepunkt und Sinn der Schöpfung ist das Volk, Israel; erst mit der Schöpfung und Ansiedlung Israels im Lande der Verheissung ist die Schöpfung vollendet... Und wie nun die Welt aus dem Wasser heraus geschaffen wurde, so ist Israel als geschichtliches Volk gleichsam aus einer grossen Wasserkatastrophe herausgerettet und als Volk geworden. Seit dem Durchgang durch den Schilfsee ist Israel auch aller Welt gegenüber das Volk Jahwä's… Durch dieses Wunder hat Jahwä sich sein Volk und Reich geschaffen; damals ist er König Israels geworden (Dtn. 33, 4²⁸; Ps. 114, 2). So werden denn auch in dem religiösen Denken und der Poesie der Drachenkampf und der Sieg über das Urmeer mit der Tradition von dem Ausgang aus Ägypten und dem wunderbaren Durchzug durch den Schilfsee kombiniert, und Rahab wird ein emblematischer Name Ägyptens (Jes. 30, 7; Ps. 87, 4). Ein hübsches Beispiel dieser Kombination bietet Deuterojesaja 51, 9 f., wo es mit Hinblick auf die Befreiung aus Ägypten heisst:

War's nicht du, der Rahab zerschellte und schändete den Drachen?
War's nicht du, der austrocknete das Meer, die Wasser der Urflut, der da Meerestiefen machte zum Wege, dass hindurchzogen die Erlösten?'²⁹

'(Die Königsherrschaft Jahwä's wird ausdrücklich genannt) in dem Hymnus Ex. 15, 1 ff., dem die Errettung aus Ägypten die Grundlage der Königsherrschaft Jahwä's, d.h. die grundlegende Heilstat, die im Kulte erneuert wird, ist. – So gipfelt der Hymnus Ex. 15… in die Ansiedlung in Kana'an und die Errichtung des Heiligtums in Jerusalem, wo seitdem Jahwä als ewiger König thront (Ex. 15, 17 f.).'³⁰

All this is written under the caption 'Der Auszugsmythus'. We must, however, keep in mind what Mowinckel understands by 'myth': 'Wenn ich hier und im Flg. den Ausdruck "Mythus" gebrauche, so ist damit kein absoluter Gegensatz zu der Geschichte gemeint. In dem Mythus findet sich manchmal viel Geschichtliches.'³¹ A myth is, according to Mowinckel, defined by its association with the cult.

That the 'exodus myth' has a historical core is stressed by Mowinckel in his criticism of Pedersen's theory of the 'Passover legend'.³² In Pedersen's opinion, the text of Ex. 1–xv is a festal legend 'die aus dem Grunde der geschichtlichen Ereignisse herausgewachsen ist'. However, Pedersen does not think it possible to reconstruct these events on the basis of the text, because its aim is not to describe historical facts, but to glorify Yhwh's triumph over his adversaries (who are personified by the pharao). 'Der Kampf Jahwes für sein Volk in Ägypten war nicht ein gewöhnliches geschichtliches Ereignis innerhalb der normalen Zeit. Es

28 In fact, 5.
29 Mowinckel (1922) 54.
30 Mowinckel (1922) 56.
31 Mowinckel (1922) 45 n. 1.
32 Pedersen (1934); Mowinckel (1952).

waren Urzeitereignisse, der konzentrierten Zeit, d.h. der Ewigkeit, angehörend. Der Kampf war identisch mit dem grossen Kampf der Urzeit, als Jahwe aus dem Chaos die geordnete Welt erschuf, indem er die Chaosdrachen erschlug.'[33] Mowinckel replies, that Pedersen underrates the importance of history in the religion of Israel. 'In letzter Instanz hat die Tradition in der tatsächlichen Frühgeschichte Israels ihren Boden; sie vertritt Israels religiöse Deutung jener Geschichte, als Fundament des Glaubens Israels.'[34] Nevertheless, one gets the impression that, in the end, Mowinckel's opinion does not differ much from that of Pedersen. It is only that Mowinckel regards the text of Ex. I–xv in its present form as a 'saga', which intends to relate Israel's history. But the exodus *tradition* functioned most positively, in Mowinckel's opinion, as a cult myth of the Enthronement Festival. (According to Pedersen, however, it concerned the festival of Passover.)

In his contribution in the *RGG*[3] [35], Mowinckel speaks of the specifically Israelite development which consists in the 'historicizing' of myth. The exodus myth is 'parallelized' to the creation myth, indeed it is almost 'identified' with it. This would appear from the fact that Egypt becomes Rahab (Is. xxx 7; li 9–10; Ps. lxxxvii 4), the pharao becomes the dragon, the Sea of Reeds becomes the Tehom (Ex. xv 8; Is. li 9–10).

Thus we see that, according to Mowinckel, 1) the story of the Reed Sea is 'mythical' as far as it is connected with the cult; 2) it has a historical basis; 3) it represents Yhwh's enemy as the power of chaos; 4) essentially, it is identical with the creation myth, because a) it concerns Yhwh's combat with chaos; b) the 'water catastrophe' results in the creation of Israel; c) in consequence of his victory, Yhwh reigns as king. That Yhwh's enemy is regarded as the power of chaos is deduced by Mowinckel from the fact that Egypt is sometimes called Rahab, and that the term *thwm* (which recalls Tiamat) is used with respect to the Sea of Reeds. It must be noted that we have thus got a double shape under which chaos appears: Egypt and the Reed Sea. As regards the Song of the Sea: it contains, in Mowinckel's view, all the elements marked by him as typical of the 'creation myth'; furthermore, it mentions the *thmt*. It does not mention Rahab, however.

That the shared concept of 'creation' contributed to the association of the Reed Sea story with the chaos myth, is the opinion of a number of

33 Pedersen (1934) 169.
34 Mowinckel (1952) 86.
35 Mowinckel (1960).

authors. Granted – L. R. Fisher writes[36] –, the creation of a people (Ex. xv) is not the same as the creation of the universe, but when the same form is used for both there is a very natural fluidity of thought. When the Hebrews looked back from the exodus to creation, they identified the god of the exodus with the god of creation. In a psalm where God controls the sea for his own purpose, leads his people to his mountain sanctuary, and reigns as king, one is dealing with the subject of creation with redemptive overtones.

M. K. Wakeman[37] regards the 'Tehom' in Ex. xv 8 as a monster which is distinguishable from, though controlling, the primeval waters. (N.B. She does not explain why Ex. xv 8 has the plural *thmt*.) This monster is split so that Israel may pass through to independent existence, which is an act of the same creative nature as the separation of heaven and earth when the cosmos was created. A few years later Wakeman writes that 'The Reed Sea is the monster which is divided into parts...; it is the symbol of the oppressive tyrant who had to be split open that Israel might be born'.[38] However, she writes in the same study that 'the association of Rahab with Egypt is explained by the fact that the creation of Israel depended on Egypt's defeat, just as the creation of the cosmos depended on the monster's defeat'.[39] Again (just like with Mowinckel) we note a certain hesitation as to which is the monster: Egypt or the sea.

Indeed it is observed by H. D. Beeby[40] that there is talk of two monsters; but he remarks that one of the characteristics of myth is the merging of apparently distinct entities. Thus, Egypt and the Reed Sea are essentially the same: they are both cosmic evil. There is in the tradition a shifting of emphasis – thus Beeby –, from the defeat of the Egyptians to Israel's crossing. The emphasis on the latter can be explained by the rôle played by the sea in the creation myth. Division of the waters is central in Enuma elish, as it is in Gen. I; similarly, the Sea of Reeds is divided, notably by Yhwh's wind (cp. Marduk's wind which he sends against Tiamat). But Egypt plays a rôle which is comparable to that of the sea: Israel had to come out of Egypt, like the world was created out of the body of Tiamat.

The creation and exodus myths are so closely related, writes H. Gott-

36 Fisher (1965).
37 Wakeman (1969).
38 Wakeman (1973) 126.
39 Wakeman (1973) 80.
40 Beeby (1970).

lieb[41], that it can at times be difficult to determine which one is meant. Both of them speak of the divine protection of organized Israelite society against all encroaching powers. Thus a gradual transition from one theme to the other is possible.

I may mention two more authors who bring up the subject of 'creation'. These differ from the above-mentioned in that they assume the Reed Sea story to have been influenced by the chaos myth only in a later period; but in their eyes, the concept of creation was at least a link between the exodus story and the myth, in as far as the influence of the myth enhanced the view of the exodus as Israel's 'creation'.

G. von Rad[42] is of the opinion, that only with Deutero-Isaiah can we speak of the identification of the exodus story with creation (see Is. LI 9–10). This procedure, Von Rad writes, was suggested by the common appearance of the catchword 'sea' both in the exodus story and the creation myth. Yhwh 'rebuked' the Sea of Reeds (Ps. CVI 9) in the same way as he had done the sea of chaos, and like the latter it 'fled' (Ps. CXIV 3). The event thus took on primeval dimensions, and was transferred from its historical setting to the beginning of history. Indeed – thus Von Rad – the event marked the beginning of Israel's existence.

Likewise, L. Hay[43] mentions Is. LI 9–10 as the text by which the association of the exodus with the creation myth is especially attested. Hay writes that the narrative was subsequently influenced by this association: the book of Exodus now tells how God created for himself a people by rescuing them from the watery chaos and abandoning their enemies to it. Originally, it was only a matter of a military encounter between the Israelites and the Egyptians, in Hay's opinion.

Although both Hay and Von Rad mention the 'creation' of Israel c.q. the 'beginning of Israel's existence', neither of them thinks, apparently, that this idea caused the association of the Reed Sea story and the chaos myth. In Hay's article, the reason for this association is not explained. Von Rad, as we saw, has the not uninteresting idea that an explanation can be found in the common appearance of the catchword 'sea'. That is of course not the same thing as the intrinsic similarity of the two stories, based on their both being a story of 'creation'.

It is time to consider for a moment what we have thus far. The idea of an intrinsic similarity between the Reed Sea story and the battle myth

41 Gottlieb (1980) 70.
42 Von Rad (1962⁴) 191.
43 Hay (1964).

raises some questions. In the view of Von Rad, the similarity is more or less superficial: because the Reed Sea reminded the Israelites of the mythical sea, their rescue and settlement came to be regarded as their 'creation' as a nation.

It could be supposed that, in Mowinckel's view, it was the other way round. The Israelites regarded their settlement as their creation. Now it so happened that some danger at a sea preceded their 'creation'; thus – possessing a myth in which a battle with chaos preceded the creation of the world – they came to regard this sea (and the enemy who was drowned in it) as the power of chaos.

As far as the Egyptians are concerned, that is as it may be; as far as the Reed Sea is concerned, we are forced to the conclusion that the Israelites, having first established that their settlement was a creation, were confronted next with the fact that a sea was involved both in the mythical and in the historical creation. Indeed it is believed by Mowinckel that some real event at a sea lies at the base of the Reed Sea story. If we distinguish between 'facts' and 'presentation of facts', the facts are, in Mowinckel's theory: rescue at a sea – settlement; the presentation is: triumph over the sea of chaos – creation of the nation – Yhwh becomes king. The features of the myth of the combat with Sea are: triumph over the sea of chaos – creation of the world – Yhwh becomes king. Thus, if we suppose the equation 'settlement = creation' to be the primary one, from which the equation 'Reed Sea = sea of chaos' and the notion of Yhwh's kingship evolved, we have to put up with the coincidence that there were two creation stories which had a sea in common – one sea being firmly anchored in the mythology of olden times, the other being firmly anchored in the facts of Israel's history.

In this respect, Von Rad's theory seems preferable; in his opinion, the two stories have only one thing in common: not creation and a sea, but only a sea – which gave rise to the metaphor that Israel's settlement was a creation.

I am not sure, however, that Mowinckel reasoned it out in the way I have suggested. Perhaps he supposed that the equations 'settlement = creation' and 'Reed Sea = sea of chaos' were both made instantaneously, not one after the other. That may be inferred from the fact, that he writes[44]: 'Wenn der Schöpfungsmythus vor unserer Betrachtung allmählich die Formen eines geschichtlichen Mythus... annimmt, so sind es ursprüngliche religiöse Gedanken und Erfahrungen, die hier eingrei-

44 Mowinckel (1922) 78.

fen. Es ist sogar wohl möglich, dass religionsgeschichtlich betrachtet der Schöpfungsmythus gar nicht die "ursprüngliche", d.h. zeitlich erstgebildete Form des Kultmythus unseres Festes gewesen, sondern dass eine ursprünglichere Form hinter einer der mythengeschichtlich "späteren", "vermenschlichten" Varianten..., etwa hinter dem Exodusmythus... stecke'. That seems to imply that the presentation of the Reed Sea story was not modelled after the myth of the battle with Sea, but that both were expressions of the same religious experience: Yhwh's triumph over chaos, his creation of cosmos and his reign as king. That belief would then have been expressed in two different ways, neither of which can, with certainty, be said to have preceded the other. Nevertheless, if it is to be assumed that something really happened at a sea, the coincidence remains. Whilst 'chaos' was pictured as a sea in the myth, there was also a real sea, which could be located somewhere in Israel's environment.

But there is another objection against Mowinckel's view. I have argued above, that the primeval battle with Sea in the OT was not a battle of creation. If that conclusion is correct, the main point of comparison between the Reed Sea story and the battle myth disappears.

In view of all this, it must be asked whether there is still sufficient reason for calling the Reed Sea c.q. Egypt a manifestation of chaos. The arguments for this viewpoint have now to be appraised without the support they received from the supposed presence of the idea of 'creation'. If it turns out that the Reed Sea was indeed identified with the mythical sea by the Israelites, we must try to establish whether this was done from the first or only at a later stage. Thirdly, we must ask what could have been the reasons for such an identification.

Thus far, we have met the following arguments. The Reed Sea was called Tehom; Egypt was called Rahab; the Reed Sea was split, like the monster; Yhwh's instrument was the wind, which recalls Marduk's weapon against Tiamat; the texts speak of Yhwh's 'rebuke' of the Reed Sea and its 'flight'; in Is. LI 9–10 the killing of the monster and the passage through the sea are mentioned in the same breath.

Now the use of the word *thwm* is not conclusive, as the term by itself does not imply a reference to the mythical combat. Egypt is called Rahab twice (Is. XXX 7; Ps. LXXXVII 4; I do not see any reason why Rahab should refer to Egypt in Is. LI 9). Moreover the pharao is called Tannim (= Tannin) in Ezek. XXIX 3, XXXII 2. The names are not used to denote Egypt or the pharao in the context of the Reed Sea story; therefore I do not think it permits us to conclude, that Egypt played the rôle of 'chaos' in that story. Apart from that, the idea that both Egypt and the Reed Sea represented Yhwh's primeval enemy at the same time, is difficult to grasp. I do not think it can have been easy to grasp for the Hebrews either.

Next, there is the 'splitting' of the Reed Sea, its 'flight' because of Yhwh's 'rebuke', and the wind as Yhwh's weapon. Now it has been remarked more than once, that the motif of the 'splitting' was introduced into the Reed Sea story only at a later date. According to A. Lauha[45], the 'miraculous' and 'cosmogonic' aspects of the event at the sea are only present in texts from the time of the exile onwards. Pre-exilic texts (Ex. XIV J; XV 21b; Dt. XI 4; Josh. II 10; IV 23; XXIV 6–7) mention only the drowning of the enemy and the drying up of the sea – which is not miraculous in Lauha's opinion, as it is caused by the wind. In the time of the exile the motif of the splitting of the sea was introduced, as appears from Ex. XIV P, Is. LXIII 12, Ps. LXXVIII 13, CXXXVI 13, Neh. IX 11. This motif was derived from other sagas, according to Lauha: an Egyptian saga tells about the high priest Zaza-em-ankh who divided the water of a lake into two halves[46]; in the Ugaritic texts it is told that El cut the sea into parts[47]; the OT tells of the dividing of the Jordan in Josh. III–IV as well as in 2 Kgs. II 8, 14. However, the increasing stress on the miraculous element in the Reed Sea story was also due to influence from the myths of Baal and Marduk, in Lauha's opinion. Thus, the sea came to be regarded as Yhwh's adversary. Lauha finds an explanation for this development in the strife between Yahwism and the surrounding religions: Yhwh was able to do what Baal and Marduk had done.

Likewise, J. Scharbert[48] concludes that the motif of the splitting of the sea dates from the time of the exile; most probably it stems from Babylonia, where the Jews had become acquainted with Enuma elish, notably the splitting of Tiamat. The sea was split in order that Israel might pass through – a motif which is lacking in the earlier texts, thus Scharbert. However, this development had already been prepared by some pre-exilic texts, which told of the passage through the Jordan (Ps. LXVI 6; in Scharbert's opinion, this text does not speak of the passage through the sea but only through the river) and of the flight of the waters of the Reed Sea (Ps. CXIV 3, 5). That the waters are represented as fleeing before Yhwh is due, Scharbert writes, to influence from the theophanic

---

45 Lauha (1963).
46 King Cheops and the Sorcerer, Erman 69.
47 *KTU* 1.23 58–59, 61, *coni.* 23.
48 Scharbert (1981).

tradition in the cult and from the tradition of the battle with chaos.

In my opinion, it is not so very important whether the verb 'to split' has been actually used or not: the idea may be there although the term is lacking. Let us consider the Song of the Sea. In Scharbert's opinion, the song (which he dates in the early monarchy) describes only natural phenomena – be it in poetical language –: the sea, which had been driven back by the wind, returned when the wind began to blow unexpectedly from the opposite direction, so that the Egyptians, unaware of the geography of the region, were drowned. (The Israelites were on the shore all the time.) This may be compared with the opinion of Lauha, that there is nothing miraculous about the drying up of the sea by the wind. Lauha, however, mentions the Song of the Sea as an example of the growing stress on the 'miraculous' and 'mythical' elements in the Reed Sea tradition (the song is counted by him among the younger texts, in view of its 'deuteronomistic atmosphere'): the waves congeal and stand like a wall; the wind is the breath of the divine anger. Now I have argued above, that the song does indeed refer to Israel's crossing of the sea. In order to enable the Israelites to cross over, Yhwh did not make the waters disappear: he made them solid – in other words, he dried them up – so that they formed a wall. Unless the Israelites travelled on the sea-bed along the shore (but that would be nonsense: why not travel on the shore, then?), we must understand this to mean that the waters formed two walls. That means that the waters were split. I do not think, therefore, that we should contrast the texts in which 'splitting' is mentioned with those in which mention is made of 'drying up'.

Moreover, I do not think Scharbert's interpretation of Ps. LXVI 6 is right. If one takes the parallelism of thought into account, one must interpret this verse as: he dried up the sea so that they crossed it on foot, he dried up the river so that they crossed it on foot.

We have met with a number of suggestions about the origin of the motif of 'splitting'. I think that an Egyptian origin is rather far-fetched. The passage in the Ugaritic texts which is thought by Lauha to mean that El cut the sea in two, very probably does not have that meaning.[49] A

---

49 The text reads *agzrym bn ym*; this has been translated by Dussaud (1937), 61, with 'je séparerai la mer d'avec la mer'. The preceding words say that 'they have borne gracious gods' (namely, Shaḥar and Shalim); the word following upon our expression reads 'who are sucking'. The meaning of *agzrym* is not clear (see Del Olmo Lete (1981), 446, for the various suggestions), but it is probably a noun in apposition to 'gracious gods'. *Bn ym* too seems to be an apposition to 'gracious gods', *bn* meaning 'sons' and *ym* either 'day' or 'sea'. Anyway, Dussaud's translation does not seem to fit at all.

more serious suggestion is, that the tale of the dividing of the Jordan at the time of the conquest (not the dividing of the Jordan by Elisha) exercised influence on the way the Reed Sea story was told. For the moment, I want to pass over this theory; we will come back to it below. First, we have to consider the possible influence of the myths of Baal and Marduk.

Especially Enuma elish has been suggested as source of the idea that the Reed Sea was split in two. (But this idea cannot have been picked up in Babylonia during the exile – as Scharbert suggests –, if the notion of 'splitting' was already present in the Song of the Sea.) Indeed it is not said in the Baal epic that Yam was split in two.[50] Neither does the OT state, in the texts about the conflict between Yhwh and Yam, that Yhwh split Yam into two halves; even of the monsters it is not stated that they were cut in two.[51] I have tried to demonstrate above, that the Israelites shared their conception of the battle of the deity with the sea with the Canaanites: in neither case does it concern a battle of creation, there is a verbal conformity in the names of the enemy, and the punishment is the same. In the OT, the ever-recurring punishment is that the waters dry up, whereas it is stated in the Baal epic that Baal dried up Yam.[52] Now if it is assumed that the Reed Sea tradition contains elements which have been derived from myth, and which were already present in an early period, it must surely have been the combat myth as it was told in Israel, that is: a myth resembling the Baal-Yam story rather than Enuma elish. In other words: 'splitting' was not a feature of the myth which presumably influenced the Reed Sea story.

I do not think that that is a problem, however. As I observed above, 'drying up' and 'splitting' must – as far as the Reed Sea story is concerned – be considered as one and the same act. The 'congealing' of the waters is a feature of the Song of the Sea, whilst 'drying up' is a feature both of the OT story about the combat with Sea and of the Ugaritic one. That fits excellently with the idea, that the Israelite-Canaanite

---

50 Therefore, Eakin (1967) does not reason correctly, when he writes that 'baalism's influence on the water-separation motif must be considered' (381). Eakin suggests that there were two exodusses; whereas the second one (the Mosaic exodus) was characterized by the motif of the drowning of the Egyptians, the first one (in the time of the Hyksos) was characterized by the water-separation motif. 'Given the Baal mythology, this (sc. a water deliverance) would naturally lead to the historization of a myth in the Yam-Baal struggle' (383). If these rather obscure words refer to the Ugaritic Baal text, it must be remarked that a 'water-separation' is nowhere to be found in this text.
51 Cp. above, p. 75–85.
52 Cp. above, p. 86–88.

myth should be the first to be taken into consideration as a possible influence on the Reed Sea story.

Thus, we should not reason: 'splitting' recalls Enuma elish; this motif was introduced in the time of the exile and was therefore most probably picked up in Babylonia; but: 'drying up' (implying 'splitting') has always been a feature of the Reed Sea story – a motif which recalls the Canaanite-Israelite myth about the combat with Yam.

When finding, over and above this, that Yhwh's rebuke (*g'r*, a topic of the combat myth[53]) of the Reed Sea and its flight are mentioned – albeit not in the Song of the Sea –, we must conclude that the Reed Sea is indeed pictured as Yhwh's adversary. That Yhwh's instrument was the wind does not, by itself, permit of any conclusion about influence from the myth – but on the other hand, it fits in well with the picture of the thunder-god who subdued Yam.

Furthermore, we may assume that the Reed Sea was regarded as Yhwh's adversary from the beginning. To be sure, the rebuke and flight occur only in texts which must be younger than the Song of the Sea; but as 'drying up' (the 'congealing' mentioned in the song) is such a prominent feature of the combat myth, I think we are justified in combining the several data, so that the 'rebuke' and 'flight' of the younger texts reinforce the conclusion about the rôle of the sea in the song.

As to the passage Is. LI 9–10: it proves the association of the combat myth and the crossing of the sea; but we need not wait until the time of Deutero-Isaiah for this association, if my assumption is right that the drying up of the Reed Sea in Ex. xv recalls the punishment of the arch-enemy Sea.

The answer to our third question (how did it come about that the Reed Sea was identified with Yhwh's arch-enemy) must wait a little longer. We must now look if there are other arguments in support of our contention, that the Song of the Sea has cast the Reed Sea in the rôle of the mythical sea.

As W. F. Albright has observed[54], the words *hr nḥltk* in Ex. xv 17 have a parallel in the Ugaritic texts. It concerns the expression *ǵr nḥlty*, which denotes Baal's 'mountain of possession' (*KTU* 1.3 III 30, IV 20). I have already drawn attention to the stylistic congruence between Ex. xv 17 and the Ugaritic texts, in that the word pair *hr nḥltk – mqdš* corresponds to *qdš – ǵr nḥlty* in the Ugaritic passages just mentioned; in

53 Cp. above, p. 50.
54 Albright (1949) 233.

addition, I have pointed to the correspondence between the word pair *hr nḥltk – mkwn lšbtk* in Ex. xv 17 and the Ugaritic *ksu ṯbth – arṣ nḥlth*.[55] The expressions used to indicate Yhwh's dwelling-place in Ex. xv 17 (to which may be added the expression *nwh qdšk* in vs. 13) have elicited endless debate. To mention some opinions: *nwh qdšk* refers to the whole land, or: to Yhwh's temple; the 'mountain' refers to the mons Casius at the Sirbonian lake, or: to the Sinai, or: to the hillcountry of Canaan, or: to mount Sion; the 'sanctuary' refers to the whole land, or: to a shrine at Gilgal; none of the expressions refers to Sion because, apart from *mqdš* in post-exilic times, they are never used to indicate the Jerusalem temple (an attempt is made to disprove that *mkwn lšbtk* in 1 Kgs. viii 13 refers to the temple). The interest taken in these questions can at least partly be explained by the wish to specify the historical circumstances in which the song must be situated.

For example, the denial that Sion is referred to is coupled with the opinion, that the song must be dated 'immediately after the event'; locating the 'sanctuary' at Gilgal is coupled with the idea that the song was connected with the Gilgal cult; the opinion that Sion is referred to is coupled with the theory that the song must be dated after the tenth century and belonged to the cult of Jerusalem.

As I remarked above, an actual mountain and sanctuary must have been intended by the expressions in vs. 17, even if they have a mythological background – but we must refrain from identifying them. If the song was composed at Jerusalem after the building of the temple, mount Sion must have been meant; if it was composed at some other place (and maybe some earlier time), it must have been another sanctuary. I only want to remark that, if *hr nḥltk* is understood as the mons Casius[56], which has been located at the western side of the lake where the miracle is thought to have taken place, Yhwh would have brought the Israelites right back into the arms of the Egyptians.

What is certain anyway, is the verbal correspondence with the Ugaritic designation of Baal's mountain. Moreover, just like Baal had a palace built on his mountain where he reigned as king, Yhwh is said to have built his sanctuary, which is his palace (*yšb* means here 'to be enthroned', in view of the kingship mentioned in vs. 18); there, he will reign as king 'forever' – which recalls Baal's 'everlasting' kingship.

I think, therefore, that Gaster has seen rightly when he writes[57], that

55 Above, p. 133.
56 Thus Norin (1977) Ch. III.
57 Gaster (1949) 43–45.

the Song of the Sea resembles the myths of Baal and Marduk in that Yhwh's victory is followed up by his enthronement as king in a new palace. (As Gaster considers the song to be 'the product of a far later age', he is thinking of a later assimilation of the Reed Sea story to the myth. 'Once again, popular fancy clothed the facts of history with the glamorous raiment of legend.' But Gaster does not try to explain why this happened.) Only, Gaster does not mention the Reed Sea as the enemy over whom Yhwh has triumphed; in his eyes, it is the Egyptians who recall the 'primeval rebels'. In a later work, however, Gaster treats the subject in a slightly different way. In general, his observations on the song have remained the same, except for his remark that 'He (Yhwh) assumes the role of the ancient warrior-god (v. 3), defeating the contumacious genius of the sea'.[58] An explanation of this change in his position is not given by Gaster.

F. M. Cross on the other hand, who also draws attention to the pattern in the Song of the Sea, writes explicitly that the Reed Sea is not regarded as Yhwh's adversary in the song: 'the sea is not personified or hostile, but a passive instrument in Yahweh's control. There is no question here of a mythological combat between two gods'.[59] Accordingly, the first element of the pattern is described by Cross as 'the combat of the Divine Warrior and his victory at the Sea'[60]; the preposition 'at' must be noted.

Cross calls the influence of the mythic pattern 'extraordinarily restrained' in the first part of the song. It is only to be seen in 'the anger and might of Yahweh, and conversely, the heaving of the sea' by the breath of the deity, as Cross and Freedman have formulated it elsewhere.[61] The sea is regarded as Yhwh's adversary only in younger texts, in Cross's opinion[62], that is, especially in texts from the time of the early monarchy (it may be remembered that Cross dates the Song of the Sea about 1100 B.C.) and in texts from the time of the exile – two periods in which the old myths became resurgent, in the view of Cross. He mentions i.a. Ps. LXXVII, where the sea is pictured as shuddering before Yhwh's thunder, Ps. LXXVIII, in which it is said that the sea is split (a motif which recalls the splitting of the dragon, according to Cross); and Is. LI 9–10, where 'the battle of creation' merges with 'the Exodus-Conquest events'. Like

58 Gaster (1969) 241.
59 CMHE 131—132.
60 CMHE 142.
61 Cross-Freedman (1955) 238a.
62 CMHE Ch. VI.

others have done before him, Cross assumes a second influence on the Reed Sea story besides that of myth, notably influence from the crossing of the Jordan (a cultic rite in his opinion).

Now it seems to me somewhat inconsequent to speak of the 'combat of the Divine Warrior' (followed up by 'the building of a sanctuary on the "mount of possession" won in battle' and 'the god's manifestation of "eternal" kingship') as an expression of 'the old mythic pattern', whilst at the same time denying the hostile character of the sea. Surely the Egyptians were no match for the 'Divine Warrior'. Moreover, Cross explains the combination of the mythical battle with the Reed Sea event in younger texts by the 'enormous power of the mythic pattern'. This power was the cause, in his opinion, of the fact that 'the episode at the sea was chosen as symbolic of Israel's redemption and creation as a community'. 'Theoretically, other episodes might have been selected just as well as this one, say the march from the southern mountains into the new land... or the Conquest proper in Canaan.'[63] In the light of these remarks, the denial that the sea was (at least vestigially) seen as a hostile power in the song seems a bit incongruous. I think that the crucial point is the translation of the verb qp' in Ex. xv 8. Once it is conceded that that means 'to dry up' (and not 'to foam', as Cross would have it), one must conclude that the sea was treated in the same way as the mythical sea. That the sea is not 'personified' does not seem to me to be relevant at all.

Thus, I think that the conclusion drawn by me above, that the sea is pictured as Yhwh's adversary in Ex. xv 1–18, is supported by the fact that the text presents the same pattern as the Baal epic, namely: triumph of the deity – palace on mountain – kingship.

Before we pass on to an examination of the possible causes of the similarity between the Reed Sea story and the myth – a similarity consisting in the enmity of the sea and in the presence of the said pattern –, I want to mention some authors who have seen a mythological reference in the term ym-swp.

J. R. Towers[64] and W. Wifall[65] are of the opinion that this name points to Egyptian influence on the Reed Sea story. According to Towers and Wifall, Egyptian mythology knows a 'lake' or 'field of reeds' in the underworld. Towers has suggested that, just like the souls of the dead were purified by passing over this lake according to Egyptian mythology, the crossing of the Reed Sea by the Israelites was consider-

63 CMHE 137.
64 Towers (1959).
65 Wifall (1980).

ed to be a purification and a transition to a new life. However, if this were the case, the absence of any indication of these ideas in the OT texts is remarkable, I should think.

Wifall has pointed out that the Egyptian sun god passed over the field of reeds every night. Now the Canaanite city states, which belonged to the Egyptian empire in the 2nd. millennium B.C., adapted the Egyptian solar mythology to the cults of El and Baal. That is why El is said to have his residence at the source of the two oceans, which recalls the watery residence of the Egyptian sun god, the 'lake' or 'field of reeds'. In Jerusalem, the cult of Yhwh replaced that of El; thus, Ps. xix can call Yhwh 'El' and relate him to the sun god whose tent is set in the waters; cp. Ps. xxix 10 and Ps. civ 3 for this location of Yhwh's residence. But Yhwh has also adopted some characteristics of Baal. In Egyptian mythology, the daily conquest of the serpent of darkness, Apophis, was performed by Seth whom the Egyptians identified with Baal. Therefore, Yhwh's battle against the serpent and the sea recalls the slaying of Apophis in the 'lake' or 'field of reeds' in the underworld – thus Wifall.

In reply, I want to remark that there is no evidence that either El or Yhwh was regarded as a sun god. Whereas El is said to live at the source of the two oceans – but not to pass over the waters of the underworld each night –, the Egyptian sun god is believed to do the latter but not to have a 'watery residence'. Neither does Yhwh cross the underworld at night. Ps. xix only states that he has put up a tent for the sun, in the heavens, it may be supposed ('in the waters' is a conjecture). Yhwh himself resides above the heavenly ocean according to Pss. xxix and civ. Furthermore, the slaying of Apophis cannot be equated to the slaying of Yam. As G. Posener[66] has pointed out, the rôle of Apophis was, in point of fact, the reverse of that of the hostile sea, as Apophis threatened to swallow up the water which was needed for the voyage of the sunbark through the underworld. And as to the Reed Sea story, I want to remark that it is definitely not about the slaying of a hostile power which tries to make the sea run dry.

N. H. Snaith[67] is of the opinion, that *ym-swp* designates 'the sea at the end of the land'. The LXX renders *ym-swp* with *eruthra thalassa*, which was used by classical authors to indicate the Red Sea, the Arabian Gulf, the Indian Ocean and the Persian Gulf, but which could also be used vaguely of far-away, remote places. Perhaps the LXX has equated *sup* with *sop*, end; or perhaps the Greek translators have read *sop* in their

66 Posener (1953) 476.
67 Snaith (1965).

text, Snaith writes. Now the verses Ex. xv 4–5 have successively *ym*, *ym-swp* and *thmt*. With *thmt*, we have passed into the realm of the creation myth. The word *thwm* does not refer to the depths of any natural sea; this is the depth of Tiamat, the great sea monster. That accords with the use of the name *ym-swp*, which was never used until the story of the crossing of the sea was interwoven with the creation myth – thus Snaith.

Snaith's idea has been taken up and worked out by B. F. Batto[68], whose article may be summarized as follows. Where the name *ym-swp* occurs in the OT outside the texts about the sea miracle, it is either certain or plausible that it refers to the Red Sea or one of its northern extensions into the gulfs of Suez and Aqabah (see e.g. 1 Kgs. ix 26). There is no reason to posit the existence of a second body of water farther north, with the homophonous name of *ym-swp* = Reed Sea. The *p³-twfy* of the Egyptian texts (designating an area where papyrus grows), which has been identified with the Reed Sea of the OT, is not a lake (it is never written with the determinative for water, but with the determinative for plant and – occasionally – with the determinative for town); thus, the main argument for positing the existence of a Reed Sea is invalidated. Despite the fact that *swp* means 'reed' in Ex. ii 3, 5 and Is. xix 6, it cannot have that meaning in the name *ym-swp*, because papyrus reed does not grow in the Red Sea.

The Song of the Sea (one of the most ancient pieces in the OT) uses the term *ym-swp*, but as the other early traditions (J; Nu. xxxiii) speak only of *ym* as the place of the miracle and not of *ym-swp*, it is unlikely that *ym-swp*, in the song, reflects the historical memory of a battle with Pharao at *ym-swp*. Rather, the name belongs to traditional mythical language.

The presence of *ym* in the Song of the Sea can be explained by the fact that the song is heavily dependent upon mythological language; it shows the same pattern as Enuma elish and the Baal cycle: the creator god overcomes the watery chaos, creates a people, and rules as king in his mountain sanctuary. This mythological language was used to express the belief that the emergence of Israel as a people was due to a creative act of Yhwh, equal to the creation of the cosmos. For that reason, the struggle against Pharao was portrayed as part of the larger battle of the deity against the powers, so that the pharao was submerged in the sea and defeated along with the sea.

68 Batto (1983).

Now *ym-swp* stands parallel to *ym*; it is thus a mythological concept, and can be rendered with: sea of end/extinction. Very appropriately the Egyptians (the evil force which threatened the new creation) were cast into the sea of extinction. This meaning of *swp* is attested by Jon. II 6, where the context (the pair *ym-nhr*, the *thwm*, the underworld) requires *swp* to have something to do with a cosmic battle against chaos. Cp. Ps. XVIII, where the psalmist is engulfed in the watery abyss (vs. 17); his rescue is told in the images of the chaos-battle (vss. 8–16).

By the time of P, the miracle at the sea has been historicized and localized at the geographical body of water we know as the Red Sea. The geographical framework of Ex. XIII 17 – XV 22 stems from the latest (P) redaction and was only secondarily joined with the tradition of the miracle at the sea. That P consciously intended to historicize and localize the miracle at the Red Sea, appears from Nu. XXXIII (a document independent of JEP, which has been used by P), where a sharp distinction is made between the sea of the miracle (vs. 8) and *ym-swp* (vss. 10–11); from the fact that P has used this document it follows that P deliberately telescoped the sea of the miracle and *ym-swp* into one.

The Israelites applied the name 'sea of end/extinction' to the Red Sea because, for them, the Red Sea was literally the sea at the end of the earth (the earth being conceived of as an island floating in the waters), a sea which in their minds was fraught with connotations of primeval chaos. Thus far Batto.

It seems to me that this theory is incorrect as far as *ym-swp* is concerned; but before going into that, an interesting point must be noted. As I have remarked above, an objection against Mowinckel's theory is the coincidence, that the myth and the Reed Sea story have two things in common: creation and a sea. In Batto's theory, that is no coincidence; the sea was introduced into the story of Israel's creation after the example of the myth of the creation of the world. Thus, the element the two stories had in common was at first only 'creation'; the actual event lying at the background of the Reed Sea story consisted only in a struggle with the pharao, but a sea was not involved.

That is, in fact, the reverse of the theory of Von Rad, according to whom the two stories shared only a sea, a common element from which the association of the Reed Sea story with creation arose secondarily.

Although I have argued that neither story is about creation, Batto's hypothesis is still of interest. There is, after all, a pattern in the song, even though 'creation' is no part of it. This pattern could be said to lie in the presentation of facts; but now the question arises: what are the facts? Has there been an event at a sea (the 'presentation' being that this sea was pictured after the manner of the mythical sea), or does the sea itself belong to the 'presentation' (the 'fact' being only a struggle with the pharao, like Batto supposes)? We have to postpone these questions for the moment; we must now examine Batto's remarks about *ym-swp*.

Now firstly, I do not believe that the Israelites knew the concept of a 'sea of extinction'. The meaning 'reed' is attested for *sup*, whilst the meaning 'end' is not. It could very well be that the Israelites were mistaken about the vegetation at the Red Sea. Moreover, it is not at all unlikely that more than one sea or lake was named *ym-swp* by the Israelites; one should not expect too much system in their geographical name-giving. The existence of an Egyptian equivalent of the Hebrew 'Reed Sea' is not required.

Furthermore, the passage in Jonah is not sufficient proof that the term *swp* was at home in the tradition of the chaos battle. True, the pair *ym/nhr* belongs to that tradition; but the prayer of Jonah is not about a battle with Sea. The presence of the pair in this passage shows that the traditions about a hostile power called Yam/Nahar were so well-known, that the word pair had become a common element of poetical speech (cp. e.g. Ps. LXXX 12, where the pair occurs outside the context of a battle with Sea; and cp. my remark on Ps. XXIV 2).[69]

As to Ps. XVIII, vss. 8–16 cannot be used to illustrate vs. 17, as they are an originally independent theophany description, which has been incorporated into the psalm.[70] Vs. 17 is in the first person singular, thus taking up vs. 7. Therefore, this verse is no proof that the image of being rescued from the waters of the underworld was associated with the tradition of the battle with Sea.

Secondly, I think that Batto's reasoning is illogical. When the 'early traditions' (J; Nu. XXXIII) mentioned *ym* as the place of the miracle, they were doing the same thing as the writer of the Song of the Sea, by speaking of a sea which had not been there (that is, if we follow Batto). Presumably, then, they also knew the concept of a 'sea of extinction': either they were following the Song of the Sea, which uses this term; or they arrived independently at the mythologization of the event, which implies that they were acquainted with the popular concepts of mythology. Indeed Nu. XXXIII mentions *ym-swp*, but – strangely enough – not as the place of the miracle. As *ym-swp* in Nu. XXXIII is not the place of

---

69 Above, p. 84 n. 192.
70 Cp. above, p. 52.

the miracle, it does not designate a purely mythical sea. It must have been the Red Sea, then. Thus, the writer of Nu. xxxiii knew of a mythical 'sea of extinction' but, although he introduced a mythical *ym* which he knew to be a *ym-swp*, he refrained from calling *ym* '*ym-swp*'; instead, he used *ym-swp* as a geographical name, to be distinguished from the place of the miracle. I find this hard to follow. It becomes even harder to follow if it is to be assumed that the Red Sea was termed *ym-swp* because it was a 'sea of chaos'. We would then have got two stations at a chaos-sea in Nu. xxxiii, only one of them being the place of the miracle.

Furthermore, we are asked to believe that *ym-swp* in the song is no geographical designation; but when P equates *ym* with *ym-swp* he is said to have 'historicized'. That implies that the Red Sea was not yet named *ym-swp* at the time of origin of the Song of the Sea; otherwise, understanding *ym-swp* in the song as the Red Sea could not have been avoided. The Red Sea was named *ym-swp* at the time of the 'early tradition' of Nu. xxxiii, however.

In short, I find Batto's theory slightly chaotic.

As against Snaith and Batto, I want therefore to keep to the meaning 'Reed Sea' for *ym-swp*. In my opinion, the term does not have a mythological connotation.

We have finally arrived at the question we have put to ourselves above: what has caused the mythological presentation of the Reed Sea story? It is a problem which has elicited much debate. The various opinions will be discussed in the next chapter.

MYTHICIZING AND HISTORICIZING

	The terms used by OT scholars to describe the relationship between the Reed Sea story and the myth of the battle with Sea are of a great diversity. This may be shown by the following examples:
Noth[1]	The myth *appears as a formulation of* historical events. The motif of the battle with the chaos monster *has been applied to* the passage through the sea. Yhwh dried up the sea *just as* he triumphed over chaos (an *image*).
Pedersen[2]	The triumph over Egypt *was identified with* creation out of chaos.
Rendtorff[3]	The myth *has been drawn into* a historical context. The myth *has been called upon for the shaping of* a historical tradition.
Mowinckel[4]	The exodus myth *has been parallelized with* the creation myth.
Widengren[5]	The myth *has been interpreted* historically (*historification*). The real event *has been exaggerated* (*mythization* of history).
Toombs[6]	Myth *was used to illuminate* historical events. The myth *has been transformed* radically (*historicizing* of myth). The exodus *has been mythologized*.
Childs[7]	The myth *was replaced by* historical events.

1 Noth (1928) 303–304.
2 Pedersen (1940) 409.
3 Rendtorff (1958) 125.
4 Mowinckel (1960) 1276.
5 Widengren (1960) 478, 481, 491 n. 58.
6 Toombs (1961) 109–110.
7 Childs (1962) 82.

Ringgren[8]	A historical event *has been interpreted* in mythical categories (*mythization* of history).
Jeremias[9]	Yhwh's triumph at the Reed Sea *has been placed in the framework of* the mythological battle.
Schmidt[10]	Historical events *are pictured with* mythical features (*historicizing*).
	History *has been mythologized.*
Cross[11]	The epic events and their interpretation *were shaped by* mythic patterns and language.
	Mythological motifs *enhanced* the redemptive events.
	Redemptive events *were assimilated to* primordial events.
	Mythic materials *were introduced into* a historical framework.
	Mythic materials *were transformed.*
	Historical episodes *were mythologized.*
Otzen[12]	Historical events *have meshed together* with mythical events.
	The destruction of the Egyptians *has been interpreted via* the categories of creation (*demythologizing*, or: *mythologizing* of history).
Gottlieb[13]	History *was integrated with* myth.
	History *was understood by means of* the categories of myth (*historicizing* of myth or *mythologizing* of reality).
	The exodus myth *is a form of* the creation myth.

Special attention must be paid to the use of the terms 'mythicizing' and 'historicizing' (and the like). Logically speaking, one would expect the term 'mythicizing' to be used for that which happened to history, and the term 'historicizing' for that which happened to the myth. Indeed we find the term 'mythicizing' used to indicate that history was pictured with mythical features, whilst we find the term 'historicizing' used to indicate that the myth was placed in a historical framework. But we also find the term 'historicizing' when it is stated that history was pictured

8 Ringgren (1963) 102.
9 Jeremias (1965) 96.
10 Schmidt (1967) 247.
11 *CMHE* VIII, 89, 90, 144.
12 Otzen (1980) 59–60.
13 Gottlieb (1980) 70, 74, 75.

with mythical features. That is perhaps not surprising, as it might be said that it concerns two sides of the same phenomenon. That must also be the reason why the two terms are sometimes used indiscriminately by one and the same author.

Nevertheless, the two processes are differently orientated: a movement from myth to history is not the same thing as a movement from history to myth. I do not think, therefore, that the terms should be used as equivalents. We should now try to make out, whether we should speak of 'mythicizing' or of 'historicizing'.

Mythicizing

The phenomenon of 'mythicizing' is extensively discussed by F. M. Cross.[14] According to Cross, the religion of Israel was characterized by a 'perennial and unrelaxed tension' between the mythical and the historical.[15] 'Myth' is, according to Cross, concerned with 'primordial events'[16]; it played an important rôle in Canaanite religion. By contrast, Israel had a 'peculiar religious concern with the "historical"'.[17] The form in which the Israelites expressed their historical experiences is called 'epic' by Cross; he writes that 'Epic... combines mythic and historical features'; 'In epic narrative, a people and their god or gods interact in the temporal course of events'.[18] The 'perennial tension' between the mythical and the historical is described by Cross as follows.

'Israel's religion in its beginning stood in a clear line of continuity with the mythopoeic patterns of West Semitic, especially Canaanite myth.'[19] The religion of the patriarchs was characterized by both historical and mythical features: there was the cult of the 'god of the Father', who guided the social group and directed its battles, and the cult of El, 'creator of heaven and earth', and leader of cosmic armies.[20] 'In the

---

14 *CMHE passim.*
15 *CMHE* viii.
16 *CMHE* viii.
17 *CMHE* ix.
18 *CMHE* viii.
19 *CMHE* 143.
20 That El was believed to be a warrior has also been defended by Miller (1967 and 1973, 48–58); but, in spite of Cross's contention, it is not proved at all. This idea has been based on Philo Byblius, who cannot be regarded as a very reliable source on early Canaanite religion. Moreover, Cross's interpretation of the name *yhwh ṣb'wt* – namely 'creator of the heavenly armies' –, which he believes to be a title of El, is purely hypothetical.

era of the league in Canaan, the historical impulse became powerful in the Mosaic faith and in the covenant festivals of the great sanctuaries... Even in the cult of the league, however, themes of mythological origin can be detected, standing in tension with themes of historical memory or enhancing redemptive events by assimilating them to primordial events.'[21] 'The thrust of historical events, recognized as crucially or ultimately meaningful, alone had the power to displace the mythic pattern. Even then we should expect the survival of some mythic forms, and the secondary mythologizing of historical experiences to point to their cosmic or transcendent meaning.'[22]

'The Canaanite mythic pattern is not the core of Israel's epic of Exodus and Conquest. On the other hand, it is equally unsatisfactory to posit a radical break between Israel's mythological and cultic past and the historical cultus of the league. The power of the mythic pattern was enormous. The Song of the Sea reveals this power as mythological themes shape its mode of presenting epic memories. It is proper to speak of this counterforce as the tendency to mythologize historical episodes to reveal their transcendent meaning.'[23]

'The overthrow of the Egyptian host in the sea is singled out to symbolize Israel's deliverance, Yahweh's victory. Later, an equation is fully drawn between the "drying up of the sea" and the Creator's defeat of Rahab or Yamm (Isaiah 51: 9–11): the historical event is thereby given cosmic or primordial meaning. As a matter of fact, the earliest sources do not equate the crossing of the sea and the killing of the Dragon by the Divine Warrior, but it is highly likely that the role of the sea in the Exodus story was singled out and stressed precisely because of the ubiquitous motif of the cosmogonic battle between the creator god and Sea in West Semitic mythology.'[24]

The cosmic elements found in the ideology of 'holy war'[25], as well as the survivals of myth, which had both continued to exist during the time of the league in spite of the force of the 'historical impulse', provided a matrix for the reintroduction of mythical motifs in the time of the monarchy: 'The institution of kingship and the inauguration of a temple in the Canaanite style in Israel obviously gave an occasion for the radical mythologizing of the "historical" festivals.'[26] 'Especially in the

21 CMHE 89.
22 CMHE 87.
23 CMHE 143–144.
24 CMHE 87–88.
25 Notably, the 'heavenly armies'.
26 CMHE 106.

royal cultus and in sixth-century prophecy... the Exodus-Conquest motif often merges with that of the battle with Sea.'[27]

In this sketch, the familiarity of the Israelites with Canaanite religious beliefs is rightly stressed. I may note in passing, that contact between the Israelites and their Canaanite surroundings is a more plausible explanation of the fact that the Israelites were acquainted with the battle myth, than Eissfeldt's theory concerning an Egyptian Baal cult.[28] According to Eissfeldt, the Israelites ascribed their rescue originally to the Baal Sapon who had his sanctuary on mount Casius near the Sirbonian lake, where the miracle (supposedly) took place; this would account for the mythological elements in the exodus tradition.[29] This theory is ingenious, but I think that it is far too hypothetical. It must then be assumed that the Israelites had become acquainted with the sanctuary and the myth while they were living in Egypt, for they would hardly have had time to get to know them on their flight. In my view, we are on safer ground if we assume, that the Israelites had become familiar with the myth in Canaan.

Nevertheless, I disagree with Cross's presentation of affairs.

Firstly, I do not find it very plausible that the mythological motifs were largely suppressed in the time of the league, to reappear only with the building of the Jerusalem temple. If 'the power of the mythic pattern was enormous', one would not expect it to have been suppressed at all. But a more important question is, how far may we speak of a 'tension' between the mythical and the historical? This brings us to the question of the definition of myth.

The 'primordial events', which are the subject of myth in Cross's view, are circumscribed by him as 'events which constitute cosmos and, hence, are properly timeless or cyclical or "eschatological" in character'.[30] Now it may hold true for a number of myths that they deal with such 'primordial events', but it certainly does not hold true as regards 'myth' in general. The Greeks used the term *muthos* in the sense of a 'tale' and of 'fiction'.[31] In modern times, the amount of literature on the subject of myth has grown to enormous proportions. It causes N. J. Ri-

---

27 *CMHE* 163.
28 Eissfeldt (1932).
29 Cp. also Gray (1953), Hillmann (1965) Part B Ch. II a, Norin (1977) Ch. III, who – though questioning the theory that the Israelites attributed their rescue to Baal – also think that the myth was adopted from the sanctuary at the Sirbonian lake.
30 *CMHE* 120.
31 See *LSJ s.v. muthos.*

chardson to speak of 'the modern obsession with the definition of
"myth"'; he adds that 'scholars seem to have created a special category
of "myths", within the general class of *muthoi* (tales), in order to mirror
their own leading pre-occupations'.[32] I shall refrain from summing up
the main theories on myth; one may find good surveys in other studies.[33] I only want to draw attention to two comparatively recent works,
by G. S. Kirk[34] and by W. Burkert.[35]. The lucid style of these authors
has made me opt for literal quotations; that is the reason why the
number of quotations on the following pages will rather exceed the
normal – for which I beg forgiveness.

Kirk attacks the idea that 'myth' is a sharply defined category: 'myth
as a general concept is completely vague'; 'it implies no more in itself
than a traditional story'.[36] Furthermore, he points to the fact that myths
need not be about gods (take, for instance, the Oedipus myth); neither
are they necessarily associated with a ritual (as is assumed in the 'Myth
and Ritual' theory, which has grown very popular among OT scholars).[37] In a paragraph titled 'A suggested typology of functions'[38], Kirk
proposes the following typology: 1) myths that are primarily narrative
and entertaining; 2) myths that are operative, iterative, and validatory;
3) myths that are speculative and explanatory. Concerning the first
type, Kirk writes that these myths are rare, 'or rather they belong to the
special genres of folktales and legends'.[39] Thus, we are confronted with
the question of the relationship between legends and myths. It is discussed by Kirk in an earlier paragraph[40], where he writes that we must
distinguish between myths and 'legends of a historical or historicizing
nature – tales, that is, that are founded, or implicitly claim to be founded, on historical persons or events'.[41] In practice, however, legend and
myth cannot always be distinguished, Kirk writes; this is shown by the
Iliad: 'the story is based on some kind of memory of the past, and... its
progress is described in largely realistic terms'[42], but 'The gods of

32 Richardson (1981).
33 E.g. Cohen (1969); Sebeok (1974). Of special interest to the OT scholar are Hartlich-
Sachs (1952) and Rogerson (1974).
34 Kirk (1970).
35 Burkert (1979).
36 Kirk (1970) 28.
37 Kirk (1970) Ch. I 2, 'Myth, religion and ritual'. See on this also Versnel (1984).
38 Kirk (1970) Ch. VI 1.
39 Kirk (1970) 254.
40 Kirk (1970) Ch. I 3, 'The relation of myths to folktales'.
41 Kirk (1970) 31.
42 Kirk (1970) 32.

Homer belong to myth; they certainly do not belong to the essence of legend or saga, which is always in some sense rooted in actuality; and therefore they represent in the Iliad the metaphysical aspect of a primarily legendary narrative'.[43] Because the gods are essential to the story, the Homeric poems are not mere legends. 'Many human episodes in... the poems have acquired archetypal mythical status largely because of the special texture impressed upon legend by the presence of the gods.'[44] That is why Kirk can speak of 'legendary myths' in his discussion of the typology. He writes that these legendary myths are sometimes purely narrative: 'they simply use traditional memories as the basis for dramatic narrative – much of the Iliad... is obviously of this kind – or elaborate a kind of historical fiction or ethnic fantasy'.[45] But, more often, legendary myths belong to the second type; 'they glorify famous leaders and tribal history by telling of wars and victories..., or disguise contradictions between national ideals and actuality'.[46]

Concerning the second type of myth, Kirk writes that these myths 'tend to be repeated regularly on ritual or ceremonial occasions; and their repetition is part of their value and meaning... Many fertility myths are of this kind'.[47] Another group of myths of the second type are myths that function as a model or charter. 'The main practical purpose of such myths is to confirm, maintain the memory of, and provide authority for tribal customs and institutions – the whole clan system, for example, or the institution of kingship and the rules for succession; and to reaffirm and institutionalize tribal beliefs. When the Trobriand islanders tell each other myths about clan origins, they are not only instructing the adolescents in the essentials of the tribal tradition; they are also restating, often on a solemn and regular occasion, their claim to particular lands and objects.'[48] 'Obviously this charter use of myths overlaps legendary types whose purpose is primarily just narrative and patriotic.'[49] 'Finally charter myths may take on a more theoretical aspect in providing emotional support for an attitude or belief.'[50]

43 Kirk (1970) 33.
44 Kirk (1970) 34.
45 Kirk (1970) 254.
46 Kirk (1970) 254.
47 Kirk (1970) 255.
48 Kirk (1970) 256. These observations are, of course, based on the famous study by Malinowski which appeared in 1926.
49 Kirk (1970) 256.
50 Kirk (1970) 257.

In a paragraph about the 'possibilities of origin'[51], Kirk writes: 'the speculative and operative functions of myths may often develop gradually out of their narrative ones; the needs of the community impress themselves on story-telling...; and the most fantastic elements of myths... are gradually and erratically accreted'.[52]

These are, I find, very illuminating remarks – although one objection may be made. Kirk classifies the Iliad as 'legend', which acquires mythical status because of the presence of the gods. The term 'legendary myth' which he uses in the following, shows that he finally chooses to classify the stories of the Iliad as 'myth'. And indeed: why not? It is, after all, quite normal for myths to refer to 'historical' persons or events, as is seen from the charter myths. I think, therefore, that Kirk's introduction of a special class consisting of 'legends', to be defined as 'tales that are founded, or implicitly claim to be founded, on historical persons or events', and to be distinguished from myths, is not justifiable. I would prefer the view of Burkert, who does not make this distinction. In the following, I want to quote some passages from Burkert's study.

W. Burkert defines 'myth' as 'a traditional tale with secondary, partial reference to something of collective importance'.[53] 'But what is a tale? If... we adopt the triple division... of 1) sign, 2) sense, and 3) reference, a tale belongs evidently to the category of sense, as against the individual text on the one side, and reality on the other. ... tales can be translated without loss or damage; they are therefore not dependent on any particular language; and even within one language the same tale can be told in quite different ways.'[54] 'A myth, qua tale, is not identical with any given text... We know... that we can remember a good tale, and a myth, by hearing it just once, without memorizing the words of a text.'[55]

'A tale, while not bound to any given text, is not bound to pragmatic reality either... In fact there is no isomorphism between reality and a tale... Reality does not automatically yield a tale... The form of the tale is not produced by reality, but by language, whence its basic character is derived: linearity. Every tale has a basic element of *poíesis*, fiction.'[56]

'All attempts to define myth from its content seem to cut through

51 Kirk (1970) Ch. VI 5.
52 Kirk (1970) 285.
53 Burkert (1979) 23.
54 Burkert (1979) 2.
55 Burkert (1979) 3.
56 Burkert (1979) 3.

living flesh, to tear apart what belongs together. If myth is defined as a tale about gods, or as a sacred tale, this would exclude central parts of Greek mythology, including Oedipus. Anthropologists have found workable a definition of myth as a tale about origins, things that happened in the remote past, *in illo tempore*.[57] But as to Greek myths, most of them are situated in an epoch which the Greeks themselves regarded as historical, the epoch of the Trojan War and a few preceding generations. In various cultures there are differentiations of tale classes, one of which may be called "myth"; none of these is universal, and hardly any are applicable to the Greek evidence. The specific character of myth seems to lie... in the use to which it is put.'[58]

'Myth is traditional tale applied; and its relevance and seriousness stem largely from this application.'[59] 'The phenomena of collective importance which are verbalized by applying traditional tales are to be found, first of all, in social life. Institutions or presentations of family, clan, or city are explained and justified by tales – "charter myths", in Malinowski's term; – or knowledge about religious ritual... and about the gods involved, is expressed and passed on in the form of such tales; then there are the hopes and fears connected with the course of nature, the seasons, and the activities of food supply; there is the desperate experience of disease. But also quite general problems of human society, such as marriage rules and incest, or even the organization of nature and the universe, may become the subject of tales applied; still it is only philosophical interest, both ancient and modern, that tends to isolate the myths of origin and cosmogony, which in their proper setting usually have some practical reference to the institutions of a city or a clan.'[60]

'There is... no reason to distinguish myth from saga in the Greek view; this distinction is rather due to the Christian tradition.'[61]

'Mythical thinking... provides... a synthesis for isolated facts. To take the simplest example, genealogy. Hellen had three sons, Dorus, Xuthus, and Aeolus; Xuthus sired two sons, Ion and Achaeus. That means: the Greek tribes know they belong together. Dorians, Aeolians, Ionians, and Achaeans: they are all Hellenes, though Ionians and Achaeans are somewhat closer to each other... Xuthus therefore must be introduced

---

57 Thus especially Eliade; see for instance Eliade (1963) 5: 'Myth narrates a sacred history ... that took place in primordial Time'.
58 Burkert (1979) 22.
59 Burkert (1979) 23.
60 Burkert (1979) 23.
61 Burkert (1979) 24.

as a filler, to produce the subclass. Evidently the question of "historical truth" is absolutely irrelevant in such a tale; it is neither more nor less effective even if it is true; in its application, it creates a system of coordinates to cope with the present or even with the future.'[62]

'This is not to forget that... there is also the function of telling a tale just for pleasure.'[63]

'What must have happened again and again to myths in history: consecutive changes of crystallization and application. A well-structured tale... may become, in a certain cultural environment, the established verbalization. ... but if retold in a new situation, it will tend to crystallize again, still preserving some elements of its former application; in its new form it can again be applied to new circumstances, and so over and over again.'[64]

I think this is a very sensible treatment of the subject of 'myth'. We should keep these observations in mind, when discussing the relationship between the 'mythical' and the 'historical' in the Reed Sea story.[65]

The narrative about the Reed Sea event is called 'epic' by Cross. Are there indeed good reasons for contrasting this 'epic' with myth? Cross writes that the composer of epic is concerned with 'the human and the temporal process'.[66] Now, as we have seen, myth may also be concerned with that. Besides, 'epic' is only the name of a form, namely, narrative poetry. A myth may be told in the epic form. I would call the Ugaritic texts about Baal and about Aqhat epics. Cross, however, speaks of the Baal *myth* and the Aqhat *epic*, apparently because Baal is a god and Aqhat is a man. But the stories should both be called myths, in my opinion.

If the Reed Sea story is a myth, we cannot speak of a 'secondary mythologizing' nor of a 'tension' between the mythical and the historical. The difference from the Baal myth would then be that human beings figure in the myth, just like, for instance, in the story of Aqhat.

The question appears to be: how much historical truth must a story contain in order to be called 'history'? A myth may contain some

---

62 Burkert (1979) 25.
63 Burkert (1979) 26.
64 Burkert (1979) 27.
65 That Kirk's and Burkert's studies have found less recognition among OT scholars than they deserve, is demonstrated by a recent work on myth, notably by C. Petersen (1982). Petersen defines myth as the portrayal of events which lie outside historical time and involve the action of deity (31).
66 *CMHE* VIII.

nucleus of historical fact. It seems as if the amount of factual truth in the story is decisive.

The Reed Sea story is, of course, fantastic; therefore, I regard it as a wholly fictive story, in other words: a myth.[67] That means, that Cross's presentation of affairs is not correct as far as the Reed Sea story is concerned.

The link between the two stories

Still, we are left with the problem, how to explain the presence of elements of the myth about the battle with Sea in a myth about Israel's history. What could have been the reason for associating the two myths?

Adherents of the 'mythicizing' theory are of the opinion, that the two stories were associated because they were believed to have the same meaning; see the quotations given by me above[68], wherein it is stated, for instance, that the historical event was 'illuminated', 'interpreted' or 'understood' by means of the myth. What is meant by that is, that the true character of Yhwh's adversary in the Reed Sea event was revealed by putting him on a par with Yhwh's mythical opponent, Yam; Yhwh's triumph at the Reed Sea was thus a triumph over 'cosmic evil', just like his triumph over Sea.

But who was Yhwh's opponent in the Reed Sea story? As we have noted above[69], both Egypt and the Reed Sea have been called 'the concrete visualization in present history' (to adopt a formula used by Widengren[70]) of the power of chaos, Yam. I have argued[71], however, that there is not sufficient reason to conclude, that Egypt played the rôle of 'chaos' in the Reed Sea story.[72] Furthermore, I have argued in the fore-going chapter that the Reed Sea has been pictured as Yhwh's adversary, in as far as this sea is treated in the same way as Yam by being dried up. Thus – if we follow the view quoted just now – the association of the Reed Sea story with the battle myth was due to the fact, that the

---

67 The question, whether the exodus is a historical fact or not, does not bear any relation to this assessment of the Reed Sea story.
68 P. 158–159.
69 P. 141–142.
70 Widengren (1960) 480.
71 Above, p. 145–146.
72 That does not mean to deny, that human enemies may be compared with the hostile Sea. A clear example is Is. XVII 12.

Israelites considered the Reed Sea to be just as much a 'power of chaos' as Yam.

Now, provided we disregard for a moment that this interpretation is coupled with a view of the Reed Sea event as history instead of myth, this idea deserves to be examined more closely. (That means, in fact, that we are still dealing with the theory of 'mythicizing'; to have rejected this term because the Reed Sea story is itself a myth, need not imply that the reasons for the association of the two stories, as they are given by the adherents of the 'mythicizing' theory, have to be rejected too.) The point of comparison between the adversaries of Yhwh in the two events would be, then, that they were both regarded as 'chaos'. Now as to the sea of the battle myth, I want to note that it cannot be called 'chaos' on the strength of its being a sea out of which the cosmos was created; as I have tried to demonstrate, the battle with Sea was not a battle of creation, neither at Ugarit nor in the OT. It has to be asked, therefore, whether there is still sufficient reason to speak of Yam as 'chaos' (a term which I have indeed used on and off in the above, following the current terminology). It seems to me, that the deity Yam represents the ordinary, earthly sea, and that the Canaanite myth about the battle with the sea must have originated among people living at the coast. To O. Kaiser[73], I owe the idea that the early winter storms must have given rise to the story of the conflict (not autumnal storms). Kaiser adduces a report about the climate at the Syrian coast by J. Weulersse[74], which is so interesting that I want to quote it in my turn:

'Passons maintenant à l'hiver; l'anticyclone des Açores rejeté vers le Sud ouvre la Méditerranée aux dépressions cyclonales venues de l'Atlantique, mais celles-ci peuvent soit emprunter la voie méditerranéenne, soit passer plus ou moins au Nord sur l'Europe. Dans le premier cas, la dépression ou le chapelet de dépressions balayent la Méditerranée de bout en bout et viennent s'installer sur son extrémité orientale. C'est alors le grand mauvais temps, la tempête aussi brutale que sur les côtes de l'Atlantique; il semble soudain que le pays ait été rejeté de 20° de latitude vers le pôle: coups de vent d'une extrême violence, mer déchaînée, averses diluviennes et continues, sautes de température avec coups de froid abaissant la température jusqu'à près de 0° sur la côte, chutes de neige énormes sur la montagne (jusqu'à 2 ou 3 m. et plus aux Cèdres du Liban, à 2000 m. d'altitude). Le pays ruisselle, les rivières débordent, les

73 Kaiser (1959) 65.
74 Weulersse (1940) 28–29.

routes sont coupées, les gens grelottent dans leur maison sans feu. Heureusement cela dure peu; quelques jours au maximum, puis la dépression se résorbe et en quelques heures le temps se transforme. L'anticyclone de l'intérieur s'étend alors vers la mer et les dépressions atlantiques sont rejetées au Nord. Le ciel redevient clair, le soleil réapparaît et aussitôt la température moyenne sur la côte remonte entre 15° et 20°; l'atmosphère est d'une clarté diaphane et la mer plate et blanche comme un lac. Ces belles périodes qui peuvent durer une ou deux semaines sont particulièrement fréquentes en novembre et décembre.'

Reading this description, one can easily imagine how the story of a battle between Baal and Yam could arise – especially if it is taken into account that the heaviest thunder-storms (the gift of Baal after he had established his kingship by defeating Yam) occur from December to February.[75] (I do not think, however, that that prevents us from assuming an autumnal festival at which the defeat of Yam was celebrated; the autumn is after all the time when the first rains occur. Moreover – although the myth must have originated at the coast – the story spread to other parts of Syria and Palestine; it must have been told and listened to by people who had perhaps never set eyes upon the sea. That must have made it all the easier to connect it with a festival in the autumn.)

Of course, the sea was a destructive power; but it is to be noted that Yam received a cult at Ugarit, as appears from offering lists. In addition, one might point to the theophoric name *ym il*.[76] That means that (at least as far as Ugarit is concerned) 'Yam' did not possess the utterly negative connotation which clings to the concept of 'chaos'. I would therefore accept the term 'chaos' as a designation of Yam with some reserve. Anyway, the negative side of Yam stands for a well-defined calamity, namely, the inundation of the land.

Now why would the Reed Sea have been equated with Yam? Is it indeed an adequate explanation, if we say that the Reed Sea was a 'cosmic evil' of the same order as total chaos? Rather, it would seem as if the fact that it concerned a sea was a reason for picturing the Reed Sea as Yam, at least as much as its 'evil' character.[77]

But now we have arrived at the point where it makes a difference, whether the Reed Sea event is regarded as (basically) historical or not. It

75 See De Moor (1971), Tables (251–269).
76 *KTU* 4.75 V 14; 4.183 II 2.
77 Cp. Von Rad's opinion, quoted above (p. 143), that the common appearance of the catchword 'sea' contributed to the association of the Reed Sea story and the battle myth.

must be kept in mind that we were dealing just now with the opinion of the adherents of the 'mythicizing' theory, that is, of those who regard the Reed Sea event as historical. My remark at the end of the last alinea was made in reply to their suggestion concerning the reason for associating the two stories; their idea was modified by me into 'the fact that it concerned a sea'. We must now consider, whether that reason is still valid if the event is not historical.

Historicizing

In the view of the adherents of the 'mythicizing' theory, the primary thing was the event; elements of the battle myth were added secondarily to the description of that event. But if the Reed Sea story is regarded as wholly fictive, another picture emerges. In that case, a story (about the Reed Sea) was made up, in which elements were used stemming from an older story (the battle myth). If we accept the reason assumed above, these elements would have been used because the younger story was also about a (dangerous) sea.

Now that is a very unsatisfactory way of putting things. If I am right in my supposition, that the 'drying up' of the Reed Sea belongs to the elements stemming from the battle myth, it would mean that a 'sea' (the 'Reed Sea') was invented first, and that the motif of the 'drying up' of that sea was added secondarily, because those who invented the Reed Sea story were reminded of the existent tale about a sea. Why not say, then, that the sea-motif *as a whole* (that is 'a sea which dried up') was taken over from the older story? Otherwise, we would have to assume a complicated process indeed, a sea being invented independently of the battle myth, and its drying up being invented in imitation of that myth. If the sea-motif as a whole was derived from the Yam myth, we could say that the motifs of this myth functioned as building-stones for the Reed Sea story.

Above, I have called 'mythicizing' a movement from history to myth, and 'historicizing' a movement from myth to history. If a historical event is pictured with mythical features, which were added secondarily for some reason or other, we have to do with mythicizing. If the motifs of a myth function as building-stones for the creation of a 'historical' narrative, we should speak of 'historicizing'. My opinion is, then, that it is a question of 'historicizing': the Reed Sea story is a myth about history, whose basic elements were derived from the myth about the battle with Sea.

OT scholars' theories on historicizing

As we have seen, the term 'historicizing' is also used by other authors; but they have used it in another sense. Whereas I understand by it that a myth was transformed into pseudo-history, it is, in the field of OT studies, generally taken to mean that the myth lost its prominent position in religion, and was replaced by the commemoration of historical events (notably, events that had actually taken place). Whilst Canaanite religion concentrated on the myth, Israelite religion concentrated on history – which implied a devaluation of the myth.

To illustrate this view by a remark made by Toombs: the myth was historicized because the Israelites could not take it seriously any longer. Concerning the exodus, Toombs speaks of 'an exclusive concentration upon this one event, the breaking and reorganizing of all mythological language to agree with it'.[78]

That explains, why scholars are able to use the terms 'mythicizing' and 'historicizing' as equivalents.[79] If 'historicizing' is taken to mean that the myth, being no longer valued, could at the most serve to furnish the phrases in which to describe history, it amounts to the same thing as 'mythicizing', which also means that history is described in phrases derived from the myth. Only – although the result may be the same – the two processes (if described in this way) are intrinsically different. If 'historicizing' implies that the myth could not be taken seriously any longer, it is in fact the opposite of 'mythicizing'; for it is to be assumed that the myth was indeed taken seriously, if it was used to elucidate the historical event.

It is an idiosyncrasy of OT scholars to define 'historicizing' in this way; outside that field, it is defined in the way I have done. Of course I cannot share the opinion that we have to do with 'historicizing' as defined by OT scholars in the present case, because I do not regard the Reed Sea event as history; but apart from that, I find the idea of this 'historicizing' as such, questionable. In the first place, it is difficult to understand why the myth should have been used at all for the shaping of a historical narrative, if it was viewed with such negative feelings; one would expect the myth to have been totally ignored in that case. In the second place, I do not believe that Israel felt so hostile towards the myth; I need only point to Ps. xxix.

78 Toombs (1961) 111.
79 Cp. above, p. 160.

I have found only one article, by R. Luyster[80], in which it is argued that Israel 'historicized' myth in the sense in which I understand the term. Apart from this general idea, however, I disagree with Luyster at many points.

Luyster starts with mentioning some authors who have questioned the historicity of the book of Exodus, namely Pedersen[81] and Engnell[82], who have seen a scenario for the Passover cult in the book. He quotes the words of Engnell, that the exodus legend is 'a historicizing representation of an original cultic myth'.[83] This raised the possibility, Luyster writes, that Yhwh's parting of the Reed Sea was merely a historicization of the myth of the struggle between a Warrior God and a Sea Dragon. As supporters of this theory Luyster mentions Pedersen[84], Gaster[85] and H. D. Beeby.[86] Luyster wants to follow up this idea by defending 1) that the main outlines of the book of Exodus as a whole were borrowed from Enuma elish; 2) that the description of the Reed Sea miracle arose out of mythical thought-forms regarding salvation and perdition.

Before we examine Luyster's argument, I want to remark that his idea is more original than he himself suspects. Unless Luyster has only the 'parting' of the Reed Sea in mind (a motif of which it has indeed been suggested that it stems from the myth), the idea that the story originated in the myth has not been defended before.[87]

Pedersen thinks it was a matter of describing history 'on a higher

---

80 Luyster (1978). Apart from Luyster's article, I have met the term 'historicizing' in the sense in which I understand it in Cross-Freedman (1955), 238a, where the idea is rejected: 'It seems necessary to conclude that we do not have a mythologically derived conflict here. It is dubious in the extreme to suppose that we have the result of the "historicizing" of myth'. In 1973, however, Cross has reverted to the use of the term in the specific sense OT scholars are wont to use it (*CMHE* 143–144). On Engnell's use of the term see below, p. 174 n. 91.

81 Pedersen (1934).

82 Engnell (1969) Chs. VIII and IX.

83 Engnell (1969) 203.

84 Pedersen (1940) 728–737.

85 Gaster (1949) 43–45; Gaster (1969) 241.

86 Beeby (1970).

87 At most, a partial derivation from the myth has been defended. I mentioned already B. F. Batto, according to whom the 'sea' was introduced into the story after the example of the myth (above, p. 154). It is assumed by Batto, however, that an actual struggle with the pharao lies at the base of the story, so that, in the end, his theory does not differ much from the ideas of those, who hold that the narrative of the event was 'mythicized'.

plane'[88], Gaster writes that, possibly, the Israelites saw in the Reed Sea
event 'a reproduction in history' of the myth, that the writer of the
Song of the Sea 'assimilated the victory at the "Red" Sea to the... myth',
and that 'popular fancy clothed the facts of history with the glamorous
raiment of legend'[89]; Beeby remarks that the possible influence of the
myth on the wording of the story 'is not of course saying that the
Exodus is myth, nor is it anyway denying historicity to the central
fact'[90]. As for Engnell, Luyster himself admits that he allows for a
nucleus of historical fact; indeed, Engnell is very outspoken on that
point. To be sure, Engnell uses the term 'historicizing'; but if I understand him correctly, he means by that, that the Passover was changed
from a nature festival into a memorial festival.[91]

As to Luyster's own argument, I think that it is not convincing. In
order to defend that the book of Exodus as a whole has been derived
from Enuma elish, he sums up 35 motifs which the two stories have
(according to him) in common. In my opinion, however, the resemblance is too remote to justify Luyster's conclusion. I do not intend to
discuss this part of Luyster's article, as I want to concentrate on the Reed
Sea story. As the Reed Sea story is part of the book of Exodus, Luyster
holds it to be a historicization of Enuma elish; but as we have seen, he
also wants to defend that it arose out of 'mythical thought-forms' found
in ancient Israel. In order to be able to combine these two explanations,
Luyster is forced to split the Reed Sea story up into different motifs:
those derived from Enuma elish, and those arising from 'mythical
thought-forms' in Israel. To begin with the latter: Luyster writes that, in
ancient Israel, 'to die' was seen as 'to sink through waters into a land of
darkness'; moreover, any experience of dread or despair was seen as,
literally, to drown in the waters of death (see e.g. Ps. LXIX 2–3, and
many similar texts). Therefore, if the Hebrews faced death at the hand
of Egypt, there was no other expression for it than that they were on the
verge of drowning; if Yhwh's anger was turned against the Egyptians,

88 Pedersen (1940) 728.
89 Gaster (1949) 43–45.
90 Beeby (1970), 'Conclusions'.
91 Once, Engnell uses the term 'historicizing' in the sense I attribute to it, but only to
deny that it took place: 'It is not very likely that we are dealing with a pure cult myth,
which did not give rise to a "historical narrative" until later by means of a historicizing
process. The reason is simply the fact that the Old Testament tradition is so unanimous
and consistent in its presentation of the origin and earliest fortunes of the people of Israel
and especially of their most prominent leading figure, Moses, whose historical existence
and contribution cannot be called into question'. See Engnell (1969) 206.

there was no other expression for it than that he brought the waters over them. Reversely, the expression for salvation was that Yhwh dried up the waters (see e.g. Josh. III–IV); therefore, if the Hebrews escaped from the Egyptians, there was no other expression for it than that the sea was dried up for them.

On the other hand, there are the motifs derived from Enuma elish. The oldest text about the Reed Sea event, Luyster writes, is the Song of the Sea. The song employs the following motifs that are borrowed from Enuma elish, in Luyster's opinion: 1) Yhwh is the champion of his people; 2) he is terrifying; 3) he wages a decisive combat with his foe; 4) his weapon is a strong wind, with which 5) he swells the body of the Sea; 6) he defeats the Sea; 7) he becomes eternal king and 8) saviour of his people; they worship him in a 9) lofty 10) sanctuary; he is the 11) supreme god.

Luyster writes that the Song of the Sea does not mention the crossing of the Hebrews on dry land. The drowning of the Egyptians is mentioned, but the question as to how the Egyptians managed to find themselves in the midst of the sea is left unanswered. The reason is, according to Luyster, that, for the mind that is authentically mythic, to die *is* to be submerged in the waters of Death; the question as to how one arrived there is meaningless. But by the time of J, it was less and less understood that the waters of the Reed Sea were the waters of Death; in that time, the question arose: how did the Egyptians happen to be in the midst of the sea? To answer that question, J invented the dry land crossing prior to the annihilation of the Egyptians. In the story of J, a strong wind makes the bed of the sea bare; Yhwh causes the Egyptians to panic and to flee onto the dry sea-bed; next, Yhwh – who has contained the sea – allows the waters to return and the Egyptians are drowned. In this story too, there are motifs derived from Enuma elish: 4) the strong wind; 12) the flight of the Egyptians; 13) the containing of the sea. Finally – thus Luyster –, P adds a new motif that was borrowed from Enuma elish, namely 14) the division of the waters (which is another way of explaining how the Egyptians came to be on the dry sea-bed, namely when they followed the Israelites who were crossing over).

I have the following objections against this theory. In the first place, I do not agree as to the 'when' and the 'whence' of the mythological influences. Luyster does not say why he thinks that the Song of the Sea does not employ the motif of the 'drying up' of the sea. Most probably, he derives his remark about the absence of this motif from Cross's study, which is mentioned by him in another context. However, as I have argued in the fore-going chapter, the drying up of the sea is narrated in vs. 8, and the crossing of the Israelites is implied in the song. Even the splitting of the sea is implied, as I have tried to demonstrate, because the waters formed a wall (that is, two walls). That means, that these motifs were already present in the oldest text about the miracle; we need not wait until the time of J and P to meet them.

Furthermore, I have argued that – if influence of the combat myth on the Reed Sea story has to be assumed – it must surely have been the myth as it was told in Israel, that is, a myth resembling the Baal-Yam story rather than Enuma elish. It is in accordance with this, that the Song of the Sea makes mention of the 'drying up' of the sea, because that is also the punishment inflicted by Baal or Yhwh upon Yam. Consequently, we should not conclude, on the basis of the 'containing' of the sea in the story of J, that the 'drying up' was added in the time of J in imitation of Enuma elish (as Tiamat was contained in a net). Neither is a derivation from Enuma elish in the time of the exile (which has been assumed because the term 'splitting' crops up in that time) a necessary conclusion: 'splitting' is merely a corollary of 'drying up' in the present case, and 'splitting by drying up' is a feature of the oldest text, the Song of the Sea. The point is, that the waters were dried up, as in the Canaanite-Israelite combat myth.

I agree with Luyster as to the significance of some of the motifs mentioned by him: the wind as weapon, the kingship, and the sanctuary on the mountain; but these motifs may just as well (or, in my opinion, better) be regarded as derivations from the Canaanite myth. As to the motifs 'champion', 'terrifying', 'decisive combat', 'saviour of his people', 'supreme god' and 'flight of the Egyptians', I do not think them to be significant if it is a matter of establishing the origin of the story. Luyster adduces the motif of the 'swelling' of the sea, which he finds in the Song of the Sea, as an argument for a derivation of the story from Enuma elish (Marduk swells the body of Tiamat by his wind) – but the song states nothing of the kind. It is merely stated that the waters were made solid, to form a mound or wall. I find it strange, by the way, that Luyster detects the motif of the defeat of the sea in Ex. xv, as he does not consider the sea to be punished by being dried up. In my opinion, the 'drying up' is crucial if one wants to maintain that the motif of the defeat of the sea is (vestigially) present in the song.

In the second place, I object to the manifold explanations given for the origin of the Reed Sea story in Luyster's theory. According to Luyster, mythical 'thought-forms' existing in ancient Israel were responsible for the creation of the story, as well as the historicizing process that transformed the (Mesopotamic) myth into pseudo-history. Now as far as the 'drying up' is concerned, affairs become very complicated indeed. This feature is explained by Luyster as 'the only way to express salvation' in ancient Israel. (It is somewhat embarrassing, then, to find that this feature is absent in the Song of the Sea – that is, if Luyster's own theory is followed.) Next, the explanation is given that J invented the drying up, as a rationalistic expansion because the mythical thought-forms were no longer understood. In addition, the 'containing' of the sea (that is, its drying up as narrated by J) is explained as a derivation from Enuma elish, where it is told that Tiamat was contained in a net. It is surely not too bold to say, that Luyster wants to have too many irons in the fire.

In short, I do not think that the idea, that Israel historicized the myth, has been properly defended by Luyster. Rather, his article does damage to this theory: an unconvincing defense does more harm than no defense at all.

A parallel in ancient Rome

In order to provide a more solid basis for my idea, that the Reed Sea story is a transformation of the myth of the battle with Sea, I now want to adduce an example taken from another culture. Thus, my approach is (for the moment) phenomenological: I want to show that the phenomenon of 'historicizing' is not an uncommon one, and that processes of the type I have suggested can indeed be demonstrated to have existed. In order to do this we shall turn for a moment to ancient Roman historiography.

It strikes us, that the ancient Romans lacked stories about their gods – a fact already noted by Dionysius of Halicarnassus.[92] On the other hand, they possessed extensive traditions concerning their national history. It is especially Georges Dumézil who has argued, that the Romans, in creating the account of their national history, drew from their Indo-European mythical heritage. To quote Dumézil:

'... des récits, des groupes de récits, qui, chez certains peuples indo-européens, garnissent la mythologie divine, se rangent, chez d'autres, dans la "mythologie humaine", dans l'histoire ancienne, dans l'épopée.

92 Dion. Hal., Ant. Rom. II 18–20.

Cela est particulièrement sensible à Rome et y constitue même un des traits fondamentaux du signalement national.'[93]

'La mythologie... est inséparable de l'épopée, c'est-à-dire de ce qui tient lieu, pour la société archaïque, de son "histoire ancienne", de ce qu'elle croit être son histoire ancienne. Il faudra donc considérer non seulement les légendes où agissent les dieux, mais les légendes où agissent les héros des origines, ceux qu'on croit avoir été les fondateurs et les grands ancêtres, et cela, même si ces légendes épiques ne sont pas proprement religieuses. Il y a des peuples, tels les Indiens, dont l'imagination est orientée vers le merveilleux, le cosmique, l'éternel; d'autres, tels les Romains, dont l'imagination se moule instinctivement dans le vraisemblable, le national, le chronologique; l'Inde a donc eu une mythologie riche et précise et peu d'histoire; Rome a eu une "histoire de ses origines" riche et précise, et peu de mythologie; mais ce qui soutient la mythologie indienne et l'histoire des origines romaines, les structures de pensée fondamentales, peuvent fort bien être les mêmes: attendons-nous, si nous cherchons à Rome l'homologue de ce qui est dans l'Inde les mythes divins, à le trouver rattaché non pas aux dieux, mais aux héros de l'époque royale.'[94]

Dumézil has devoted a lifetime to tracing the religious and social concepts shared by the peoples whose languages are of Indo-European stock. The underlying idea is, that there is necessarily a genetic relationship between the ideologies of those who speak genetically related languages.

I want to remark at once, that I am not an adherent of Dumézil's tripartition-theory.[95] It is perfectly possible, however, to reject this mainstay of Dumézil's comparative mythology, whilst retaining at the same time part of the ideas of that highly intelligent scholar. Very rightly, F. B. J. Kuiper has remarked that the fervent antagonism and the just as ardent adherence with which Dumézil's work has been greeted should make place for a more deliberate judgment.[96] I think, then, that Dumézil is right in seeing an inherited Indo-European motif in the Roman stories of Horatius Cocles and Mucius Scaevola. It is true that

---

93 Dumézil (1949) 117.
94 Dumézil (1949) 38.
95 This theory assumes, that the mythology of the Indo-European peoples reflects a tripartite social structure, by which Indo-European society was characterized in pre-historic times, viz 'la fonction de souveraineté' (comprising kingship and religion), 'la fonction guerrière' and 'la fonction de fécondité'; the gods are classified in accordance with this tripartite order.
96 Kuiper (1961).

Dumézil fits the case into his tripartition-theory; but we will leave that aspect aside, as the argumentation can do without it.

As a basis, we will take the stories of Horatius Cocles and Mucius Scaevola as they are told by Livy.[97] The scene is the first war of the Roman republic, when Rome was attacked by the Etruscan chieftain Porsenna.

On the approach of the Etruscan army, the Romans fortified their city with garrisons; but an especially vulnerable point was the bridge spanning the Tiber, the pons Sublicius. Horatius Cocles[98] was guarding the bridge at the outer end, when the enemies came pouring down the Janiculum. The Roman soldiers quitted their posts and fled towards the city, but Horatius reproached them, saying that they must not leave the bridge open in their rear. Thereupon he urged them to destroy the bridge behind them, while he himself would stay at his post and hold up the Etruscan army alone. He prepared himself for close combat, stupefying the enemy by the sheer miracle of his courage. At first, two men stayed with him, but he sent them away, and confronted the Etruscans with glaring and menacing glances (*circumferens truces minaciter oculos*), heaping abuse upon them. The Etruscans hesitated, but finally shame overcame them and they hurled their weapons at him. Horatius caught them all on his shield. Then the Etruscans pushed forward, but at the same moment the crash of the falling bridge was heard, and the triumphant shouts of the Roman soldiers, so that their advance was checked. With a prayer to father Tiber, Horatius sprang fully armed into the river and swam to the other side, under a hail of missiles. He reached the city in safety, and was awarded as much land as he could drive a plough round in a day; moreover, a statue of him was placed at the Comitium.

Next, Porsenna laid siege to the city. Food was becoming scarce, when a young aristocrat, Gaius Mucius, presented himself to the senate, saying that he wanted to penetrate into the enemy's camp. The senate granted him permission and he went on his way, a dagger concealed in his clothing. Having arrived there, he took his stand in the crowd, close to the platform where Porsenna was seated. It was pay-day, and a secretary was sitting next to him. Mucius feared to inquire which of the two was Porsenna, and at a venture he stabbed the secretary.

Mucius was seized and brought before Porsenna. He said: 'I am a Roman; my name is Gaius Mucius. I came here to kill you; but I am as much prepared to die as to kill: that is our Roman way. Nor am I the

97 Livy II 10, 12–13.
98 The *cognomen* means 'one-eyed'.

only one to lay a plot against your life: there is a long line of men behind me, eager for the same honour. Gird yourself for the struggle – a struggle for your life from hour to hour, with an armed enemy always at your door'.

Porsenna ordered the prisoner to be burnt alive unless he at once divulged the plot thus obscurely hinted at; but Mucius, saying 'see how cheap men hold their bodies when they care only for honour', thrust his right hand into the fire which had been kindled for the sacrifice. He let it burn there as if he were unconscious of the pain, whereupon Porsenna, astonished by the miracle, ordered him to be removed from the altar and released him. Mucius – as if thanking him for his generosity – said: 'I will tell you as a favour what you could not force from me by threats. There are three hundred young men in Rome, who have sworn an attempt on your life in this way. I drew the first lot; the others will be here each in his turn, until we have got you'.

The release of Mucius (who got the *cognomen* Scaevola – left-handed one – from the loss of his right hand) was followed by the arrival in Rome by envoys from Porsenna, who was very much shaken by the attempt on his life and the prospect of having to face the same thing again. Porsenna offered peace. The conditions were established and peace was concluded. The senate rewarded Mucius with a grant of land across the Tiber, which was afterwards known as the *prata Mucia*.

In 1940, Dumézil advanced his theory about the Indo-European background of the figures of Cocles and Scaevola.[99] Afterwards, he has reverted to the subject many times.[100] As I said above, I shall leave out those elements of Dumézil's argumentation which have to do with tripartition; what remains is the following.

Cocles and Scaevola constitute a pair: their *cognomina* are parallel, both having been derived from a mutilation; their mutilations are also parallel: the loss of a part of the body which is one of a pair; they fight in the same war; both offer themselves as volunteers; both act alone; they are both rewarded with a gift of land.[101] Now we find a similar pair in

99 I have used the revised edition of 1948; see Dumézil (1948) Ch. IX.
100 See e.g. Dumézil (1949) 159–169; Dumézil (1951) 111–115; Dumézil (1968) 424–428; Dumézil (1973) 267–283; Dumézil (1974).
101 Delcourt (1957), who is opposed to Dumézil's explanation, tries to detract from the idea of Cocles and Scaevola as a pair by saying that they symbolize republican heroism together with Cloelia (see e.g. Livy II 13). I want to remark, however, that the association of Cocles and Scaevola was so firmly rooted in consciousness, that the literature of the empire features a one-eyed centurio and a one-handed soldier in Caesar's army, in such a way as to remind the reader of the earlier couple. See Capdeville (1972).

Scandinavian mythology: the god Odin is one-eyed, the god Tyr loses his right hand. Neither is this the only resemblance between the two couples.[102] We will take the case of Odin first.

In one of the poems of the Edda, the Voluspá, we read: 'I know, Odin, where you hid your eye: in the famous well of Mimir'.[103] The so-called prose-Edda, by the Icelandic scholar Snorri Sturluson (1179–1241), tells us more:

In the well of Mimir, science and intelligence are hidden; the master of the well, Mimir, is full of knowledge, because he drinks daily from it. One day, Odin came an asked for a draught, but he was only permitted after having left one of his eyes there.[104] In fact, Odin is a god who is versed in magic, especially war-magic. Snorri writes that he could make his enemies blind or deaf, or paralyzed by fear, so that their weapons became ineffective.[105] In the Eddic poem called Hávamál, Odin says that he can make the arrows of the enemy stop in their flight, merely by looking at them.[106]

The resemblance to Cocles is obvious. Dumézil draws attention to the fact, that the hero carries the whole thing off by his terrible glances[107], by which the enemy is paralyzed – if we follow the account of Livy. Cp. Polybius: the enemies were astounded (*katapeplègmenoon*), not so much by his strength, as by his confidence and his daring[108]; Dion. Hal.: the Etruscans dared not approach him, considering him raving mad and about to die (*hoos memènoti kai thanatoonti*)[109]. This means that Cocles's battle was viewed as something superhuman.

I do not quite understand why Dumézil expresses a certain reserve as to the parallelism Odin-Cocles.[110] Dumézil writes that Odin sacrifices an eye in order to acquire supernatural knowledge, whereas Cocles does

---

102 Contra Scott Littleton (1966), 85–87, who writes that the only common denominators seem to be the absence of an eye and a hand and a concern for the maintenance of sovereignty.

103 Voluspá 28–29. (For the Edda, I have followed the numbering of the strophes as it is given by Gering.)

104 Gylfaginning 15.

105 Ynglingasaga 6.

106 Hávamál 149.

107 That is surely the meaning of *oculos*; contra Delcourt (1957), who maintains, on the ground of this plural form, that Livy does not picture Horatius as one-eyed.

108 Pol. VI 55. (Polybius, by the way, is the only one according to whom Cocles drowns in the Tiber.)

109 Dion. Hal., Ant. Rom. V 24.

110 Dumézil (1974).

nothing of the sort[111]; moreover, Odin's power to paralyze the enemy – a power which he has in common with Cocles – is not the result of his mutilation (the two-eyed Berserkir also had the power to make the weapons of their adversaries ineffective, according to Scandinavian mythology).

It seems to me that Dumézil has been too critical of his own position – perhaps out of a desire to forestall possible objections. In the first place I would remark that Odin's power to paralyze the enemy should surely not be disconnected from his magical powers in general, which he acquired by the sacrifice of his eye. Indeed Dumézil writes elsewhere[112] that Odin's powers all result, directly or indirectly, from his mutilation. But apart from that, I think that the *condition* of being one-eyed (as opposed to the story of the loss) should be the point of comparison. The condition of one-eyedness – in which state he performed his miraculous deed – is the only datum we possess about Horatius; of course we can hardly expect a story about the acquisition of supernatural powers in exchange for the loss of an eye in the case of a Roman citizen. Now it is surely not accidental that one-eyedness goes hand in hand with (war-) magic in the present case. The fact that there are other cases where we find these two things combined makes it probable that, according to a wide-spread belief, one-eyedness made one especially qualified for the exercise of magic. Dumézil himself points to the case of the hero Cúchulainn, a prominent figure in Old-Irish literature. When Cúchulainn is seized with battle fury, this is shown by a special distortion of his body, called *riastrad*. In his *riastrad*, Cúchulainn lets one eye protrude, enlarging it to the size of a bowl, whilst he withdraws the other eye far into his head.[113] F. le Roux[114] stresses the point that this was understood as real one-eyedness, because the reference to Cúchulainn's *riastrad* in Serglige Con Culaind is given as an explanation of the words that 'every woman who loved Cúchulainn lost an eye in order to resemble him'.

In this state, Cúchulainn is possessed of superhuman strength. Although that is not exactly the same thing as Odin's magical power to

---

111 According to Dion. Hal., Ant. Rom. V 23, Horatius had lost an eye in a former battle. Plutarch, Publicola 16, also gives this explanation, adding that, according to others, he was called Cocles because his nose was flat and his eyebrows grew together. Livy does not give an explanation of the name Cocles; neither does Polybius.
112 Dumézil (1973) 275.
113 See Maccgnimrada Con Culaind, *LU* fol. 59; Serglige Con Culaind, *LU* fol. 43a – 50b 14. In translation: Gantz 136 and 156.
114 Le Roux (1961) 333.

make weapons stop in their flight, I think we may nevertheless speak of war-magic. (Moreover, we are told in Maccgnimrada Con Culaind that Cúchulainn remained unhurt although many weapons were thrown at him; this was immediately before his *riastrad* seized him. This miraculous invulnerability may surely be termed 'war-magic'. Admittedly, it does not coincide with the *riastrad*; but it shows, anyway, that Cúchulainn possessed magical powers.)

Dumézil also adduces the case of the viking Egil, who made one of his eyebrows jump down to his cheek and the other to the roots of his hair[115]; according to Dumézil this was a traditional heroic gesture through which Egil was characterized as a warrior. The context however makes clear that Egil did this out of sorrow.

In his article of 1974, Dumézil quotes a publication by J. Heurgon[116], in which a case of magic in Rome is discussed. It concerns the barrister M. Aquilius Regulus, who is described by his contemporary Pliny the Younger as being very superstitious. This man used to paint round his right or his left eye (according to whether he had to plead for the accuser or for the defendant), whilst he covered the eyebrow of his other eye with a white patch.[117] In this way, Heurgon remarks, he produced the effect of being one-eyed. This is explained by Heurgon as casting the evil eye. Dumézil thinks that it is rather a magical protection: Regulus merely wanted to make himself impressive and terrifying, to protect himself against the opposite party and keep them – morally – at a distance and on the defensive. However that may be – the association of one-eyedness with magic is apparently also found in Rome.[118]

Thus, we have got a good correspondence between Odin and Cocles, in my opinion: in both cases it concerns a one-eyed figure exercising war-magic, as a concomitant of his one-eyedness.

Next, we have the case of Tyr. The Eddic poem Lokasenna refers to the wolf Fenrir, which robbed Tyr of his right hand, but which will remain chained till the end of the world.[119] The full story is given by Snorri[120]:

---

115 Egil's Saga Skallagrímssonar 55.
116 Heurgon (1969).
117 Pliny, Ep. VI 2.
118 Cp. also Africa (1970), who points to the fact that there were several one-eyed war-chiefs in classical antiquity (e.g. Hannibal, Sertorius, Julius Civilis); these were invested with a shamanistic aura in the tales that were told about them.
119 Lokasenna 38–39.
120 Gylfaginning 34.

The gods, having a presentiment that the wolf Fenrir would destroy them, wanted to bind it while it was still small. They made therefore a magic tie, which, though looking like a thread of silk, was in fact unbreakable. They challenged the wolf to let itself be bound, so that they might see if it could free itself. The wolf accepted, on the condition that one of the gods should put his right hand into its mouth, as a guarantee that it would be fair play. The other gods refused, but Tyr offered to put his hand into the wolf's mouth. The wolf was bound, and when it turned out that it could not free itself, it bit off the right hand of Tyr.

In order to appreciate the correspondence between the stories of Tyr and Scaevola, we must submit the latter story to a closer inspection. Why does Mucius sacrifice his right hand? In Livy's account it is simply a proof of heroism – but a rationalist might ask whether such a proof was still needed after his heroic attempt on Porsenna's life. I do not believe in the explanation of M. Delcourt[121], who thinks that the burnt hand symbolized freedom. This is based by her on a text of Pseudo-Plutarch[122], where Mucius says, whilst letting his hand burn: 'barbarian, I am free, whether you like it or not'. The underlying idea is, according to Delcourt, that the burning of the hand served to free it from its fetters. In my opinion, this explanation is rather far-fetched. Even if this is indeed the meaning of the text, it only shows that the author did not quite know what to make of Mucius's act. The same perplexity is found with other authors, who ascribe the motivation to Mucius, that he wanted to punish himself for his error.[123]

Now Dumézil draws attention to the following. In the cult of Fides, the three *flamines maiores* performed the rites with their right hands swathed.[124] E. Pais[125] has advanced the idea, that a connection of some sort must have existed between this custom and the story of Mucius Scaevola. Perhaps, Pais writes, Mucius's act was originally conceived as an ordeal. Referring to this hypothesis, F. Münzer writes[126]: Dionysius of Halicarnassus, who, from lack of comprehension, has suppressed the

---

121 Delcourt (1957).
122 Ps. Plut., Parallela Minora 2; these parallels are incorporated in the Moralia (the text in question is Mor. 306 A).
123 See e.g. Valerius Maximus III 3, 1: *perosus enim, credo, dexteram suam, quod eius ministerio in caede regis uti nequisset, iniectam foculo exuri passus est*; the word *credo* is to be noted.
124 See e.g. Livy I 21.
125 Pais (1915) 117–118.
126 Münzer, *PWR.*

self-mutilation of Mucius, stresses the point that Mucius binds himself by oath to reveal the truth to Porsenna, but that he deceives Porsenna and that the oath is a ruse[127] – something about which most authors are vague, avoiding to specify whether Mucius's disclosures are true or false. The reason why Mucius lost his hand was perhaps originally, that he swore a false oath and accepted voluntarily the punishment for perjury. In later times, however, the perjury was felt to be a vile deed and was passed by in silence; thus, Mucius's act had to go without a proper motivation.

After having quoted these remarks, Dumézil observes that, any-how,the resemblance to the story of Tyr is obvious. In the case of Tyr, the hand is a guarantee that the gods, in saying that the cord is not magical, are speaking the truth; in the case of Mucius, the burning of the hand is a proof of heroism, but the result is the same: the hand is a guarantee of an affirmation which, without it, would not have been believed, and which, through it, is believed and works on the mind of the enemy.

I think that Dumézil brushes away the difficulties a bit too easily. The present form of the story does not permit of calling the burning of Mucius's hand a guarantee of his affirmation: it is merely an act by which Porsenna is so much impressed that he releases Mucius. Plu-tarch[128] gives as his opinion, that Porsenna's offer of peace was not so much inspired by fear of the conspiracy as by admiration of the courage of the Romans; but even then the burning of the hand only serves as an incitement for Porsenna to conclude peace, not as a way to make him believe the story of the conspiracy.

However, it does indeed seem likely that the burning of Mucius's right hand was originally connected with the taking of an oath. Livy continues his information concerning the cult of Fides[129] with saying that troth must be preserved and that its seat, even in the right hand, was sacred.[130] That the right hand was consecrated to Fides (c.q. connected with *fides*) is attested by many other texts.[131] In view of this, it does not

127 Dion. Hal., Ant. Rom. V 29.
128 Plut., Publicola 17.
129 See above, p. 184 n. 124.
130 Boyancé (1964) comments: 'la protection donnée à l'une (sc. the right hand) est la traduction matérielle, le symbole du respect qu'il convient d'assurer à l'autre (sc. the deity Fides)' (1972, 122).
131 E.g. Servius ad Aen. III 607. For further references, see W. F. Otto (*PWR*) and Boyancé (1964).

seem too bold to suppose that the belief existed, that one could lose one's right hand in the case of perjury.[132] The connection between *fides* and the oath is demonstrated by P. Boyancé with the aid of a great number of texts.[133]

That Mucius's statement was a lie, is not only the opinion of Dionysius of Halicarnassus. Florus[134] and Cassius Dio[135] add explicitly, that he deceived Porsenna. As a matter of fact, we do not hear anything about a conspiracy in the part of Livy's story, where Mucius lays his plan before the senate.

It seems therefore to be the obvious conclusion – if we want to make sense of the story – that Mucius wanted to lend force to his words by putting his hand into the fire, and was punished for his perjury. We must assume that, in an older form of the tradition, Mucius told the whole story of the conspiracy at once (not first the general outline and afterwards, out of gratitude, the specification – as in Livy). Münzer[136] is surely right in writing: 'Die Teilung des Geständnisses des M. in die unheimliche Einschüchterung und in die Enthüllung ist gewiss nicht ursprünglich; die Motivierung der Selbstverstümmelung gewinnt nicht dadurch, dass zuerst die Verachtung des Todes überhaupt angegeben wird und dann noch besonders die des Flammentodes, und dass dazu noch die Ruhmbegier tritt'. It seems as if Livy was forced to split Mucius's disclosures into two parts in order to furnish a motivation for Mucius's act (namely, his proud contempt of the threat that he would be burnt alive unless he told more about the plot).

But now a curious fact presents itself. If Mucius's statement were to carry conviction, his hand would have had to remain unburnt. Dumézil has failed to notice this point; but I think that it may reinforce his theory. The very strangeness of the story seems to suggest that the historians worked with a traditional motif, which was adapted by them as best they might. In other words, I do indeed believe that the stories of

132 One is reminded of a popular belief in present times, connected with the so-called Bocca della Verità in Rome. This marble slab, in the portal of the church of Santa Maria in Cosmedin, represents a monstrous face with open mouth. Popular fancy has it that, whoever puts his hand into the mouth, will lose his hand if he is guilty of a lie. (It may be noted, that that is exactly what happened to Tyr.)
133 Boyancé (1962). I may mention as an example Livy I 21: *ut fides ac ius iurandum ... civitatem regerent.*
134 Florus I 10.
135 Cassius Dio ap. Tzetzem, Chiliades VI 214.
136 Münzer, *PWR*.

Scaevola and Tyr are both rooted in the common Indo-European set of myths to which the Romans and the Scandinavians were heirs.

This idea receives support from the following argument, furnished by Dumézil in his article of 1974. By that time, Dumézil had discovered another variant of the one-handedness motif within the Indo-European area. It concerns an Iranian story, which has been preserved in a comparatively recent text[137], but whose origin is probably very much older. In fact, the Avesta already makes mention of the tradition that the mythic world-king Taḫma Urupi (= Taḫmorup) rode Ahra Mainyu (= Ahriman), transformed into a horse, for thirty years, from one end of the world to the other.[138] The text in question runs as follows. Taḫmorup succeeded in binding Ahriman and kept him in this condition for thirty years. Three times a day the king saddled him like a horse and rode through the world. At home, he kept him firmly bound. After thirty years, the devil found out, by bribing Taḫmorup's wife, that Taḫmorup always suffered from a short fit of fear at a certain point of the journey. The next day, on arriving there, Ahriman unsaddled Taḫmorup and devoured him.

Taḫmorup's brother Yim-shed went in search of him, but in vain. When he had lost all hope, the angel Srosh came to him and told him what had happened. Yim-shed asked Srosh for a device by which he might retrieve the body of his brother from the devil's belly. Srosh told him that Ahriman was very sensitive to singing and to homosexual pleasures. Accordingly, Yim-shed sang for Ahriman, till the latter got excited and wanted to have sexual intercourse. This was granted by Yim-shed on the condition, that he was permitted first to retrieve the body of Taḫmorup. He put his hand into Ahriman from behind and extracted the body. Thereupon, he fled. When the devil saw the deceit, he dived into hell. But Yim-shed's hand, with which he had extracted the body, shrivelled up. He went to live as a recluse; later on, his hand was healed because a bull made water on it.

As Dumézil has pointed out, we have here the same elements as in the story of Tyr, be it in another sequence. It is to be noted, that the wolf Fenrir will get loose at the end of time, when it will devour Odin, according to Scandinavian mythology.[139] The common elements are,

---

137 Sagas of Taḫmorup and of Yim-shed; edition: Spiegel, translation: Christensen. According to Christensen, the text dates from ± the 16th century A.D.

138 Yašt 15, 11–13; Yašt 19, 27–29.

139 Vafthrúdnismál 53; Gylfaginning 51.

then: binding of monster – monster frees itself and devours god c.q. mythical king – putting of hand into monster in a saving act – perjury – loss of hand. In Scandinavia, the perjury and the loss of the hand occur between the binding of the monster and its getting loose; in Iran only after its getting loose. The shared elements are sufficiently characteristic to permit of the conclusion, that the Scandinavian and Iranian stories both stem from a common source. To be sure, swearing by the right hand (and losing it in the case of perjury) is not an exclusively Indo-European theme. In his study *Der Eid bei den Semiten*, Pedersen writes that the motif 'dass die Hand als Folge eines Fluches oder Falschschwurs gelähmt oder angegriffen wird' occurs frequently.[140] But the Scandinavian and Iranian stories have more in common than that: the hand was lost after it had been put into a monster, with the intention to save.

It is precisely this latter feature, which is also shown by the story of Scaevola: he sacrificed his hand in order to save the Romans from Porsenna.

Thus, we may reason as follows. The assumption that the Roman story is based on inherited material may be made the more readily, if there is an indication that this material existed indeed in pre-historic times; now we have found such an indication in the correspondence between the Scandinavian and Iranian stories. That implies at the same time, that the story of Tyr and the story of Scaevola owe certain shared elements to a common prototype. But in the case of Scaevola, the traditional material became very much distorted. Naturally, the saving of his own party (the Romans) ought to have taken place *before* the perjury became manifest, not after. Apparently, the re-telling of the story in the context of Roman history presented no small difficulty, if the central motif (loss of hand as a consequence of perjury) had to remain unchanged. That accounts for the illogical element in the story of Scaevola.

I have remarked above, that the couple Odin–Tyr can be compared with the couple Cocles–Scaevola, in that it concerns a one-eyed and a one-handed figure in both cases. Next, we have discussed the closer resemblances between Odin–Cocles and Tyr–Scaevola respectively. I want to return now to the phenomenon of a one-eyed figure in close proximity to a one-handed one.

It is Dumézil himself who has pointed to the occurrence of such a couple in the Old-Irish literature; but in his article of 1974, he writes that

140 Pedersen (1914) 225.

he has stopped thinking it a good parallel of Cocles-Scaevola and Odin-Tyr. Let us consider the facts.

According to the Lebor Gabála (the Book of Invasions, dating from the 12th century A. D. but containing material which is much older), Ireland was subjected to six invasions, the fifth being that of the Túatha Dé Danann, the People of the Goddess Danu. On their arrival, they had to do battle with the Fir Bolg, who were defeated in the first battle of Mag Tured. The leader of the Túatha Dé Danann in this battle was their king Núada. Afterwards, the Túatha Dé Danann were oppressed by the Fomóre; from this ensued the second battle of Mag Tured, in which the Fomóre were defeated. At that time, the king of the Túatha Dé Danann was Lug.

Now Núada lost a hand in the battle, Lug made himself one-eyed.

Not in the Lebor Gabála, but in other texts[141], we find a full account of these occurrences. In the first battle of Mag Tured, Núada's right arm is cut off by Streng. The following day, Streng challenges Núada to single combat. Núada answers that the duel will only be fair if Streng does not use his right arm, but Streng replies that he is under no obligation, as their first combat was on fair terms. This induces the Túatha Dé Danann to conclude peace with the Fir Bolg. (Núada gets a silver arm and is since called: Núada Airgetlám, Núada with the silver hand.[142]) When the second battle of Mag Tured is about to begin, Lug makes use of a magic device. He sings a war-song, circling the army on one foot and with one eye.[143] In the battle, he causes the Túatha Dé Danann to win, by killing the most dangerous adversary, Balor with the evil eye.

In *Mitra-Varuna*, Dumézil stresses the point that Streng makes use of a juridical argument; that would link the story to that of Tyr, because Tyr loses his hand in a legal procedure. But in his article of 1974, he drops this point; moreover, he remarks about Lug that he was after all not really one-eyed. In my opinion, however, the couple Núada-Lug forms an interesting parallel. As Dumézil himself also realizes, the Túatha Dé Danann are ancient gods. The texts have 'historicized' them, so that they are turned into invaders of Ireland; but it is apparent in the tales that they are not ordinary human people.

As for Núada, he is the same as the god Nodons, whom we meet in inscriptions found in a temple in Lydney Park, Gloucestershire (prob-

---

141 See Fraser (text and translation); Stokes (text and translation).
142 See e.g. Stokes § 133.
143 Cp. the temporary one-eyedness of Cúchulainn.

ably 4th century A.D.).[144] The inscriptions read *D.M. Nodonti, Deo Nudente* and *Devo Nodenti*. The oldest Irish form of Núada is Núado ⟨*Núadont-s; the first syllable must have had a diphtongue: eu or ou⟩ ō⟩ Ir. úa, Brit. u.[145]

As for Lug, we meet his name in the placename Lugdunum. According to J. de Vries[146], there were no less than fifteen towns bearing this name, among which – as is well-known – Lyon in France. Furthermore, Carlisle was called Luguvallum in Roman times. Lug's festival in Ireland was Lugnasad, on the 1st of August.

I do not think we should stress the 'juridical' aspect of Núada's encounter with Streng; the important thing is, that the Celts knew a one-handed god – even if the story about the loss of his hand differs from that of Tyr or Scaevola. In addition, they knew a god who was at least temporarily one-eyed. The function of Lug's grimace was the exercise of war-magic; that makes him comparable with Odin, notwithstanding the fact that his one-eyedness was not permanent.

To sum up, we have two Indo-European mythologies in which a one-eyed god is found next to a one-handed one. The function of the one-eyed god is the same in both cases: he is versed in war-magic. The stories about the loss of the hand differ; but Tyr's story appears to draw upon a common Indo-European motif: to lose one's hand in a perjury, which is committed in a good cause.

I think, therefore, that Dumézil's insight was right. The data which we have discussed above, combined with the a-priori unlikeliness that the ancient mythology disappeared in Rome without a trace, lead to the conclusion that the tales of Cocles and Scaevola are historicizations. The divine mythology was transformed into national history by the Romans, because a concern for their own past prevailed upon their interest in purely superhuman matters.

That is exactly the process which I assume to have taken place in Israel in the case of the Reed Sea story.

144 *CIL* VII 138–140.
145 I owe this to the friendly information of dr. R. S. P. Beekes, professor of Indo-European comparative linguistics at Leyden University. Prof. Beekes thinks it possible that the forms with – *ent* – have to be explained by *Ablaut*.
146 De Vries (1961) 50.

III

TRANSFORMATION OF THE TALE OF THE SEA

Our chapter titled 'The Song of the Sea' ended with the question: what has caused the mythological presentation of the Reed Sea story? In the chapter on 'mythicizing and historicizing', I have rejected the idea that this presentation was due to the 'mythicizing' of historical facts: the fantastic character of the Reed Sea event tells against its historicity. I have concluded that it must be a matter of 'historicizing'; if the Reed Sea event is regarded as fictive, and if certain elements of the Reed Sea story (such as the drying up of the sea) stem from the myth of the battle with Sea, the idea suggests itself that the very notion of a 'Reed Sea', as the scene of an event in Israel's past, goes ultimately back to that myth. Thus, the myth of the battle with Sea was transformed into a myth about Israel's national history.

In the present chapter, I want to state my argument in more detail; in order to do so, I shall first give a survey of the texts concerning the Reed Sea event. A few texts will be included, containing oracles about future happenings which will be like the miracle at the Reed Sea.

Texts

Ex. XIV   16 *w'th hrm 't-mṭk wnṭh 't-ydk 'l-hym wbq'hw, wyb'w bny-yśr'l btwk hym bybš.*

21 *wyṭ mšh 't-ydw 'l-hym wywlk yhwh 't-hym brwḥ qdym 'zh kl-hlylh wyśm 't-hym lḥrbh, wybq'w hmym.*

22 *wyb'w bny-yśr'l btwk hym bybš, whmym lhm ḥmh mymynm wmśm'lm.*

23 *wyrdpw mṣrym wyb'w 'ḥryhm kl sws pr'h rkbw wpršyw, 'l-twk hym.*

26 *wy'mr yhwh 'l-mšh nṭh 't-ydk 'l-hym, wyšbw hmym 'l-mṣrym 'l-rkbw w'l-pršyw.*

27 *wyṭ mšh 't-ydw 'l-hym wyšb hym lpnwt bqr l'ytnw wmṣrym nsym lqr'tw, wyn'r yhwh 't-mṣrym btwk hym.*

28 *wyšbw hmym wyksw 't-hrkb w't-hpršym lkl ḥyl pr'h hb'ym 'ḥryhm bym, l'-nš'r bhm 'd-'ḥd.*

29 *wbny yśr'l hlkw bybšh btwk hym, whmym lhm ḥmh
mymynm wmśm'lm.*

16 And you, lift up your rod and stretch out your hand over the sea and split it, so that the Israelites may go through the sea on dry ground.

21 And Moses stretched out his hand over the sea, and Yhwh drove the sea back all night by a strong east wind and turned the sea into dry land, and the waters were split.

22 And the Israelites went through the sea on dry ground, and the waters formed a wall for them on their right hand and on their left.

23 And the Egyptians went in pursuit and came after them, all the horses of the pharao, his chariots and his horsemen, far into the sea.

26 And Yhwh said to Moses: stretch out your hand over the sea, so that the waters flow back over the Egyptians, over their chariots and over their horsemen.

27 And Moses stretched out his hand over the sea, and at daybreak the sea returned to its accustomed place; and the Egyptians fled into it, and Yhwh shook off the Egyptians in the midst of the sea.

28 And the waters returned and covered the chariots and the horsemen of the entire army of the pharao, who had pursued them through the sea; not one of them was left.

29 And the Israelites went on dry ground through the sea, and the waters formed a wall for them on their right hand and on their left.

Ex. xv   For the Song of the Sea, I may refer to the chapter in question; it will be remembered that the song makes mention of the drowning of the enemy, whilst stating furthermore that the waters were heaped up by the blast of Yhwh's nostrils, the floods stood like a mound, and the deeps congealed in the heart of the sea.

Ex. xv   19 *ky b' sws pr'h brkbw wbprśyw bym wyśb yhwh 'lhm 't-my hym, wbny yśr'l hlkw bybšh btwk hym.*

19 For the horses of the pharao, with his chariots and

192

his horsemen, went through the sea, and Yhwh brought back the waters of the sea over them; but the Israelites went on dry ground through the sea.

Nu. xxxiii   8a *wys'w mpny (l. mpy) hḥyrt wy'brw btwk-hym hmdbrh,*
...
8a And they set out from Pi Haḥirot, and they passed through the sea into the wilderness, ...

Dt. xi   4 *w'šr 'śh lḥyl mṣrym lswsyw wlrkbw 'šr hṣyp 't-my ym-swp 'l-pnyhm brdpm 'ḥrykm, wy'bdm yhwh 'd hywm hzh.*
4 And what he did to the army of the Egyptians, to its horses and to its chariots, how he caused the waters of the Reed Sea to flow over them as they pursued you; and Yhwh has destroyed them (and so things remain) to this day.

Josh. ii   10a *ky šm'nw 't 'šr-hwbyš yhwh 't-my ym-swp mpnykm bṣ'tkm mmṣrym,* ...
10a For we have heard how Yhwh dried up the waters of the Reed Sea before you when you came out of Egypt, ...

Josh. iv   23b *k'šr 'śh yhwh 'lhykm lym-swp 'šr-hwbyš mpnynw 'd-'brnw.*
23b Just as Yhwh your god did to the Reed Sea, which he dried up before us until we had crossed.

Josh. xxiv   6 *w'wṣy' 't-'bwtykm mmṣrym wtb'w hymh, wyrdpw mṣrym 'ḥry 'bwtykm brkb wbpršym ym-swp.*
7aα *wyṣ'qw 'l-yhwh wyśm m'pl bynykm wbyn hmṣrym wyb' 'lyw 't-hym wykshw,* ...
6 And I brought your fathers out of Egypt, and you came to the sea; and the Egyptians pursued your fathers with chariots and horsemen to the Reed Sea.
7aα And they cried to Yhwh, and he put darkness between you and the Egyptians and brought the sea over them, and it covered them, ...

Is. xi   15 *whḥrym* (LXX *erèmoosei*; Targ. Pesh. *hḥryb*) *yhwh 't lšwn ym-mṣrym/whnyp ydw ʿl-hnhr bʿym (l. bʿṣm? LXX biaiooi) rwḥw,/whkhw lšbʿh nḥlym whdryk bnʿlym.*

16 *whyth mslh lšʾr ʿmw ʾšr yšʾr mʾšwr,/kʾšr hyth lyśrʾl bywm ʿltw mʾrṣ mṣrym.*

15 And Yhwh will ban (cut off?) – *l. cum* LXX, Targ., Pesh. dry up – the tongue of the sea of Egypt, and will fling his hand against the river, breathing his powerful breath, and he will beat it, to form seven rivulets, so that men may cross dryshod.

16 And there will be a road for the remnant of his people which has been rescued from Assur, as there was a road for Israel when they came up from the land of Egypt.

Is. XLIII

16 *kh ʾmr yhwh hnwtn bym drk, wbmym ʿzym ntybh.*

17 *hmwṣyʾ rkb-wsws ḥyl wʿzwz, yḥdw/yškbw bl-yqwmw dʿkw kpšth kbw.*

16 Thus speaks Yhwh, who made a road through the sea and a path through mighty waters,

17 who made chariot and horse set out, an army of strong men, together; they lie down, they cannot rise, they are extinguished, quenched like a wick.

Is. LI

9 *ʿwry ʿwry lbšy-ʿz zrwʿ yhwh/ʿwry kymy qdm drwt ʿwlmym,/hlwʾ ʾt-hyʾ hmḥṣbt rhb mḥwllt tnyn.*

10 *hlwʾ ʾt-hyʾ hmḥrbt ym my thwm rbh,/hśmh mʿmqy-ym drk lʿbr gʾwlym.*

9 Awake, awake, put on strength, arm of Yhwh, awake as in the days of old, the generations of long ago. Was it not you who slew Rahab, who pierced Tannin,

10 was it not you who dried up the sea, the waters of the great deep, who made the depths of the sea into a road for the rescued to pass over?

Is. LXIII

11bα *ʾyh hmʿlm mym ʾt rʿy ṣʾnw, ...*

12 *mwlyk lymyn mšh zrwʿ tpʾrtw,/bwqʿ mym mpnyhm lʿśwt lw šm ʿwlm.*

13 *mwlykm bthmwt, ksws bmdbr/lʾ ykšlw.*

11bα Where is he who brought them up from the sea, the shepherds of his flock, ...

12 who made his glorious arm go at the right hand of Moses, splitting the waters before them, to make for himself an everlasting name,

13 who made them go through the depths? Like a horse in the wilderness they did not stumble.

Zech. x

11a *w'br bym ṣrh (l. mṣrym?) whkh bym glym whbyšw kl mṣwlwt y'r, ...*

11a They will pass through the sea in distress (of Egypt?), they will beat the waves in the sea, and all the depths of the Nile will run dry, ...

Ps. LXVI

6a *hpk ym lybšh bnhr y'brw brgl, ...*

6a He turned the sea into dry land; they passed through the river on foot, ... (The second part of the half-verse refers to the crossing of the Jordan; but in view of the parallelism, the crossing of the sea is also inferred.)

Ps. LXXVII

16 *g'lt bzrw' 'mk, bny-y'qb wywsp slh.*

17 *r'wk mym 'lhym r'wk mym yḥylw, 'p yrgzw thmwt.*

18 *zrmw mym 'bwt qwl ntnw šḥqym, 'p-ḥṣṣyk ythlkw.*

19 *qwl r'mk bglgl h'yrw brqym tbl, rgzh wtr'š h'rṣ.*

20 *bym drkk wšbylyk bmym rbym, w'qbwtyk l' nd'w.*

21 *nḥyt kṣ'n 'mk, byd-mšh w'hrn.*

16 You rescued your people with your arm, the sons of Jacob and Joseph. Selah.

17 The waters saw you, o god, the waters saw you, they trembled, yes, the depths shuddered.

18 The clouds poured out water, the skies thundered, yes, your arrows flashed around.

19 The sound of your thunder was in the whirlwind (?), the lightnings lit up the world, the earth shuddered and shook.

20 Your road was in the sea and your paths were in the mighty waters, and your tracks were not known.

21 You guided your people like a flock, through the hand of Moses and Aaron.

Ps. LXXVIII

13 *bq' ym wy'byrm, wyṣb-mym kmw-nd.*

53 *wynḥm lbtḥ wl' pḥdw, w't-'wybyhm ksh hym.*

13 He split the sea and made them pass through, and made the waters stand like a mound.

53 He led them in safety and they were not afraid; but the sea covered their enemies.

Ps. CVI

9 *wyg'r bym-swp wyḥrb, wywlykm bthmwt kmdbr.*

11 *wyksw-mym ṣryhm, 'ḥd mhm l' nwtr.*

9 He rebuked the Reed Sea so that it dried up, and he made them go through the depths as through the wilderness.

11 But the waters covered their adversaries; not one of them was left.

Ps. CXIV

1 *bṣ't yśr'l mmṣrym, byt y'qb m'm l'z.*

2 *hyth yhwdh lqdšw, yśr'l mmšlwtyw.*

3 *hym r'h wyns, hyrdn ysb l'ḥwr.*

4 *hhrym rqdw k'ylym, gb'wt kbny-ṣ'n.*

1 When Israel came out of Egypt, the house of Jacob from a people with a strange language,

2 Judah became its sanctuary, Israel its dominion.

3 The sea saw it and fled, the Jordan receded.

4 The mountains skipped like rams, the hills like lambs.

Ps. CXXXVI

13a *lgzr ym-swp lgzrym, ...*

14a *wh'byr yśr'l btwkw, ...*

15a *wn'r pr'h wḥylw bym-swp, ...*

(Praise)

13a him who cut the Reed Sea in pieces, ...

14a and let Israel pass through it, ...

15a and shook off the pharao and his army in the Reed Sea, ...

Neh. IX

11 *whym bq't lpnyhm wy'brw btwk-hym bybš, w't-rdpyhm hšlkt bmṣwlt kmw-'bn bmym 'zym.*

11 And you split the sea before them, and they passed through the sea on dry ground; but you cast their pursuers into the depths, like a stone into mighty waters.

Jdt. v   13 *kai katexèranen ho theos tèn eruthran thalassan empros-*
then autoon.
13 And God dried up the Red Sea before them.

Sap. Sal. x   18 *diebibasen autous thalassan eruthran/kai diègagen autous*
di' hudatos pollou.
19 *tous de echthrous autoon kateklusen/kai ek bathous abus-*
sou anebrasen autous.
18 She (sc. Wisdom) brought them over the Red Sea,
and led them through much water.
19 But she drowned their enemies, and cast them up
from the depth of the ocean.

Sap. Sal. xix   7 *hè tèn parembolèn skiazousa nephelè,/ek de prouphestoo-*
tos hudatos xèras anadusis gès etheoorèthè,/ex eruthras tha-
lassès hodos anempodistos/kai chloèphoron pedion ek kludoo-
nos biaiou.
8 *di' hou panethnei dièlthon hoi tèi sèi skepazomenoi cheiri/*
theoorèsantes thaumasta terata.
7 The cloud was seen overshadowing the camp, and
dry land emerging where water had stood before, an
unhindered way out of the Red Sea, and a grassy plain
out of the raging waves,
8 where those protected by your hand passed through
as one nation, having gazed on marvellous wonders.

Midrash Ex.   1 (ad Ex. xv 22). Quotation of Ps. cvi 7 'they were
Rabbah xxiv   rebellious at the sea, at the Reed Sea'.
b'wth š'h ntml' 'lyhm ḥymh śr šl ym wbqš lštpn 'd šg'r bw
hqbh wybšw.
At that moment the prince of the sea was filled with
anger against them and sought to overflow them, until
the Holy One, blessed be He, rebuked him and made
him dry. Quotation of Nah. 1 4 'He rebukes the sea and
makes it dry' and Ps. cvi 9 'He rebuked the Reed Sea
and it dried up'. Cp. Midrash Rabbah ad Nu. xviii 22
śr šl ym rhb šmw, the prince of the sea is called Rahab.

Further argumentation

The acceptance of my idea, that the Reed Sea story is a transformation of the battle myth, does not only require a recognition of the fantastic (ergo fictive) character of the event[1]; it is crucial that it be conceded, that the feature of the 'drying up' of the Reed Sea belonged to the elements which were derived from the older myth.

According to the adherents of the 'mythicizing' theory, the derivations consist merely of some poetic embellishments, like Yhwh's rebuke of the sea or its fear. The 'drying up', on the contrary, constitutes the kernel of the Reed Sea story; thus, my theory could be reformulated as follows: if the Reed Sea event is regarded as fictive, and if the *kernel* of the story stems from the myth of the battle with Sea, the conclusion must be that the story as a whole has sprung from that myth. The difference from the 'mythicizing' theory is thus not only, that this theory reckons with a historical fundament of the Reed Sea miracle; another difference lies in the weight of the element that was borrowed from the battle myth.

In order to substantiate my point, I want to present two diagrams. The first diagram shows six elements, found in the texts about the battle with Sea, namely:

1 drying up of the waters;
2 rebuke of the waters;
3 wind/thunder, lightning;
4 flight/fear of the waters;
5 anxiety of nature;
6 (slaying of) monsters.

---

1 Continual endeavours have been made to make plausible, that the Reed Sea event could actually have happened. Gaster, after having quoted some stories (one of African provenance, the other two told by classical authors) about waters miraculously ebbing away, writes that cases are indeed recorded of a sudden recession of waters due to the action of strong winds; one of the instances mentioned by Gaster concerns lake Menzaleh in the vicinity of the Suez canal. See Gaster (1949) 42–43; Gaster (1969) 238–240. Recently, M. Dayan has done extensive oceanographic research in the region of the Suez canal; he believes that the Reed Sea event can be proved to have been entirely possible. Dayan reckons with a rare combination of winds, ebb and flood tides, which could have created the necessary fluctuation to bring about the two events of the crossing and drowning. See Dayan (1978). I would only reply that, according to the proverb, man may believe the impossible, but not the improbable. I, for my part, am very little inclined to do the latter.

The second diagram shows some elements found in the texts about the Reed Sea event, that were quoted by me above:

A a drowning of the enemy;
B a road through the sea;
C splitting of the sea.

The numbers 1, 2, 3, 4, 5, 6 indicate the same things as in the first diagram.

	I *Battle with Sea*					
	1	2	3	4	5	6
Is. XIX 5	+					
Is. XXVII 1						+
Is. XLIV 27	+					
Is. L 2	+	+				
Jer. L 38	+					
Jer. LI 36	+					
Ezek. XXX 12	+					
Nah. I 3–6	+	+	+		+	
Hab. III 8–15		(+)	+	+	+	
Ps. XVIII 8–16	(+)	+	+		+	
Ps. XXIX 3–9		(+)	+		+	
Ps. LXXIV 13–15	+					+
Ps. LXXXIX 11						+
Ps. CIV 7		+	+	+		
Job IX 13						+
Job XII 15	+					
Job XXVI 11–13		+				+
Or. Sib. V 447	+					
Aeth. Hen. CI 7	+	+				
Rev. XXI 1	(+)					

In Ps. XVIII and in Rev. XXI, it is not literally said, that the waters dry up; Ps. XVIII: their beds become visible; Rev. XXI: the sea exists no more.

Hab. III and Ps. XXIX do not speak literally of Yhwh's rebuke; Hab. III: Yhwh's anger against the waters; Ps. XXIX: Yhwh's voice against the waters.

II *Reed Sea event*

	A	B	C	1	2	3	4	5	6
Ex. xiv 16–29	+	+	+	+		+			
Ex. xv 1–18, 21	+			+		+			
Ex. xv 19	+	+							
Nu. xxxiii 8		+							
Dt. xi 4	+								
Josh. ii 10				+					
Josh. iv 23		+		+					
Josh. xxiv 6–7	+								
Is. xi 15–16		+	(+)	+?		+			
Is. xliii 16–17	+	+							
Is. li 9–10		+		+					+
Is. lxiii 11–13		+	+						
Zech. x 11		+		+					
Ps. lxvi 6		+		+					
Ps. lxxvii 16–21		+?				+	+	+	
Ps. lxxviii 13, 53	+	+	+						
Ps. cvi 9,11	+	+		+	+				
Ps. cxiv 3–4							+	+	
Ps. cxxxvi 13–15	+	+	(+)						
Neh. ix 11	+	+	+						
Jdt. v 13				+					
Sap. Sal. x 18–19	+	+							
Sap. Sal. xix 7–8		+		+					
Midr. Ex. xv 22			+	+					+

In Is. xi and in Ps. cxxxvi, the term *bq'* is not used to indicate the splitting. Ps. cxxxvi has: to cut in pieces; Is. xi does not picture a split from shore to shore, but a number of splits parallel to the shore; in this way, small streams are formed which may easily be crossed. The 'drying up' in Is. xi is not the reading of the MT.

In Ps. lxxvii 20, it is not clear whether the 'road' refers to the road to be taken by the Israelites; it might merely refer to Yhwh's rule over the sea, which is sometimes expressed by saying that he treads upon it (Hab. iii 15; Job ix 8).

Unquestionably, the motifs 1, 2, 3, 4, 5, 6 belong together: each of them occurs in combination with some of the others. If it is readily conceded, that Yhwh's rebuke of the Reed Sea or its flight are motifs which stem from the battle myth, it is not reasonable to repudiate this in the case of motif number one: the drying up of the sea. We might also put it this way: if the 'rebuke' and 'flight' of the Reed Sea are regarded as a poetic embellishment of the actual event, its 'drying up' should also be regarded as such. But if this were the case, what would be left of the 'actual event'? If the 'drying up' of the Reed Sea is to be discarded – being a mere festoon –, the 'body' is taken out of the story.

Of course, the drowning of the Egyptians might be considered equally important to the tale; but as the story stands, that mishap could only befall the Egyptians because the sea was dried up first.

Unless one were to maintain that the similarities between the Reed Sea story and the battle myth are completely fortuitous – which does not seem very likely –, the conclusion urges itself, that the Reed Sea story has developed out of the myth of the battle with Sea.

Changes in the Reed Sea story?

I am not able to detect a development within the Reed Sea story itself. Above, I have mentioned the opinion, that the idea that the Reed Sea was split in two emerged only in later times.[2] One of the advocates of this opinion is F. M. Cross, to whose discussion of the matter[3] we should turn our attention for a moment.

As we have seen above, Cross is of the opinion that the Song of the Sea (which according to him preserves the oldest version of the event) does not refer to the drying up of the sea or Israel's crossing. However, the later story of the episode of the sea was reshaped because two factors exercised their influence upon it. The first of these factors was the old mythic pattern of Canaan: the myth of creation came to be identified with the historical battle. A clear example is Is. LI 9–11, where the main theme is the way which splits through the Sea(-dragon), along which Yhwh leads his people. Cross also adduces the texts in which the term *bq'* is used, a term which is called by him 'more appropriate to the smiting of the Sea-dragon than to the drying up of the sea'.

The second factor was, according to Cross, the cult at the early league shrine at Gilgal. Cross deduces from Josh. III–v that the ark was borne across the Jordan in solemn procession at a covenant-renewal festival, for which occasion the Jordan was 'divided', i.e. dammed. This was

2 Above, p. 146.
3 *CMHE* Ch. VI.

understood as a dramatic reenactment of the crossing of the sea as well as the crossing over to the new land in the conquest. The sea-crossing from Egypt and the river-crossing of the conquest were ritually fused in these cultic acts. Yhwh dried up River as he had dried up Sea – a cultic identity which lay close at hand, because Prince Sea and Judge River were a formulaic pair in Canaanite myth. This cultic repetition of the crossing of River-Sea at Gilgal had a reflex effect on the historical traditions of the exodus – thus Cross.

This presentation of affairs is rather complicated. If I understand it correctly, the Canaanite myth worked upon the Reed Sea story in two ways, a direct and an indirect one. The direct influence is mainly to be observed in later times; it is then, that the verb *bq'* crops up in the texts: a direct reminiscence of the killing of the sea-monster. Indirect influence was exercised via the early cult at Gilgal, where the drying up of the Jordan was thought to symbolize the drying up of the Reed Sea, because the myth paired Yam with Nahar; consequently, it was believed that the sea had been dried up too. It is to be noted, however, that the idea of 'drying up' did not stem from the myth, but from the actual dividing of the Jordan, in Cross's theory.

If it is kept in mind, that the passages about the battle with Sea do not use the term *bq'*[4], not even when there is talk of monsters, and that they do employ the term 'to dry up', in the Baal epic as well as in the OT, one is amazed to find that Cross ignores this fact. Instead, he explains the 'drying up' of the Reed Sea by a cultic rite which is purely hypothetical, combined with the acquaintance of the Israelites with the formula found in the battle myth. The battle myth was thus not followed where the principal action was concerned – because, by a happy coincidence, this action actually took place at Gilgal –, but only as far as it concerned the object(s) of the action. But afterwards, the battle myth came to be followed even where its action was concerned: 'splitting' – a term not used by it, but which amounts to the same thing as 'drying up' – was introduced into the Reed Sea story purely in imitation of the said myth.

I think that, if one theorizes, one should do it in a more economical way. It is admitted by Cross, that the 'drying up' is an early feature of the Reed Sea story (Cross mentions i.a. Ex. xiv 21a, which he assumes to date from the tenth century B.C.) – even though he denies that the Song of the Sea refers to it (as I am convinced it does). If Cross assumes the 'splitting' to be derived from the myth, he should do the same in the

4 On Ps. LXXIV 15, see above, p. 79–80.

case of 'drying up' (it concerns two aspects of the same phenomenon, after all[5]). Cross does not want to admit this, however, because the actual drying up of the Jordan (represented as a miracle by the OT, but reshaped into a commonplace event by Cross[6]) is in his eyes the source of the belief in the Reed Sea's desiccation. Thus, we would have to reckon with an actual as well as a mythical drying up, the first concerning only *nhr*, the second concerning *nhr/ym*.

It is much simpler to explain the drying up of the Jordan by the same process by which I have explained the Reed Sea story.

The quintessence of the Jordan miracle, as it is described in Josh. III–IV, is the following:

Josh. III	16 *wy'mdw hmym hyrdym mlm'lh qmw nd-'ḥd ... whyr-dym 'l ym h'rbh ... tmw nkrtw, wh'm 'brw ...*
	17 *wy'mdw hkhnym nś'y h'rwn bryt-yhwh bḥrbh btwk hyrdn hkn, wkl-yśr'l 'brym bḥrbh ...*
Josh. IV	18 *wyhy b'lwt hkhnym nś'y 'rwn bryt-yhwh mtwk hyrdn ntqw kpwt rgly hkhnym 'l hḥrbh, wyšbw my-hyrdn lmqwmm ...*
Josh. III	16 The water coming down from above stood still; it stood up like a mound ... and the water flowing down towards the sea of the Arabah ... was completely cut off, and the people crossed over ...
	17 And the priests carrying the ark of the covenant of Yhwh stood firm on dry ground in the Jordan, and all Israel crossed on dry ground ...
Josh. IV	18 And when the priests carrying the ark of the covenant of Yhwh came up from the Jordan, they had no sooner set foot on dry land than the water of the Jordan returned to its place ...
	Furthermore, the miracle is referred to in the words of Joshua:
Josh. IV	22b *bybšh 'br yśr'l 't-hyrdn hzh.*

---

5 Cp. above, p. 147.

6 The event would be even more commonplace if a crossing without a dam is assumed. There were fords in the Jordan (see e.g. Josh. II 7), which could be crossed in spite of the spring floods, according to the story of the spies. But of course, the hypothesis that the river was dammed (i.e. dried up) is necessary, if one postulates an actual event at the basis of the tradition.

23 *'šr hwbyš yhwh 'lhykm 't-my hyrdn mpnykm 'd-'brkm,*
k'šr 'śh yhwh 'lhykm lym-swp 'šr-hwbyš mpnynw 'd-
'brnw.

22b Israel crossed this Jordan on dry ground.

23 For Yhwh, your god, dried up the water of the
Jordan before you until you had crossed, as Yhwh,
your god, did to the Reed Sea, which he dried up
before us until we had crossed.

The same wordings as in Josh. IV 23 are used in Josh.
V I.

Finally, two psalms make mention of the Jordan
miracle:

Ps. LXVI   6a *hpk ym lybšh bnhr y'brw brgl,* ...

6a He turned the sea into dry land; they passed
through the river on foot, ...

Ps. CXIV   1 *bṣ't yśr'l mmṣrym, byt y'qb m'm l'z.*

2 *hyth yhwdh lqdšw, yśr'l mmšlwtyw.*

3 *hym r'h wyns, hyrdn ysb l'ḥwr.*

4 *hhrym rqdw k'ylym, gb'wt kbny-ṣ'n.*

1 When Israel came out of Egypt, the house of Jacob
from a people with a strange language,

2 Judah became its sanctuary, Israel its dominion.

3 The sea saw it and fled, the Jordan receded.

4 The mountains skipped like rams, the hills like
lambs.

The texts themselves couple river and sea. Just as with the Reed Sea, the
term 'drying up' is used (in Ps. LXVI, the 'turning into dry land' of the
river may of course be inferred from the parallelism). In Ps. CXIV, the
parallelism requires that the 'receding' of the Jordan is understood as its
'flight'; moreover, the anxiety of nature concerns also the Jordan miracle.

I think, therefore, that a double historicization has occurred: the
drying up is told of Yam as well as of Nahar, the *zbl ym ṭpṭ nhr* of the
Ugaritic texts, whose title had firmly taken root in Hebrew speech.[7] I
would regard the Reed Sea story as the primary tradition; the story was
probably told first of all of Yam himself – and besides, the historiciza-

7 Cp. above, p. 84 n. 192.

tion is easiest to demonstrate in the Song of the Sea, which does not mention the Jordan crossing.[8] But because the notion existed, that Yam was also Nahar, the tale must have been brought into circulation, that the same thing happened to the river: it was dried up in order that it could be crossed by Israel.

To put it schematically, we do not have:

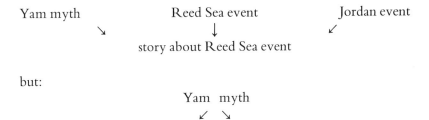

As I remarked, I cannot detect a development in the tale of the Reed Sea. Even if it were possible to arrange the texts of diagram II in a precise chronological order, the strewing of the motifs does not permit any conclusions about such a development. To be sure, the term bq' occurs only in (post)exilic texts (unless Ps. LXXVIII should be pre-exilic); but then, as I have argued, the 'splitting' is implied by the 'drying up' – a notion which was present from the beginning. The Yam myth used the term 'to dry up', not 'to split'. It is in accordance with this, that diagram II shows a more frequent use of 'to dry up' than of 'to split'. A shift of emphasis, as is discovered by some[9], from the drowning of the Egyptians to the crossing of the Israelites, cannot be concluded from the diagram. The texts are eclectic in their choice of the several motifs; and indeed, there is no reason why they should give a full report.

The transformation in concreto

I shall now attempt to describe the transformation which I assume to have taken place.

I have already mentioned the fact, that the Baal epic and the Song of the Sea present a common pattern.[10] If we put the elements constituting

8 Cp. above, pp. 135 and 139.
9 E.g. Beeby; see above, p. 142.
10 Above, p. 150–152.

the pattern in these two texts side by side, it can easily be seen that the transformation, which the tale has undergone in Israel, consists of certain additions.

Baal epic	Song of the Sea
The deity triumphs over Sea, making it dry.	The deity manipulates the sea, making it dry for his people and drowning their enemies in it.
The deity acquires a palace on his mountain.	The deity acquires a palace on a mountain, to which he guides his people.
The deity is king till eternity.	The deity is king till eternity.

The additions are: 1 the people of the deity;
2 their enemies.

1 Above, I have mentioned the so-called 'charter myths'.[11] If a tale about the origins of a tribe functions as a legitimation of certain claims in present days, we have to do with this type of myth. It seems to me that the Reed Sea story must be classified as a charter myth. The tale sanctions a reality (by telling how it came into existence in the distant past), namely: that the Israelites have their domicile around a particular mountain, on which their god, Yhwh, resides as king. This state of affairs is due to the fact that *Yhwh acquired* his people, his territory and his kingship; it is these events, which are narrated in the Reed Sea story.

Yhwh acquired his people and his territory. That is explicitly stated in the Song of the Sea, by the expressions '*m-zw qnyt*, the people which you acquired (vs. 16) and *hr nhltk*, the mountain which fell to your share (vs. 17). *KBL* writes *s.v. nhlh*: '*nhlh* ist der bei Erbteilung, Eroberung, Beute dem Einzelnen (der Familie) zufallende Besitz(-anteil) an Boden, Habe und sonstigem Gut, share of possession of landed property, inheritance, or any goods apportioned to an individual (or family)'. The combination of the words *qnh*, *nhlh* and *hr* is also found in Ps. LXXIV 2:

11 P. 164.

206

zkr ʿdtk qnyt qdm gʾlt šbṭ nḥltk, hr-ṣywn zh šknt bw.

Remember your congregation, which you acquired in ancient times – the tribe that fell to your share, which you rescued –, and mount Sion, your dwelling-place.

Ps. CXIV, which, as we have seen, speaks of the 'flight' of the sea and the Jordan, associates these occurrences with Israel's acquisition of a territory: When Israel came out of Egypt, the house of Jacob from a people with a strange language, Judah became its sanctuary, Israel its dominion (vss. 1–2).

Evidently, the belief existed, that Yhwh did not possess his territory from the beginning of the world.

Now we find a remarkable confirmation of this thought in the book of Deuteronomy. Dt. XXXII 8–9 read as follows:

8 *bhnḥl ʿlywn gwym bhprydw bny ʾdm, yṣb gblt ʿmym lmspr bny yśrʾl (l. ʾl[12]).*

9 *ky ḥlq yhwh ʿmw, yʿqb ḥbl nḥltw.*

8 When Elyon allotted peoples[13], at the time when he was dispersing mankind, he set boundaries between the nations corresponding to the number of gods.

9 Truly, Yhwh obtained his people[14], Jacob was the land which fell to his share.

Although Elyon came to be regarded as a title of Yhwh, we cannot assume that it referred originally to Yhwh in this passage, for that would make nonsense of vs. 9. I take it to be a reference to El in the present case. It is true that Elyon is an independent deity in the first Sefire inscription (*KAI* 222 I A 11), where the pair *ʾl w ʿlyn* is found; but Gen. XIV 19 (*ʾl ʿlywn*) pleads for it having been an epithet of El as well.

Thus, Yhwh is pictured as a subject of El in this passage, as one of the *bny ʾl* (cp. Ex. XV 11, where Yhwh is said to be the greatest among the *ʾlm*). That the cult of El stretched down to the south is proved by the Proto-Sinaitic inscriptions, where the name *ʾl ḏ ʿlm* is found[15]; cp. also the Jerusalem inscription mentioned by me above[16].

El has allotted each of the gods his proper dominion; again, we note

12 The LXX reads *aggeloon theou*; a text from cave four at Qumran has *bny ʾlwhym* (see Skehan (1959) 21). Most probably, the original text read *ʾl*, of which *yśrʾl* is a corruption, due to misunderstanding or censure. The *bny ʾl* are the gods (cp. Ps. XXIX 1).

13 Viz. to the gods.

14 This half-verse means: Yhwh obtained us, Israel.

15 Mine M no. 358; see Cross, *CMHE* 19.

16 P. 113 n. 57.

the term *nḥlh*, a share one receives at a distribution of property. One will remember, that the same term is used of Baal's mountain.[17]

If the passage in Deuteronomy is combined with the Song of the Sea, it may be concluded that Yhwh's domain, which he acquired according to the song, was believed to have been granted him by El. That is a datum which we have to keep in mind, when passing on to the subject of Yhwh's kingship.

I may recall how Baal acquired his kingship. When El favours Yam, granting him a palace and declaring Baal to be his servant, Baal enters into single combat with Yam and is victorious. This earns him his kingship, whereupon El lets himself be persuaded to grant him a palace. It is built on Baal's mountain, the *ǵr nḥlty*. Ergo: Baal is entitled to the kingship, because he has shown himself capable of it by being victorious over Yam; these things come to pass under the supervision of El.

I think that the Song of the Sea tells exactly the same story: Yhwh has earned his kingship, because he has shown himself capable of drying up the sea.[18] Accordingly, he acquires a palace (vs. 17). This palace is situated on the mountain, which was given Yhwh by El as his *nḥlh*, his proper share. Contrary to the Baal epic, the Song of the Sea stresses the fact that Yhwh acquires a people at the same time, whose king he is to be.

Yhwh's newly acquired domain is also destined for his people. Yhwh dried up the sea in order to establish his dominion, but also for the benefit of his people. It is not such a big step from here to the fantasy, that the people have crossed that sea. It is, after all, typical of a dry sea-bed that it can be trodden.

2 Whereas we might speak of a 'natural' extension of the tale in as far as it concerns the deity's people, the introduction of an 'enemy' is less self-evident. I would not conclude from that, however, that the drowning of the enemy constitutes the historical core of the story. The drowning is a miraculous event, of which the miracle of the 'drying up' forms an

17 See above, p. 149.

18 It could be argued, that Yam was a *person* in the Ugaritic myth, a deity who was slain by Baal in single combat, with the aid of maces which hit him 'between his arms' and 'between his eyes'. It might be considered too big a step from here to the Israelite story, which is about a mass of water, a real sea. If that would indeed be an objection to my theory, I would like to draw attention to the statement in the Ugaritic text, that Yam was 'dried up' by Baal (cp. above, p. 86–88). The shift from an anthropomorphic deity to a literal sea is thus already found at Ugarit. It is noteworthy, that the Midrash exhibits the same wavering between an anthropomorphic deity and a literal sea, by stating that Yhwh dried up the prince of the sea (see above, p. 197).

essential part: that was the reason why the enemy found himself on the sea-bed. Of course, one may indulge in all kinds of 'reconstructions' of the event, in which the drowning occurs in a perfectly naturalistic way; but I think we should only reckon with the story as it stands. Otherwise, one would have to assume a historical 'drowning', the cause of which had fallen into oblivion, it having been replaced by a fictive cause which was derived from the old myth. Although that is not entirely impossible, I think that, as a hypothesis, it is not satisfactory. I would prefer my own hypothesis because it is simpler. In my theory, the occurrence as it is told us is taken for granted; an intricate mixture of fact and fantasy is not needed for its explanation.

Enemies are a likely feature of a story about a journey to a safe destiny. What is more, I consider the Reed Sea tale to be a fine specimen of story-telling. It is quite thrilling to have one's enemy, close upon one's heels, drowned in the sea which one has safely crossed only a moment before.

If one should object, that the exodus from Egypt is a historical fact all right, I want to reply that it is practically impossible for us to retrace this 'ancient history'.[19] Of course, we may assume that, with the continuous movements of groups and splinter-groups caused by the ecological conditions, there have also been migrations from the south (even as far as Egypt) into Palestine. As Zuber remarks: under those difficult climatic conditions, practically everybody (the inhabitants of the cities excepted) has 'come from somewhere' – which may have found expression in the traditions of the group. However, these fluctuations of the population, from nomadism to a sedentary life and vice versa, do not lead to the assumption that an entire people – Israel – made their entry into the 'promised land' as one nation, as the OT would have it.

To be sure, a tradition about a flight before the Egyptians existed when the Reed Sea story was coined – unless one were to regard the mentioning of the pharao in the Song of the Sea as an interpolation, for which I cannot find any grounds. But even if that tradition is rooted in history, we do not have reason to regard the Reed Sea story as (basically) historical. We may only say, that the Reed Sea myth has been attached to the tradition of a flight before the Egyptians.

It is not impossible, that Israelites have fled before Egyptians at some time or other. Moreover, we must reckon with real experiences of

19 See on this the fundamental study by Zuber (1976, especially Ch. III, 'Die mündliche Tradition', and Ch. IV, 'Nomadentum und Sesshaftigkeit'), with whose observations I heartily agree.

wandering, of skirmishes, and of pursuit, at all times. Thus, the historicized version of the Yam myth has been placed in the framework of actual experiences.

It is noteworthy, that the process of historicizing has taken the same course in Rome. 'Cocles' and 'Scaevola' have been placed in a historical setting: the war between Rome and the Etruscans. Although we cannot point to such a definite historical event as setting of the Reed Sea miracle, we must note that it is the same process in both cases: the historicized myth has been situated in 'real life'. Again, we find that the thought-process, which led to the shaping of the Reed Sea story, is not exceptional.

The fate of the enemy shows, by the way, that Yhwh has not dried up the Reed Sea for good and all. That is not as surprising as it may seem: the story merely wants to say, that Yhwh is able to dry up the sea when it is necessary. That is in accordance with the general picture we have got of Yhwh's combat with Sea: the sea was regarded as a perennial enemy.[20] At Ugarit, it was known by experience that the sea continued to exist; but when the dangerous winter-storms came on, it was 'dried up' by Baal.

It is likewise in agreement with beliefs about Baal, that Yhwh uses the Reed Sea as an instrument, with which to punish Israel's pursuers. The treaty of Asarhaddon with king Baal of Tyre contains the following passage: 'May Baal Shamem, Baal Malage and Baal Sapon raise an evil wind against your ships, to undo their moorings, tear out their mooring-pole, may a strong wave sink them in the sea, a violent tide (   ) against you'.[21] Thus, Baal has the sea at command; he may use it as a means of punishing transgressors. Such is his power over the sea, that he makes it dry or he makes it stormy at will.

This double aspect of Yhwh's power over the sea is not only evidenced by the Reed Sea story. Job XII 15 states that, if Yhwh withholds the waters, they dry up; if he sends them out, they overwhelm the land. A curious passage is found in Jer. LI. Babylon is threatened by Yhwh, with the words that he will dry up its sea (vs. 36). This sort of oracle originates in the mythological concept of Sea as a dangerous power, which has to be dried up. Babylon is, as it were, identified with this tyrant (otherwise, it would only be to the profit of Babylon, that its sea was to be dried up, as it was to the profit of Israel where its own sea was concern-

20 Cp. above, p. 85.
21 *ANET*³ 534.

ed). But in vs. 42, it is said that the sea has come up over Babylon. In a moment, the image has switched from the elimination of the sea to its use as an instrument of revenge.

I want to adduce one more example of Yhwh's using his adversary as an instrument of vengeance. It concerns the flood-story in the book of Genesis, where the flood is, of course, a means of punishing mankind, but where some traces testify to its being Yhwh's opponent as well. In other words: the flood was Yam himself.

Earlier on, I have set out my argument concerning the flood-story in *ZAW*.[22] I will repeat the essence of my article here.

In 1974, P. A. H. de Boer has offered an interesting explanation of Gen. IX 8–17.[23] De Boer's hypothesis starts from the meaning of *qšt* and the wording of Gen. IX 16. Hebrew does not know a separate term for 'rainbow'; in fact *qšt* usually indicates the bow as a weapon. Moreover, the bow in Gen. IX is bent, which points to a situation of war. Every time Elohim puts his bow in the clouds, he shows that he maintains his *bryt*, apparently by subduing an enemy. As for vs. 16, if Elohim is the subject of *wr'ytyh*, the words *bryt byn 'lhym* etc. are remarkable: one would expect 'between *me* and ...' – which is in fact the reading of the LXX. If the MT is retained, it follows that the subject of *r'ytyh* is not Elohim. Now the sentence reads quite fluently, if we suppose the *mbwl* to be the subject of this verb: every time the Flood sees the bow, he is reminded of the *bryt* between Elohim and all flesh. In other words: the *mbwl* is the enemy who is subdued by Elohim; when he sees the weapon, he is reminded of his forced obedience.

From this, De Boer draws the conclusion that there may have been an old myth, lost to us except for the traces just mentioned. That myth must have included a *bryt*, that is to say, a decree by which God instituted the laws of nature. In connection with the hypothetical myth, the name 'Yam' is mentioned only once by De Boer, and in an indirect way at that: he remarks that the enemy of Elohim must have been 'a power like Yam'. I have tried to demonstrate in my article, 1) that De Boer has not made plausible, that there has been a myth about the institution of the laws of nature; 2) that the flood was identified with Yam by the OT writer. The second conclusion was based on De Boer's observation, that the flood was an enemy (as appears from the bow), an independent power which submitted to God (as appears from Gen. IX 16). I have

22 Kloos (1982).
23 De Boer (Louvain 1974).

remarked that this implies that, even in the time of the priestly writer, two traditions were flourishing: the flood-story (of Mesopotamic origin), in which the flood is caused by the gods, and the tradition of the Water as the defeated arch-enemy of God. My conclusion was, that the priestly writer has brought the concept of the flood as an instrument of God into accord with the concept of Yam as God's defeated enemy, by conceiving of the Flood as a power which was temporarily let loose by God to punish mankind, and which, its rôle being fulfilled, was forced to renewed obedience.[24] – Thus far my article.

Thus, the picture presented by the Reed Sea story does not stand by itself. The hostile power is checked by Yhwh: it is dried up; but it is also used as an auxiliary force, by whose aid the enemy is eliminated.

Conclusion

I hope to have demonstrated in this part of my study, that.the Reed Sea story is a transformation of the myth of the battle with Sea. As Burkert has written[25]: 'what must have happened again and again to myths in history: consecutive changes of crystallization and application'. The combat myth found a new application in Israel, where it was converted into a charter myth.

24 That does not contradict my conclusion on p. 88, that the *mbwl* cannot be regarded as a hostile power. In that section, we had to do with *mbwl* in the sense of 'heavenly ocean', whereas our present argument is concerned with the deluge in Noah's days.
25 See above, p. 167.

CONCLUSION

In Psalm XXIX, Yhwh is pictured as a thunder-god who threatens the mighty waters, thereby causing nature to tremble with fear. Consequently, he receives homage from the other gods in his palace upon the heavenly ocean. His eternal kingship ensures the well-being of his people, who are blessed by him with the fertilizing rain.

Thus, the Old Testament contains a hymn of praise, in which Yhwh is wholly represented as Baal. We can hardly avoid concluding, that the Israelites truly credited their god with the qualities and deeds, which were ascribed to Baal in the Ugaritic myth of Baal and the sea.

A deity who could ensure sufficient rainfall was, of course, of vital importance to the population of Syria and Palestine, who were dependent on the rain for their sustenance. The Ugaritans were acquainted with the phenomenon, that a time of abundant rainfall was preceded by a short period of violent turbulence of the sea. They put this experience into words in the myth of Baal, who had to conquer Yam before he could exercise his kingly power – a power which found expression in the thunder-storms.

Apparently, the triumph over Sea had come to be so fixedly bound up with the gift of the rain, that a people living farther inland – the Israelites – adopted this mythology lock, stock and barrel.

There is yet another text in the Old Testament – a self-contained unity, like Psalm XXIX –, in which Yhwh functions as Baal. The Song of the Sea in Exodus XV displays the same pattern as the myth of Baal and Yam: having dried up the sea, Yhwh acquires a palace on the mountain which has been allotted to him, where he will reside as king till eternity.

The Old Testament testifies to the deep concern of the Israelites in their national history; we may say that the account of their own past has taken the place of myths about gods, of which only slight traces subsist (the battle with Sea being an outstanding exception). In this respect, the Israelites resembled the ancient Romans. As the interest of both Israelites and Romans was focussed on human instead of purely superhuman matters, it is not surprising that we meet a similar phenomenon in the writings of both, namely, the transformation of a tale about gods into a tale about human people. In the case of Horatius Cocles and Mucius Scaevola, the gods have totally disappeared from the scene: they have been transformed into Roman citizens. In the case of the Reed Sea story, the gods have remained (although Yam has been deprived of his divine character); but human actors have made their entrance on the scene as well.

The Reed Sea myth must have played an important rôle in Israelite thought. That is not only evidenced by the frequent references to the miracle in the Old Testament; it may also be deduced from the content of the tale. The myth functions as a charter, legitimizing the claim of the Israelites to their domicile around the mountain of their god, Yhwh, as well as Yhwh's kingship over Israel. This corroborates the conclusion which was drawn from Psalm xxix: that the Baal traits formed an essential part of the Israelite conception of Yhwh – instead of their being a mere 'figure of speech', employed by poets who had recourse to a stock of traditional phrases.

I do not assert, of course, that there has been no evolution in religious beliefs. Mythological elements have been discarded in the course of time – although, to my knowledge, the belief in Yhwh's drying up of the Reed Sea has survived in certain circles to the present day. It is difficult to make out, at what time precisely the combat with Sea came to be regarded with disbelief. What I am interested in, however, is the early conception of Yhwh. In an early period (which is when the Song of the Sea must have been composed), Yhwh's Baal traits must have formed part of the living creed of Israel.

Thus, the conclusion to be drawn from the present study is, that the Baal religion has influenced the conception of Yhwh at essential points. Acting, as it were, as an 'Israelite Baal', Yhwh fulfilled, for his people, two fundamental needs: he sanctioned their claim to a special territory, and he blessed them with the rain. He could do these things in virtue of his kingship, which he had won by his victory over Yam. Yhwh's combat with the sea played indeed an important rôle in the religion of ancient Israel.

BIBLIOGRAPHY

The titles mentioned in the bibliography are mostly referred to by the author's name plus the year of publication. In a few cases, the reference consists of the author's name plus an abbreviation indicating a multi-author work, in a few other cases of an abbreviation only; one should consult the list of abbreviations.

The list of abbreviations contains moreover – apart from periodicals – editions of sources (either in the original language, or in translation, or both) and dictionaries. The abbreviation may consist of only an author's name; these names are neither included in the bibliography, nor in the index of authors.

I regret not having been able to discuss the following two books, which only reached me after the completion of my manuscript:
J. Day, *God's Conflict with the Dragon and the Sea. Echoes of a Canaanite Myth in the Old Testament*, Cambridge 1985.
O. Loretz, *Psalm 29. Kanaanäische El- und Baaltraditionen in jüdischer Sicht*, Altenberge 1984.

Th. W. Africa, 'The one-eyed Man against Rome: An Exercise in Euhemerism', *Hist* 19 (1970), 528–538.
B. Albrektson, *History and the Gods. An Essay on the Idea of Historical Events as Divine Manifestations in the Ancient Near East and in Israel*, Lund 1967.
W. F. Albright, 'The Psalm of Habakkuk', *Studies in Old Testament Prophecy presented to Professor Theodore H. Robinson*, ed. H. H. Rowley, Edinburgh 1946, 1–18.
W. F. Albright, *The Archeology of Palestine*, Harmondsworth 1949.
A. Angerstorfer, 'Ašerah als "consort of Jahwe" oder Aširtah?', *BN* 17 (1982), 7–16.
Y. Avishur, 'Addenda to the Expanded Colon in Ugaritic and Biblical Verse', *UF* 4 (1972), 1–10.
B. F. Batto, 'The Reed Sea: Requiescat in pace'. *JBL* 102 (1983), 27–35.
W. W. Baudissin, *Kyrios als Gottesname im Judentum und seine Stelle in der Religionsgeschichte*, Giessen 1929.

H. D. Beeby, 'The Exodus Against the Background of Mythology', *SEAJT* 11 (1970), 94–100.

J. Begrich, 'Mabbūl. Eine exegetisch-lexikalische Studie', *ZS* 6 (1928), 135–153.

M. Ben-Asher, 'The Gender of Nouns in Biblical Hebrew', *Sem* 6 (1978), 1–14.

A. Berlin, 'On the Meaning of *rb*', *JBL* 100 (1981), 90–93.

P. A. H. de Boer, 'The Son of God in the Old Testament', *OTS* 18 (1973), 188–207.

P. A. H. de Boer, *Fatherhood and Motherhood in Israelite and Judean Piety*, Leiden 1974.

P. A. H. de Boer, 'Quelques remarques sur l'Arc dans la Nuée (Genèse 9, 8–17)', *Questions disputées d'Ancien Testament: méthode et théologie*, ed. C. Brekelmans, Louvain 1974, 105–114.

P. A. H. de Boer, 'Cantate Domino: An Erroneous Dative?', *OTS* 21 (1981), 55–67.

P. Boyancé, '*Fides* et le serment', *Hommages à Albert Grenier*, ed. M. Renard, Bruxelles 1962, I 329–341 (= P. Boyancé, *Études sur la religion romaine*, Rome 1972, 91–103).

P. Boyancé, 'La main de *Fides*', *Hommage à Jean Bayet*, ed. M. Renard – R. Schilling, Bruxelles 1964, 101–113 (= P. Boyancé, *Études sur la religion romaine*, Rome 1972, 121–133).

L. Bronner, *The Stories of Elijah and Elisha as Polemics against Baal Worship*, Leiden 1968.

W. Burkert, *Structure and History in Greek Mythology and Ritual*, Berkeley-Los Angeles-London 1979.

M. Buttenwieser, *The Psalms, Chronologically treated with a New Translation*, New York 1969[2] (Chicago 1938).

G. Capdeville, 'Le centurion borgne et le soldat manchot', *MEFRA* 84 (1972), 601–621.

A. Caquot, 'In splendoribus sanctorum', *Syr* 33 (1956), 36–41.

A. Caquot – M. Sznycer – A. Herdner, *Textes Ougaritiques* I, *Mythes et Légendes*, Paris 1974 (*CSH*).

E. Cassin, *La splendeur divine. Introduction à l'étude de la mentalité mésopotamienne*, Paris 1968.

U. Cassuto, *The Goddess Anath. Canaanite Epics of the Patriarchal Age*, Jerusalem 1971 (translation of *Ha-elah Anath*, Jerusalem 1951).

H. Cazelles, 'Une relecture du psaume XXIX?', *À la rencontre de Dieu, Mémorial Albert Gelin*, Le Puy 1961, 119–128.

B. S. Childs, *Memory and Tradition in Israel*, London 1962.

R. J. Clifford, 'The Temple in the Ugaritic Myth of Baal', *Symposia celebrating the seventy-fifth anniversary of the founding of the American Schools of Oriental Research (1900–1975)*, ed. F. M. Cross, Cambridge (MA) 1979, 137–145.

G. W. Coats, 'The Song of the Sea', *CBQ* 31 (1969), 1–17.

P. S. Cohen, 'Theories of Myth', *Man* 4 (1969), 337–353.

G. Cooke, 'The Sons of (the) God(s)', *ZAW* 76 (1964), 22–47.

P. C. Craigie, 'Psalm xxix in the Hebrew Poetic Tradition', *VT* 22 (1972), 143–151.

P. C. Craigie, 'The Problem of Parallel Word Pairs in Ugaritic and Hebrew Poetry', *Sem* 5 (1977), 48–58.

P. C. Craigie, 'Parallel Word Pairs in Ugaritic Poetry: A Critical Evaluation of their Relevance for Psalm 29', *UF* 11 (1979), 135–140.

F. M. Cross, 'Notes on a Canaanite Psalm in the Old Testament', *BASOR* 117 (1950), 19–21.

F. M. Cross, *Canaanite Myth and Hebrew Epic. Essays in the History of the Religion of Israel*, Cambridge (MA) 1973 (*CMHE*).

F. M. Cross – D. N. Freedman, 'The Song of Mirjam', *JNES* 14 (1955), 237–250.

J. L. Cunchillos, *Estudio del Salmo 29. Canto al Dios de la fertilidad-fecundidad. Aportación al conocimiento de la Fe de Israel a su entrada en Canaan*, Valencia 1976.

A. H. W. Curtis, 'The "Subjugation of the Waters" Motif in the Psalms; Imagery or Polemic?', *JSS* 23 (1978), 244–256.

M. Dahood, 'Hebrew-Ugaritic Lexicography I', *Bibl* 44 (1963), 289–303.

M. Dahood, *Psalms* I, New York 1966.

M. Dahood, 'Hebrew-Ugaritic Lexicography VI', *Bibl* 49 (1968), 355–369.

É. Dantinne, 'Création et Séparation', *Mus* 74 (1961), 441–451.

M. Dayan, 'The Dividing of the Red Sea According to Natural Sciences', *BethM* 73 (1978), 162–176.

A. Deissler, 'Zur Datierung und Situierung der "kosmischen Hymnen" Ps. 8; 19; 29', *Lex tua Veritas, Festschrift für H. Junker*, ed. H. Gross – F. Mussner, Trier 1961, 47–58.

M. Delcor, 'Les allusions à Alexandre le Grand dans Zach. ix 1–8', *VT* 1 (1951), 110–124.

M. Delcourt, 'Horatius Coclès et Mucius Scaevola', *Hommages à Waldemar Déonna*, Bruxelles 1957, 169–180.

G. Del Olmo Lete, 'Review of J. L. Cunchillos, *Estudio del Salmo 29*', *UF* 12 (1980), 473–474.

G. Del Olmo Lete, *Mitos y leyendas de Canaan*, Madrid 1981.

W. G. Dever, 'Recent Archaeological Confirmation of the Cult of A-sherah in Ancient Israel', *HS* 23 (1982), 37–43.

M. Dietrich – O. Loretz, 'Baal *rpu* in *KTU* 1.108; 1.113 und nach 1.17 VI 25–33', *UF* 12 (1980), 171–182.

M. Dietrich – O. Loretz – J. Sanmartín, 'Die Götterliste RS 24.246 = UG. 5, S. 594 NR. 14', *UF* 7 (1975), 545–546.

H. Donner, 'Ugaritismen in der Psalmenforschung', *ZAW* 79 (1967), 322–350.

G. R. Driver, 'Studies in the Vocabulary of the Old Testament II', *JThS* 32 (1931), 250–257.

G. R. Driver, *Canaanite Myths and Legends*, Edinburgh 1956 (*CML*).

B. Duhm, *Die Psalmen*, Tübingen 1922² (1899).

G. Dumézil, *Mitra-Varuna. Essai sur deux représentations indo-européennes de la souveraineté*, Paris 1948² (1940).

G. Dumézil, *L'Héritage indo-européen à Rome*, Paris 1949.

G. Dumézil, 'Mythes romains', *RevPar* 58 (1951), 105–118.

G. Dumézil, *Mythe et épopée I, L'idéologie des trois fonctions dans les épopées des peuples indo-européens*, Paris 1968.

G. Dumézil, *Mythe et épopée III, Histoires romaines*, Paris 1973.

G. Dumézil, '"Le Borgne" and "Le Manchot": the State of the Problem', *Myth in Indo-European Antiquity*, ed. G. J. Larson, Berkeley-Los Angeles-London 1974, 17–28.

R. Dussaud, *Les Découvertes de Ras Shamra (Ugarit) et l'ancien Testament*, Paris 1937.

F. E. Eakin, 'The Reed Sea and Baalism', *JBL* 86 (1967), 378–384.

O. Eissfeldt, 'Jahve und Baal', *PrJ* 155 (1914), 257–270 (= O. Eissfeldt, *Kleine Schriften* I, Tübingen 1962, 1–12).

O. Eissfeldt, *Baal Zaphon, Zeus Kasios und der Durchzug der Israeliten durchs Meer*, Halle 1932.

M. Eliade, *Myth and Reality*, New York 1963.

J. A. Emerton, '"Spring and Torrent" in Psalm LXXIV 15', *SVT* 15 (1966), 122–133.

J. A. Emerton, 'New Light on Israelite Religion: The Implications of the Inscriptions from Kuntillet 'Ajrud', *ZAW* 94 (1982), 2–20.

I. Engnell, *A Rigid Scrutiny. Critical Essays on the Old Testament*, translated and edited by J. T. Willis, Nashville 1969.

F. C. Fensham, 'Psalm 29 and Ugarit', *OTWSAP* 6 (1963), 84–99.

L. R. Fisher, 'Creation at Ugarit and in the Old Testament', *VT* 15 (1965), 313–324.

A. Fitzgerald, 'A Note on Psalm 29', *BASOR* 215 (1974), 61–63.

D. N. Freedman, 'Archaic Forms in Early Hebrew Poetry', *ZAW* 72 (1960), 101–106.

D. N. Freedman – C. F. Hyland, 'Psalm 29: A Structural Analysis', *HThR* 66 (1973), 237–256.

V. Fritz, 'Kadesch Barnea – Topographie und Siedlungsgeschichte im Bereich der Quellen von Kadesch und die Kultstätten des Negeb während der Königszeit', in: V. Fritz – M. Görg – H. F. Fuhs, 'Kadesch in Geschichte und Überlieferung', *BN* 9 (1979), 45–70.

Th. H. Gaster, 'Notes on "the Song of the Sea"', *ExTim* 48 (1936/37), 45.

Th. H. Gaster, 'Psalm 29', *JQR* 37 (1946/47), 55–65.

Th. H. Gaster, *Passover – its History and Traditions*, New York 1949.

Th. H. Gaster, *Thespis. Ritual, Myth and Drama in the Ancient Near East*, Garden City 1961² (New York 1950).

Th. H. Gaster, *Myth, Legend and Custom in the Old Testament*, New York-Evanston 1969.

G. Gerleman, '*šlm* genug haben', *ThHAT* II, 919–935.

H. Gese, 'Die Religionen Altsyriens', in: H. Gese – M. Höfner – K. Rudolph, *Die Religionen Altsyriens, Altarabiens und der Mandäer*, Stuttgart 1970, 5–232.

S. Gevirtz, 'The Ugaritic Parallel to Jeremiah 8:23', *JNES* 20 (1961), 41–46.

M. Gilula, 'To Yahweh Shomron and His Asherah', *Shnaton* 3 (1978/79), 129–137, XV–XVI.

H. L. Ginsberg, 'A Phoenician Hymn in the Psalter', *Atti XIX CongrOr*, 472–476 (= H. L. Ginsberg, *Kitve Ugarit*, Jerusalem 1936, 129–131).

H. L. Ginsberg, 'A Strand in the Cord of Hebraic Hymnody', *ErIs* 9 (1969), 45–50.

E. M. Good, 'Exodus XV 2', *VT* 20 (1970), 358–359.

C. H. Gordon, *Ugaritic Textbook*, Roma 1965.

H. Gottlieb, 'Myth in the Psalms', in: B. Otzen – H. Gottlieb – K. Jeppesen, *Myths in the Old Testament*, London 1980 (translation of *Myter i Det gamle Testamente*, Copenhagen 1973, 1976²), Ch. III.

F. Gradl, 'Abermals Überlegungen zu Struktur und Finalität von Ps. 29', *SBFLA* 29 (1979), 91–110.

J. Gray, 'Canaanite Mythology and Hebrew Tradition', *GUOST* 14 (1953), 47–57.

J. Gray, *The Biblical Doctrine of the Reign of God*, Edinburgh 1979.

J. Gray, 'The Blood Bath of the Goddess Anat in the Ras Shamra Texts', *UF* 11 (1979), 315–324.

E. L. Greenstein, 'The Snaring of Sea in the Baal Epic', *Maarav* 3 (1982), 195–216.

O. Grether, *Name und Wort Gottes im Alten Testament*, Giessen 1934.

J. H. Grønbaek, 'Jahves kamp med dragen. Om baggrunden for kampmotivet i de gammeltestamentlige skabelsesforestillinger', *DTT* 47 (1984), 81–108.

H. Gunkel, *Schöpfung und Chaos in Urzeit und Endzeit*, Göttingen 1895.

H. Gunkel, *Die Psalmen*, Göttingen 1926⁴.

C. Hartlich – W. Sachs, *Der Ursprung des Mythosbegriffes in der modernen Bibelwissenschaft*, Tübingen 1952.

B. Hartmann, 'Monotheismus in Mesopotamien?', *Monotheismus im Alten Israel und seiner Umwelt*, ed. O. Keel, Fribourg 1980, 50–81.

L. Hay, 'What really happened at the Sea of Reeds?', *JBL* 83 (1964), 397–403.

M. Held, 'The YQTL—QTL (QTL—YQTL) Sequence of Identical Verbs in Biblical Hebrew and in Ugaritic', *Studies and Essays in Honor of Abraham A. Neuman*, Leiden 1962, 281–290.

W. Herrmann, 'Die Göttersöhne', *ZRGG* 12 (1960), 242–251.

W. Herrmann, 'Die Frage nach Göttergruppen in der religiösen Vorstellungswelt der Kanaanäer', *UF* 14 (1982), 93–104.

J. Heurgon, 'Les sortilèges d'un avocat sous Trajan', *Hommage à Marcel Renard*, ed. J. Bibauw, Bruxelles 1969, 443–448.

R. Hillmann, *Wasser und Berg. Kosmische Verbindungslinien zwischen dem kanaanäischen Wettergott und Jahwe*, Halle 1965.

J. Hoftijzer, *A Search for Method. A study in the syntactic use of the H-locale in classical Hebrew*, Leiden 1981.

H. D. Hummel, 'Enclitic Mem in Early Northwest Semitic, especially Hebrew', *JBL* 76 (1957), 85–107.

L. Jacobs, 'Jewish Cosmology', *Ancient Cosmologies*, ed. C. Blacker – M. Loewe, London 1975, 66–86.

K. Jaroš, 'Zur Inschrift Nr. 3 von Ḥirbet el-Qōm', *BN* 19 (1982), 31–40.

E. Jenni, *Das hebräische Pi'el. Syntaktisch-semasiologische Untersuchung einer Verbalform im Alten Testament*, Zürich 1968.

J. Jeremias, *Theophanie. Die Geschichte einer alttestamentlichen Gattung*, Neukirchen-Vluyn 1965.

A. Jirku, 'Kanaanäische Psalmenfragmente in der vorisraelitischen Zeit Palestinas und Syriens', *JBL* 52 (1933), 108–120.

A. R. Johnson, *Sacral Kingship in Ancient Israel*, Cardiff 1955.

P. Joüon, *Grammaire de l'Hébreu Biblique*, Rome 1923.

O. Kaiser, *Die mythische Bedeutung des Meeres in Ägypten, Ugarit und Israel*, Berlin 1959.

A. S. Kapelrud, *Baal in the Ras Shamra Texts*, Copenhagen 1952.

A. S. Kapelrud, *The Ras Shamra Discoveries and the Old Testament*, Oxford 1965.

A. S. Kapelrud, 'Ba'al, Schöpfung und Chaos', *UF* 11 (1979), 407–412.

A. S. Kapelrud, 'Die Theologie der Schöpfung im Alten Testament', *ZAW* 91(1979), 159–170.

E. Kautzsch – A. E. Cowley ed., *Gesenius' Hebrew Grammar*, Oxford 1910² (*GK*).

C. A. Keller – G. Wehmeier, '*brk* pi. segnen', *ThHAT* I, 353–376.

G. S. Kirk, *Myth: Its Meaning and Functions in Ancient and Other Cultures*, Berkeley-Los Angeles-Cambridge 1970.

E. J. Kissane, *The Book of Psalms* I, Dublin 1953.

K. A. Kitchen, 'Egypt, Ugarit, Qatna and Covenant', *UF* 11 (1979), 453–464.

C. J. L. Kloos, 'The Flood on Speaking Terms with God', *ZAW* 94 (1982), 639–642.

K. Koch, 'Zur Entstehung der Ba'al-Verehrung', *UF* 11 (1979), 465–475.

H. J. Kraus, *Die Psalmen*, Neukirchen-Vluyn 1978⁵ (1961).

F. B. J. Kuiper, 'Some Observations on Dumézil's Theory (with reference to Prof. Frye's article)', *Numen* 8 (1961), 34–45.

C. J. Labuschange, '*qōl* Stimme', *ThHAT* II, 629–634.

W. G. Lambert, 'The Great Battle of the Mesopotamian Religious Year. The Conflict in the Akītu House', *Iraq* 25 (1963), 189–190.

W. G. Lambert, 'The Cosmology of Sumer and Babylon', *Ancient Cosmologies*, ed. C. Blacker – M. Loewe, London 1975, 42–62.

B. Lang ed., *Der einzige Gott. Die Geburt des biblischen Monotheismus.* Mit Beiträgen von B. Lang, M. Smith und H. Vorländer, München 1981.

E. Laroche, 'Documents en langue Hourrite provenant de Ras Shamra', *Ugaritica* V, 447–544.

K. Latte, *Römische Religionsgeschichte*, München 1960.

A. Lauha, 'Das Schilfmeermotiv im Alten Testament', *SVT* 9 (1963), 32–46.

I. O. Lehman, 'A Forgotten Principle of Biblical Textual Tradition Rediscovered', *JNES* 26(1967), 93–101.

A. Lemaire, 'Les inscriptions de Khirbet el Qôm et l'Ashérah de YHWH', *RB* 84 (1977), 595–608.

C. E. L'Heureux, *Rank among the Canaanite Gods El, Ba'al, and the Repha'im*, Missoula 1979.

E. Lipiński, *La royauté de Yahwé dans la poésie et le culte de l'Ancien Israel*, Brussel 1965.

S. E. Loewenstamm, 'The Expanded Colon in Ugaritic and Biblical Verse', *JSS* 14 (1969), 176–196.

S. E. Loewenstamm, 'The Lord is my Strength and my Glory', *VT* 19 (1969), 464–470.

S. E. Loewenstamm, 'The Ugaritic Myth of the Sea and its Biblical Counterparts', *ErIs* 9 (1969), 96–101.

S. E. Loewenstamm, 'Grenzgebiete Ugaritischer Sprach- und Stilvergleichung: Hebräisch des Zweiten Tempels, Mittelhebräisch, Griechisch', *UF* 3 (1971), 93–100.

S. E. Loewenstamm, 'The Expanded Colon, Reconsidered', *UF* 7 (1975), 261–264.

S. E. Loewenstamm, 'Die Wasser der biblischen Sintflut: ihr Hereinbrechen und ihr Verschwinden', *VT* 34 (1984), 179–194.

N. Lohfink, 'De Moysis Epinicio (Ex. 15, 1–18)', *VD* 41 (1963), 277–289.

O. Loretz, 'Psalmenstudien III', *UF* 6 (1974), 175–210.

O. Loretz, 'Ugarit-Texte und israelitische Religionsgeschichte', *UF* 6 (1974), 241–248.

R. Lowth, *De sacra poesi Hebraeorum praelectiones academicae*, Oxonii 1753.

R. Luyster, 'Myth and History in the Book of Exodus', *Rel* 8 (1978), 155–170.

R. Luyster, 'Wind and Water: Cosmogonic Symbolism in the Old Testament', *ZAW* 93 (1981), 1–10.

B. Malinowski, *Myth in Primitive Psychology*, London 1926 (= B. Malinowski, *Magic, Science and Religion*, ed. R. Redfield, Garden City 1948, 93–148).

B. Margulis, 'A Ugaritic Psalm (RS 24.252)', *JBL* 89 (1970), 292–304.

B. Margulis, 'The Canaanite Origin of Psalm 29 reconsidered', *Bibl* 51 (1970), 332–348.

H. G. May, 'Some Cosmic Connotations of Mayim Rabbim, "Many Waters"', *JBL* 74 (1955), 9–21.

D. J. McCarthy, '"Creation" Motifs in Ancient Hebrew Poetry', *CBQ* 29 (1967), 393–406.

Z. Meshel, 'Did Yahweh Have a Consort?', *BAR* 5 (1979), 24–35.

Z. Meshel – C. Meyers, 'The Name of God in the Wilderness of Zin', *BA* 39 (1976), 6–10.

T. N. D. Mettinger, *The Dethronement of Sabaoth. Studies in the Shem and Kabod Theologies*, Gleerup 1982.

F. de Meyer, '*kbd* comme nom divin en éblaïte, ougaritique et hébreu', *RThL* 11 (1980), 225–228.

P. D. Miller, 'El the Warrior', *HThR* 60 (1967), 411–431.

P. D. Miller, *The Divine Warrior in Early Israel*, Cambridge (MA) 1973.

P. D. Miller, 'El, The Creator of Earth', *BASOR* 239 (1980), 43–46.

S. Mittmann, 'Komposition und Redaktion von Psalm xxix', *VT* 28 (1978), 172–194.

S. Mittmann, 'Die Grabinschrift des Sängers Uriahu', *ZDPV* 97 (1981), 139–152.

J. A. Montgomery, 'Ras Shamra Notes IV: The Conflict of Baal and the Waters', *JAOS* 55 (1935), 268–277.

J. C. de Moor, 'Studies in the new alphabetic Texts from Ras Shamra II', *UF* 2 (1970), 303–327.

J. C. de Moor, 'The Semitic Pantheon of Ugarit', *UF* 2 (1970), 187–228.

J. C. de Moor, *The Seasonal Pattern in the Ugaritic Myth of Ba'lu*, Kevelaer–Neukirchen-Vluyn 1971.

J. C. de Moor, 'Contributions to the Ugaritic Lexicon', *UF* 11 (1979), 639–653.

S. Mowinckel, *Psalmenstudien II. Das Thronbesteigungsfest Jahwäs und der Ursprung der Eschatologie*, Kristiania 1922.

S. Mowinckel, 'Die vermeintliche "Passahlegende" Ex. 1–15 in Bezug auf die Frage: Litterarkritik und Traditionskritik', *StTh* 5 (1952), 66–88.

S. Mowinckel, 'Psalm Criticism between 1900 and 1935 (Ugarit and Psalm Exegesis)', *VT* 5 (1955), 13–33.

S. Mowinckel, 'Mythos und Mythologie. III. Im AT', *RGG*[3] IV (1960), 1274–1278.

S. Mowinckel, *The Psalms in Israel's Worship*, Oxford 1962 (translation of *Offersang og Sangoffer*, Oslo 1951).

M. J. Mulder, *Ba'al in het Oude Testament*, 's-Gravenhage 1962.

M. J. Mulder, 'Der Gott Hadad im nordwestsemitischen Raum', *Interaction and Acculturation in the Mediterranean*, ed. J. G. P. Best – N. M. W. de Vries, Amsterdam 1980, 69–83.

E. Th. Mullen, *The Assembly of the Gods. The Divine Council in Canaanite and Early Hebrew Literature*, Chico 1980.

H.-P. Müller, 'Gott und die Götter in den Anfängen der biblischen Religion. Zur Vorgeschichte des Monotheismus', *Monotheismus im Alten Israel und seiner Umwelt*, ed. O. Keel, Fribourg 1980, 100–142.

F. Münzer, 'Mucius 10', *PWR* XVI 1, 416–423.

J. Naveh, '*lĕmakbirām* or *lammĕkabbĕdîm?*', *ErIs* 15 (1981), 301–302.

S. I. L. Norin, *Er spaltete das Meer. Die Auszugsüberlieferung in Psalmen und Kult des alten Israel*, Lund 1977.

M. Noth, 'Die Historisierung des Mythus', *CuW* 4 (1928), 265–272, 301–309 (= M. Noth, *Gesammelte Studien zum Alten Testament* II, ed. H. W. Wolff, München 1969, 29–47).

W. O. E. Oesterley – Th. H. Robinson, *Hebrew Religion, Its Origin and Development*, London 1937² (1930).

E. Otto, 'Silo und Jerusalem', *ThZ* 32 (1976), 65–76.

E. Otto, 'El und Jhwh in Jerusalem. Historische und theologische Aspekte einer Religionsintegration', *VT* 30 (1980), 316–329.

W. F. Otto, 'Fides', *PWR* VI, 2281–2286.

B. Otzen, 'The Use of Myth in Genesis', in: B. Otzen – H. Gottlieb – K. Jeppesen, *Myths in the Old Testament*, London 1980 (translation of *Myter i Det gamle Testamente*, Copenhagen 1973, 1976²), Ch. II.

E. Pais, *Storia critica di Roma durante i primi cinque secoli* II, Roma 1915.

S. B. Parker, 'Exodus xv 2 again', *VT* 21 (1971), 373–379.

E. Pax, 'Studien zur Theologie von Psalm 29', *BZ Neue Folge* 6 (1962), 93–100.

J. Pedersen, *Der Eid bei den Semiten*, Strassburg 1914.

J. Pedersen, 'Passahfest und Passahlegende', *ZAW* 52 (1934), 161–175.

J. Pedersen, *Israel, Its Life and Culture* III–IV, London-Copenhagen 1940.

C. Petersen, *Mythos im Alten Testament. Bestimmung des Mythosbegriffs und Untersuchung der mythischen Elemente in den Psalmen*, Berlin 1982.

E. Podechard, *Le Psautier. Traduction littérale et explication historique* I. *Psaumes 1–75; Notes critiques* I. *Psaumes 1–75*, Lyon 1949.

M. H. Pope – J. H. Tigay, 'A Description of Baal', *UF* 3 (1971), 117–130.

G. Posener, 'La légende égyptienne de la mer insatiable', *AIPhHOS* 13 (1953), 461–478.

G. von Rad, *Theologie des Alten Testaments* I, München 1962⁴ (1957).

A. F. Rainey, 'The Ugaritic Texts in *Ugaritica* 5', *JAOS* 94 (1974), 184–194.

S. C. Reif, 'A Note on g‘r', *VT* 21 (1971), 241–244.

R. Rendtorff, 'Kult, Mythos und Geschichte im alten Israel', *Festschrift für H. Rendtorff*, Berlin 1958, 121–129 (= R. Rendtorff, *Gesammelte Studien zum Alten Testament*, München 1975, 110–118).

R. Rendtorff, 'El, Ba‘al und Jahwe. Erwägungen zum Verhältnis von kanaanäischen und israelitischen Religion', *ZAW* 78 (1966), 277–292 (= R. Rendtorff, *Gesammelte Studien zum Alten Testament*, München 1975, 172–187).

S. Ribichini – P. Xella, 'Milk 'Aštart, *mlk(m)* e la tradizione siro-palestinese sui Refaim', *RivSF* 7 (1979), 145–158.

N. J. Richardson, 'Review of W. Burkert, *Structure and History in Greek Mythology and Ritual*', *ClassRev* 31 (1981), 63–64.

N. H. Ridderbos, 'Enkele aspecten van Psalm 29', *GThT* 60 (1960), 64–69.

H. Ringgren, *Israelitische Religion*, Stuttgart 1963.

H. Ringgren, 'Jahvé et Rahab-Léviatan', *Mélanges bibliques et orientaux en l'honneur de M. Henri Cazelles*, ed. A. Caquot – M. Delcor, Kevelaer – Neukirchen-Vluyn 1981, 387–393.

D. A. Robertson, *Linguistic Evidence in Dating Early Hebrew Poetry*, Missoula 1972.

J. W. Rogerson, *Myth in Old Testament Interpretation*, Berlin-New York 1974.

F. le Roux, 'Le guerrier borgne et le Druide aveugle: La cécité et la voyance', *Ogam* 13 (1961), 331–342.

H. W. F. Saggs, *The Encounter with the Divine in Mesopotamia and Israel*, London 1978.

J. Scharbert, 'Das "Schilfmeerwunder" in den Texten des Alten Testaments', *Mélanges bibliques et orientaux en l'honneur de M. Henri Cazelles*, ed. A. Caquot – M. Delcor, Kevelaer – Neukirchen-Vluyn 1981, 419–438.

J. Schildenberger, 'Bemerkungen zum Strophenbau der Psalmen', *Est Ecl* 34 (1960), 673–687.

W. Schlisske, *Gottessöhne und Gottessohn im Alten Testament. Phasen der Entmythisierung im Alten Testament*, Stuttgart 1973.

H. H. Schmid, *"aeraeṣ* Erde, Land', *ThHAT* I, 228–236.

W. H. Schmidt, *Königtum Gottes in Ugarit und Israel. Zur Herkunft der Königsprädikation Jahwes*, Berlin 1961.

W. H. Schmidt, 'Mythos im Alten Testament', *EvTh* 27 (1967), 237–254.

G. Schmitt, *Du sollst keinen Frieden schliessen mit den Bewohnern des Landes. Die Weisungen gegen die Kanaanäer in Israels Geschichte und Geschichtsschreibung*, Stuttgart 1970.

C. Scott Littleton, *The New Comparative Mythology. An anthropological assessment of the theories of G. Dumézil*, Berkeley – Los Angeles 1966.

F. A. Sebeok, *Myth: A Symposium*, Indiana 1974.

A. van Selms, 'A Systematic Approach to *CTA* 5, I, 1–8', *UF* 7 (1975), 477–482.

P. W. Skehan, 'Qumran and the Present State of Old Testament Text Studies: the Masoretic Text', *JBL* 78 (1959), 21–25.

N. H. Snaith, '*yam-sop*: The Sea of Reeds: The Red Sea', *VT* 15 (1965), 395–398.

L. I. J. Stadelmann, *The Hebrew Conception of the World. A Philological and Literary Study*, Rome 1970.

W. Staerk, '*Zu Habakuk 15–11*. Geschichte oder Mythos?', *ZAW* 51 (1933), 1–28.

D. M. G. Stalker, 'Exodus', *Peake's Commentary on the Bible*, ed. M. Black – H. H. Rowley, Edinburgh 1962, 208–240.

J. J. Stamm, 'Erwägungen zu RS 24.246', *UF* 11 (1979), 753–758.

F. Stolz, *Strukturen und Figuren im Kult von Jerusalem. Studien zur altorientalischen, vor- und frühisraelitischen Religion*, Berlin 1970.

F. Stolz, 'Monotheismus in Israel', *Monotheismus im Alten Israel und seiner Umwelt*, ed. O. Keel, Fribourg 1980, 144–189.

F. Stolz, 'Funktionen und Bedeutungsbereiche des Ugaritischen Ba'alsmythos', in: J. Assmann – W. Burkert – F. Stolz, *Funktionen und Leistungen des Mythos. Drei altorientalische Beispiele*, Freiburg (Schw.)-Göttingen 1982, 83–118.

H. Strauss, 'Zur Auslegung von Psalm 29 auf dem Hintergrund seiner kanaanäischen Bezüge', *ZAW* 82 (1970), 91–102.

E. F. Sutcliffe, 'A Note on Psalm CIV 8', *VT* 2 (1952), 177–179.

J. M. de Tarragon, *Le culte à Ugarit d'après les textes de la pratique en cunéiformes alphabétiques*, Paris 1980.

C. Toll, 'Ausdrücke für 'Kraft' im Alten Testament mit besonderer Rücksicht auf die Wurzel *BRK*', *ZAW* 94 (1982), 111–123.

L. E. Toombs, 'The Formation of the Myth Patterns in the Old Testament', *JBR* 29 (1961), 108–112.

R. Tournay, 'En marge d'une traduction des Psaumes', *RB* 63 (1956), 161–181.

J. R. Towers, 'The Red Sea', *JNES* 18 (1959), 150–153.

M. Tsevat, *A Study of the Language of the Biblical Psalms*, Philadelphia 1955.

H. S. Versnel, 'Religious Mentality in Ancient Prayer', *Faith, Hope and Worship. Aspects of Religious Mentality in the Ancient World*, ed. H. S. Versnel, Leiden 1981, 1–64 (translation of 'Van onderen....... Antiek gebed in kelderlicht', *Lampas* 12 (1979), 7–49).

H. S. Versnel, 'Gelijke monniken, gelijke kappen: Myth and Ritual, oud en nieuw', *Lampas* 17 (1984), 194–246.

C. Virolleaud, 'Les nouveaux textes mythologiques et liturgiques de Ras Shamra (xxive campagne, 1961)', *Ugaritica* V, 546–595.

L. Vosberg, *Studien zum Reden vom Schöpfer in den Psalmen*, München 1975.

J. de Vries, *Keltische Religion*, Stuttgart 1961.

M. K. Wakeman, 'The Biblical Earth Monster in the Cosmogonic Combat Myth', *JBL* 88 (1969), 313–320.

M. K. Wakeman, *God's Battle with the Monster. A Study in Biblical Imagery*, Leiden 1973.

W. G. E. Watson, 'Reversed Word-Pairs in Ugaritic Poetry', *UF* 13 (1981), 189–192.

G. Wehmeier, *Der Segen im Alten Testament. Eine semasiologische Untersuchung der Wurzel brk*, Basel 1970.

M. Weinfeld, '*kabod*', *ThWAT* IV, 23–40.

C. Westermann, *Isaiah 40–66: A Commentary*, London 1969 (translation of *Das Buch Jesaja (Kapitel 40–66)*, Göttingen 1966).

C. Westermann, '*kbd* schwer sein', *ThHAT* I, 794–812.

C. Westermann, *Genesis 1–11*, Neukirchen-Vluyn 1974.

J. Weulersse, *Le pays des Alaouites*, Tours 1940.

G. Widengren, 'Myth and History in Israelite-Jewish Thought', *Culture in History, Essays in Honor of Paul Radin*, ed. S. Diamond, New York 1960, 467–495.

W. Wifall, 'The Sea of Reeds as Sheol', *ZAW* 92 (1980), 325–332.

T. Worden, 'The Literary Influence of the Ugaritic Fertility Myth on the Old Testament', *VT* 3 (1953), 273–297.

N. Wyatt, 'Some Observations on the Idea of History among the West Semitic Peoples', *UF* 11 (1979), 825–832.

P. Xella, *I testi rituali di Ugarit* I, Roma 1981.

E. Zenger, 'Tradition und Interpretation in Exod. xv 1–21', *SVT* 32 (1981), 452–483.

B. Zuber, *Vier Studien zu den Ursprüngen Israels. Die Sinaifrage und Probleme der Volks- und Traditionsbildung*, Freiburg (Schw.)-Göttingen 1976.

ABBREVIATIONS

AIPhHOS	*Annuaire de l'Institut de Philologie et d'Histoire Orientales et Slaves*, Bruxelles.
ANET	*Ancient Near Eastern Texts Relating to the Old Testament*, ed. J. B. Pritchard, Princeton 1950, 1955[2], 1969[3].
Atti XIX CongrOr	*Atti del XIX Congresso Internazionale degli Orientalisti (Roma 1935)*, Roma 1938.
Avigad	N. Avigad, 'Excavations in the Jewish Quarter of the Old City of Jerusalem, 1971 (Third Preliminary Report)', *IEJ* 22(1972), 193–200.
BA	*The Biblical Archaeologist*, New Haven.
BAR	*Biblical Archaeology Review*, Washington.
BASOR	*Bulletin of the American Schools of Oriental Research*, New Haven.
Bauer	Th. Bauer, 'Ein viertes altbabylonisches Fragment des Gilgameš-Epos', *JNES* 16 (1957), 254–262.
BdJ	*La Sainte Bible, traduite en français sous la direction de l'École Biblique de Jérusalem*, Paris 1972.
Benz	F. L. Benz, *Personal Names in the Phoenician and Punic Inscriptions*, Rome 1972.
BethM	*Beth Mikra*, Jerusalem.
BHK	*Biblia Hebraica*, ed. R. Kittel, Stuttgart 1951[7].
Bibl	*Biblica. Commentarii periodici ad rem biblicam scientifice investigandam*, Roma.
BN	*Biblische Notizen. Beiträge zur exegetischen Diskussion*, Bamberg.
Borger	R. Borger, *Die Inschriften Asarhaddons Königs von Assyrien*, Graz 1956.
BZ	*Biblische Zeitschrift*, Paderborn.
CBQ	*The Catholic Biblical Quarterly*, Washington.
Christensen	A. Christensen, *Les types du premier homme et du premier roi dans l'histoire légendaire des Iraniens* I, Stockholm 1917, 184–189.

CIL	*Corpus Inscriptionum Latinarum*, Berolini 1863 sqq.
CIS	*Corpus Inscriptionum Semiticarum*, Parisiis 1881 sqq.
ClassRev	*Classical Review*, Oxford.
CMHE	See Bibliography, Cross.
CML	See Bibliography, Driver.
CSH	See Bibliography, Caquot-Sznycer-Herdner.
CuW	*Christentum und Wissenschaft*, Leipzig.
DISO	C. Jean – J. Hoftijzer, *Dictionnaire des Inscriptions Sémitiques de l'Ouest*, Leiden 1965.
Docs	M. Ventris – J. Chadwick, *Documents in Mycenaean Greek*, Cambridge 1959, 1973².
DTT	*Dansk Teologisk Tidsskrift*, København.
EA	J. A. Knudtzon, *Die El-Amarna Tafeln*, Leipzig 1915.
ErIs	*Eretz-Israel. Archaeological, historical and geographical Studies*, Jerusalem.
Eriu	*Eriu. The Journal of the School of Irish Learning*, Dublin.
Erman	A. Erman, *Die Literatur der Ägypter. Gedichte, Erzählungen und Lehrbücher aus dem III. und II. Jahrtausend v. Chr.*, Leipzig 1923.
EstEcl	*Estudios Eclesiásticos*, Madrid.
EvTh	*Evangelische Theologie*, München.
ExTim	*The Expository Times*, Edinburgh.
Fraser	J. Fraser, 'The First Battle of Moytura', *Eriu* 8 (1916), 1–63.
Gantz	J. Gantz, *Early Irish Myths and Sagas*, Harmondsworth 1981.
Gelb	I. J. Gelb, *Computer-aided Analysis of Amorite*, Chicago 1980.
Gering	H. Gering, *Die Edda*, Leipzig-Wien 1892.
Gesenius	Wilhelm Gesenius' *Hebräisches und Chaldäisches Handwörterbuch über das Alte Testament*, Leipzig 1878⁸.
GK	See Bibliography, Kautzsch-Cowley.
GSAI	*Giornale della Società Asiatica Italiana*, Firenze.
GThT	*Gereformeerd Theologisch Tijdschrift*, Aalten.
GUOST	*Glasgow University Oriental Society Transactions*, Glasgow.
HAL	*Hebräisches und Aramäisches Lexikon zum Alten Tes-*

	tament von L. Köhler – W. Baumgartner, neu bearbeitet von W. Baumgartner, mit Mitarbeitern, Leiden 1967 sqq.
Hist	*Historia. Zeitschrift für alte Geschichte*, Wiesbaden.
HS	*Hebrew Studies. A Journal devoted to the Hebrew Language, the Bible and related Areas of Scholarship*, Louisville.
HThR	*Harvard Theological Review*, Cambridge (MA).
Huffmon	H. Huffmon, *Amorite Personal Names in the Mari Texts*, Baltimore 1965.
IDAM	Israel Department of Antiquities and Museums.
IEJ	*Israel Exploration Journal*, Jerusalem.
Iraq	*Iraq. British School of Archaeology in Iraq*, London.
JAOS	*Journal of the American Oriental Society*, Baltimore.
JBL	*Journal of Biblical Literature*, Philadelphia.
JBR	*Journal of Bible and Religion*, Boston.
JNES	*Journal of Near Eastern Studies*, Chicago.
JQR	*Jewish Quarterly Review*, London.
JSS	*Journal of Semitic Studies*, Manchester.
JThS	*Journal of Theological Studies*, Oxford.
KAI	H. Donner – W. Röllig, *Kanaanäische und aramäische Inschriften*, Wiesbaden 1962, 1968², *Texte* 1971³, *Kommentar* 1973³.
KBL	L. Köhler – W. Baumgartner, *Lexicon in Veteris Testamenti Libros*, Leiden 1958.
Kramer	S. N. Kramer, *Sumerian Mythology. A Study of Spiritual and Literary Achievement in the Third Millennium B.C.*, Philadelphia 1944.
KTU	M. Dietrich – O. Loretz – J. Sanmartín, *Die keilalphabetischen Texte aus Ugarit. Einschliesslich der keilalphabetischen Texte ausserhalb Ugarits*, Kevelaer – Neukirchen-Vluyn 1976.
Lampas	*Lampas. Tijdschrift voor Nederlandse classici*, Muiderberg.
Lindsay	W. M. Lindsay, *Nonius Marcellus* I, Lipsiae 1903.
LSJ	H. G. Liddell – R. Scott, *A Greek-English Lexicon*, New Edition by H. S. Jones, Oxford 1940⁹.
LU	R. I. Best – O. Bergin, *Lebor na hUidre*, Dublin 1929.
Maarav	*Maarav. A Journal for the Study of the Northwest Semitic Languages and Literatures*, Guilford.

Man	Man. A monthly Record of anthropological Science, London.
MEFRA	Mélanges d'archéologie et d'histoire. École française de Rome, Antiquité, Paris.
Meshel	Z. Meshel, Kuntillet 'Ajrud. A religious Centre from the Time of the Judaean Monarchy on the Border of Sinai, Jerusalem 1978.
Mus	Le Muséon. Revue d'études orientales, Louvain.
NBG	De Bijbel in de Nieuwe Vertaling door het Nederlands Bijbelgenootschap, Amsterdam 1951.
NEB	The New English Bible. Old Testament, Oxford – Cambridge 1970.
Numen	Numen. International Review for the History of Religions, Leiden.
Ogam	Ogam. Tradition celtique. Histoire, langue, archéologie, religion, numismatique. Bulletin des amis de la tradition celtique, Rennes.
OTS	Oudtestamentische Studiën, Leiden.
OTWSAP	Papers read at the Meeting of Die Ou Testamentiese Werkgemeenskap in Suid-Afrika, Pretoria.
PrJ	Preussische Jahrbücher, Berlin.
PTU	F. Gröndahl, Die Personennamen der Texte aus Ugarit, Rom 1967.
PWR	Pauly-Wissowa, Real-Encyclopädie der classischen Altertumswissenschaft, Stuttgart 1894 sqq.
RB	Revue biblique, Paris.
Rel	Religion, London.
RevCelt	Revue Celtique, Paris.
RevPar	Revue de Paris, Paris.
RGG³	Die Religion in Geschichte und Gegenwart, Tübingen 1957 sqq.
RHR	Revue de l'Histoire des Religions, Paris.
RivSF	Rivista di Studi Fenici, Roma.
RSP	Ras Shamra Parallels. The Texts from Ugarit and the Hebrew Bible, Roma, ed. L. R. Fisher I 1972, II 1975; ed. S. Rummel III 1981.
RSV	The Oxford Annotated Bible with the Apocrypha. Revised Standard Version, New York – Oxford 1965.
RThL	Revue Théologique de Louvain, Louvain.
SBFLA	Studii Biblici Franciscani Liber Annuus, Jerusalem.

SEAJT	*The South East Asia Journal of Theology*, Singapore.
Sem	*Semitics*, Pretoria.
Shnaton	*Shnaton. An Annual for Biblical and Ancient Near Eastern Studies*, Jerusalem.
Spiegel	F. Spiegel, *Einleitung in die traditionellen Schriften der Parsen* II, *Die traditionelle Literatur der Parsen*, Wien – Leipzig 1860, 317–332.
Stokes	W. Stokes, 'Second Battle of Moytura', *RevCelt* 12 (1891), 52–130.
StTh	*Studia Theologica. Scandinavian Journal of Theology*, Lund.
SVT	*Supplements to Vetus Testamentum*, Leiden.
Syr	*Syria. Revue d'Art Oriental et d'Archéologie*, Paris.
Thesaurus	E. Ben Yehuda, *Thesaurus totius hebraitatis et veteris et recentioris*, Berlin – Jerusalem 1911 sqq.
ThHAT	*Theologisches Handwörterbuch zum Alten Testament*, ed. E. Jenni – C. Westermann, München – Zürich I 1971, II 1976.
ThWAT	*Theologisches Wörterbuch zum Alten Testament*, ed. G. J. Botterweck – H. Ringgren – H.-J. Fabry, Stuttgart IV 1984.
ThZ	*Theologische Zeitschrift*, Basel.
UF	*Ugarit Forschungen*, Neukirchen.
Ugaritica V	*Ugaritica* V, ed. C. F. A. Schaeffer, Paris 1968.
VD	*Verbum Domini. Commentarii de re biblica*, Roma.
VT	*Vetus Testamentum*, Leiden.
WUS	J. Aistleitner, *Wörterbuch der Ugaritischen Sprache*, Berlin 1967³ (1963).
ZAW	*Zeitschrift für die alttestamentliche Wissenschaft und die Kunde des nachbiblischen Judentums*, Berlin.
ZDPV	*Zeitschrift des Deutschen Palästina-Vereins*, Wiesbaden.
ZRGG	*Zeitschrift für Religions- und Geistesgeschichte*, Köln.
ZS	*Zeitschrift für Semitistik und verwandte Gebiete*, Leipzig.

INDEX OF AUTHORS

INDEX OF TEXTS

236

COLOPHON

This first impression of *Yhwh's Combat with the Sea. A Canaanite Tradition in the Religion of Ancient Israel* by Carola Kloos was set up in Bembo and printed by the Royal Printers G. J. Thieme Ltd. in Nijmegen, the Netherlands, by authorization of G. A. van Oorschot, publisher in Amsterdam. The cover was designed by Gerrit Noordzij. The book is distributed by E. J. Brill Publishing Company.